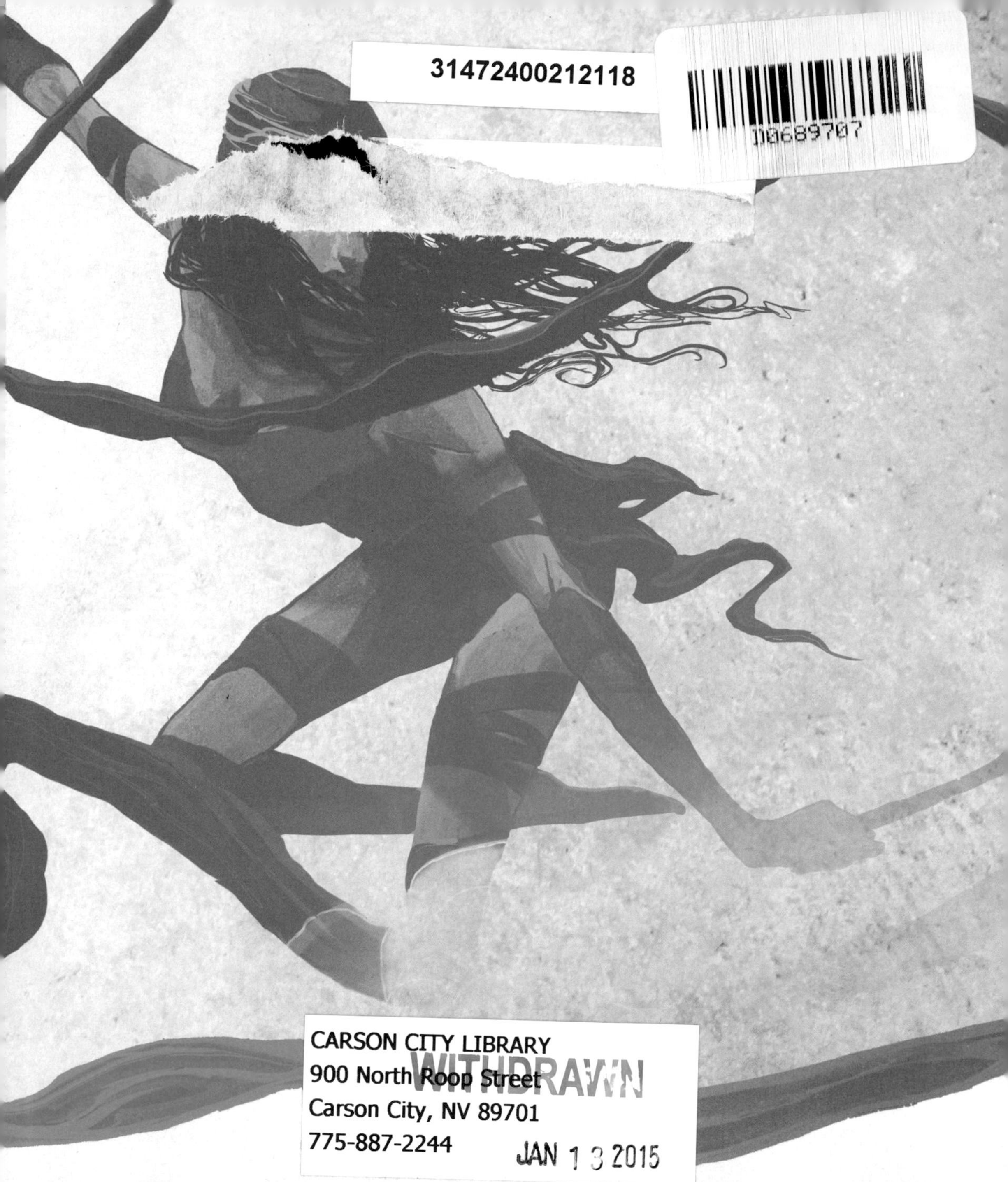

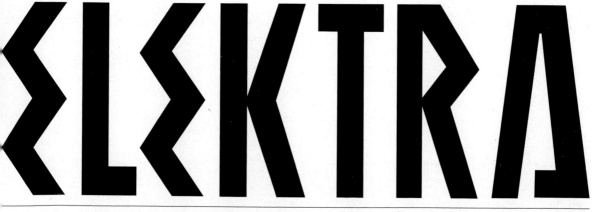

ELEKTRA

BLOODLINES

ELEKTRA

WRITER:
W. HADEN BLACKMAN

ARTIST:
MICHAEL DEL MUNDO

COLOR ARTISTS:
MICHAEL DEL MUNDO WITH MARCO D'ALFONSO

LETTERER:
VC'S CLAYTON COWLES

COVER ART:
MICHAEL DEL MUNDO

ASSISTANT EDITOR:
DEVIN LEWIS

EDITOR:
SANA AMANAT

SENIOR EDITORS:
NICK LOWE & STEPHEN WACKER

COLLECTION EDITOR: **JENNIFER GRÜNWALD**   ASSISTANT EDITOR: **SARAH BRUNSTAD**
ASSOCIATE MANAGING EDITOR: **ALEX STARBUCK**   EDITOR, SPECIAL PROJECTS: **MARK D. BEAZLEY**
SENIOR EDITOR, SPECIAL PROJECTS: **JEFF YOUNGQUIST**   SVP PRINT, SALES & MARKETING: **DAVID GABRIEL**
BOOK DESIGNER: **RODOLFO MURAGUCHI**

EDITOR IN CHIEF: **AXEL ALONSO**   CHIEF CREATIVE OFFICER: **JOE QUESADA**
PUBLISHER: **DAN BUCKLEY**   EXECUTIVE PRODUCER: **ALAN FINE**

ELEKTRA VOL. 1: BLOODLINES. Contains material originally published in magazine form as ELEKTRA #1-5. First printing 2014. ISBN# 978-0-7851-5406-8. Published by MARVEL WORLDWIDE, INC., a subsidiary of MARVEL ENTERTAINMENT, LLC. OFFICE OF PUBLICATION: 135 West 50th Street, New York, NY 10020. Copyright © 2014 Marvel Characters, Inc. All rights reserved. All characters featured in this issue and the distinctive names and likenesses thereof, and all related indicia are trademarks of Marvel Characters, Inc. No similarity between any of the names, characters, persons, and/or institutions in this magazine with those of any living or dead person or institution is intended, and any such similarity which may exist is purely coincidental. **Printed in Canada.** ALAN FINE, EVP - Office of the President, Marvel Worldwide, Inc. and EVP & CMO Marvel Characters B.V.; DAN BUCKLEY, Publisher & President - Print, Animation & Digital Divisions; JOE QUESADA, Chief Creative Officer; TOM BREVOORT, SVP of Publishing; DAVID BOGART, SVP of Operations & Procurement, Publishing; C.B. CEBULSKI, SVP of Creator & Content Development; DAVID GABRIEL, SVP Print, Sales & Marketing; JIM O'KEEFE, VP of Operations & Logistics; DAN CARR, Executive Director of Publishing Technology; SUSAN CRESPI, Editorial Operations Manager; ALEX MORALES, Publishing Operations Manager; STAN LEE, Chairman Emeritus. For information regarding advertising in Marvel Comics or on Marvel.com, please contact Niza Disla, Director of Marvel Partnerships, at ndisla@marvel.com. For Marvel subscription inquiries, please call 800-217-9158. **Manufactured between 9/12/2014 and 10/20/2014 by SOLISCO PRINTERS, SCOTT, QC, CANADA.**

10 9 8 7 6 5 4 3 2 1

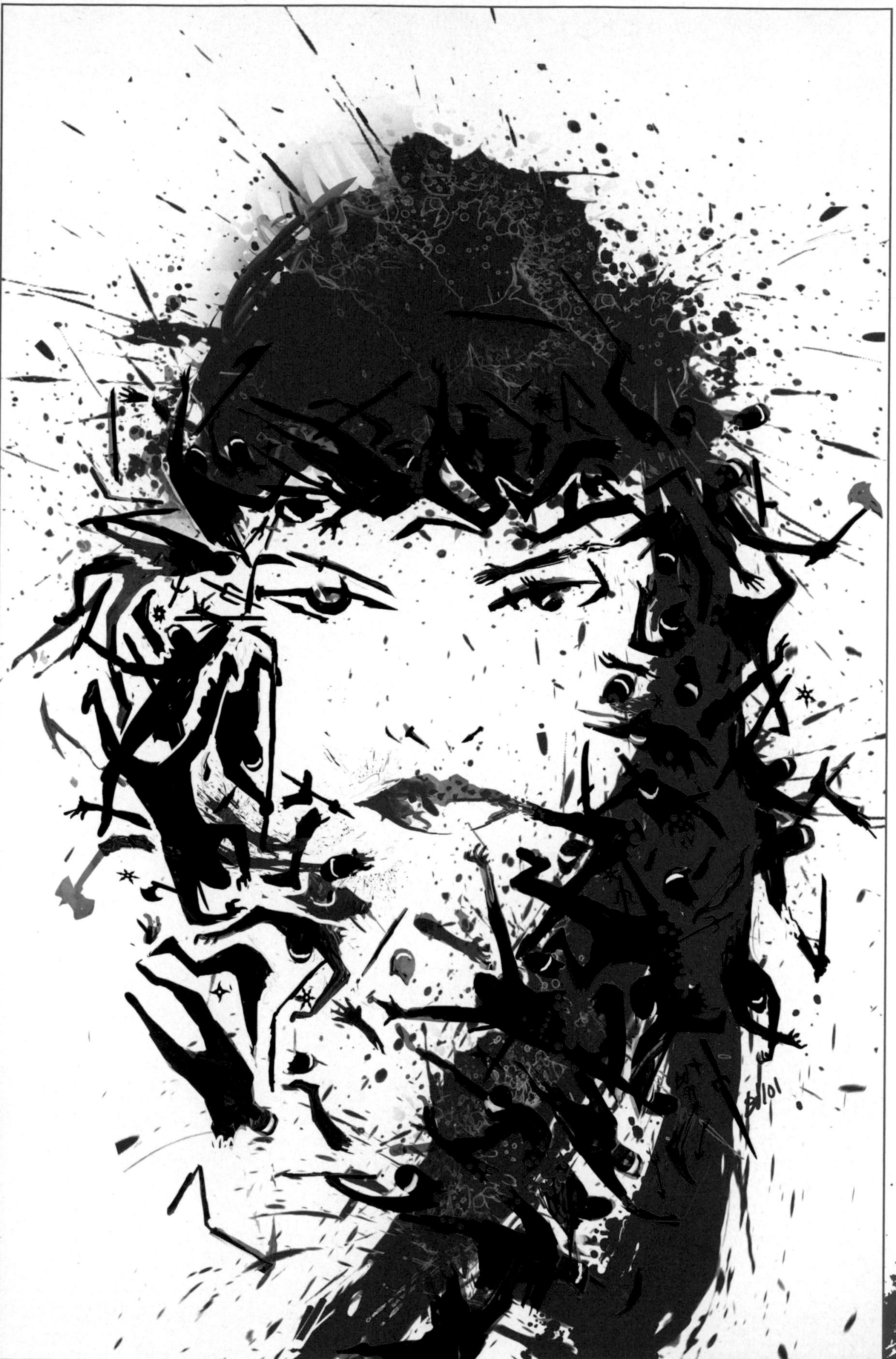

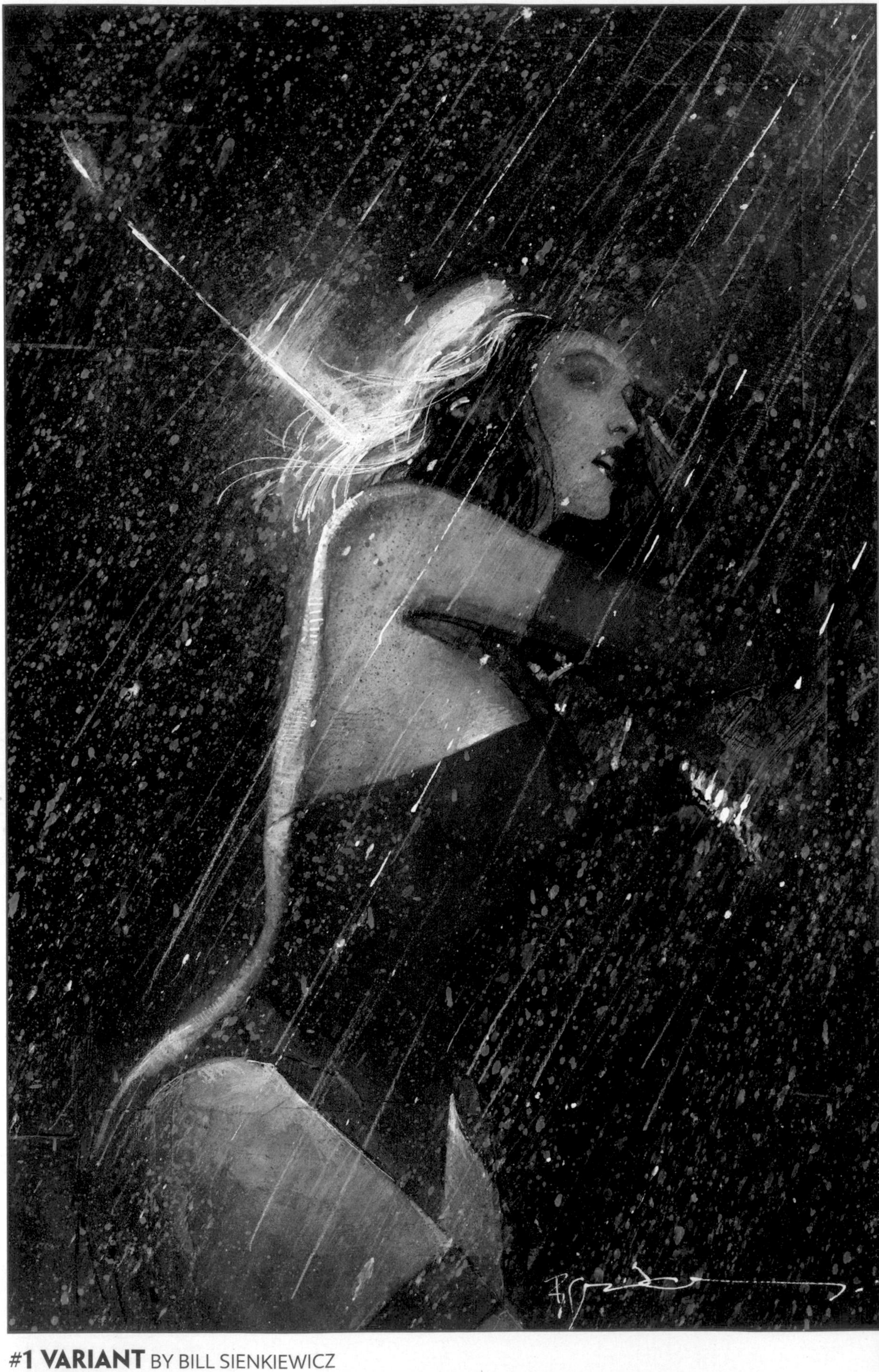

#1 VARIANT BY BILL SIENKIEWICZ

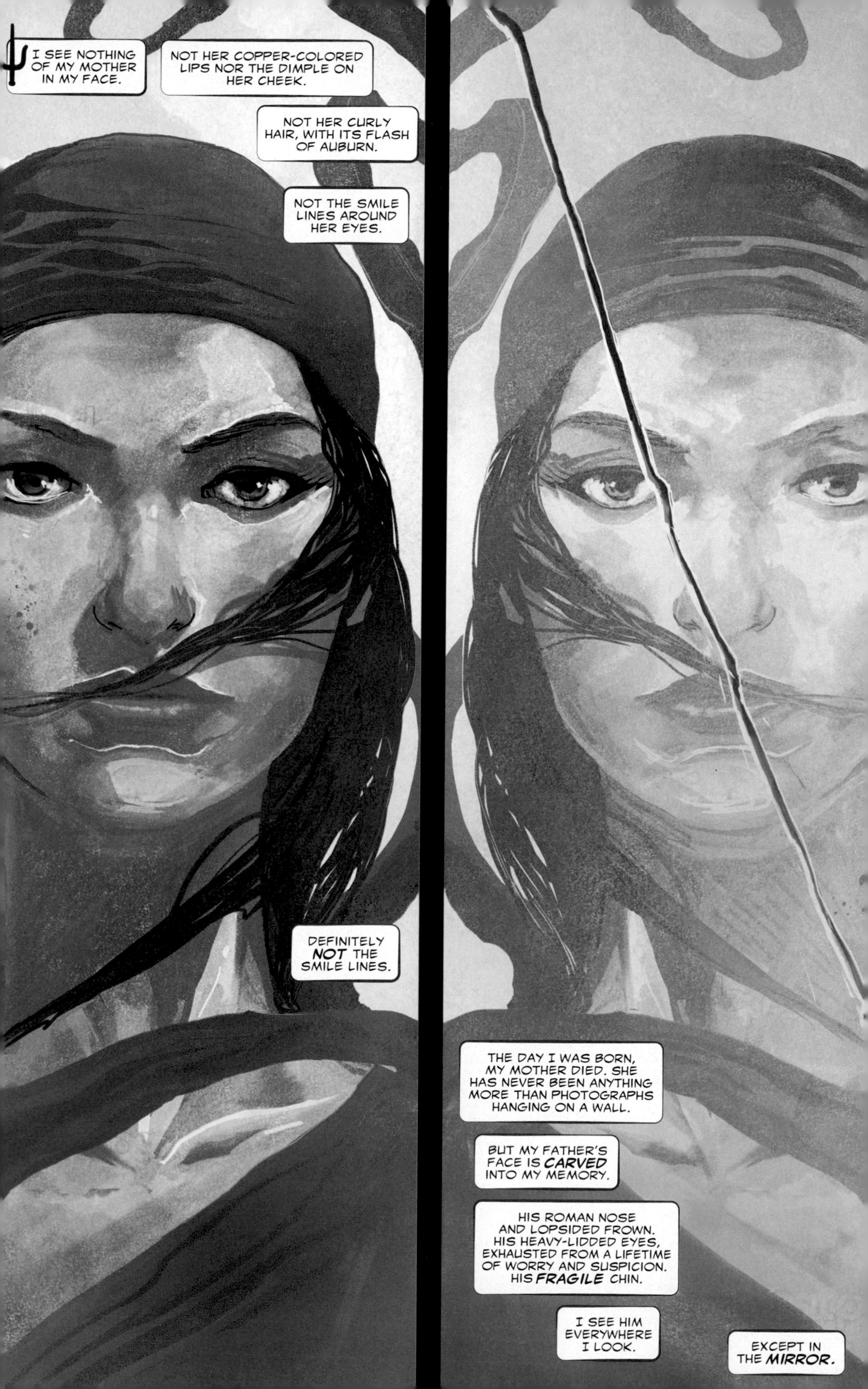
I SEE NOTHING OF MY MOTHER IN MY FACE.
NOT HER COPPER-COLORED LIPS NOR THE DIMPLE ON HER CHEEK.
NOT HER CURLY HAIR, WITH ITS FLASH OF AUBURN.
NOT THE SMILE LINES AROUND HER EYES.
DEFINITELY NOT THE SMILE LINES.
THE DAY I WAS BORN, MY MOTHER DIED. SHE HAS NEVER BEEN ANYTHING MORE THAN PHOTOGRAPHS HANGING ON A WALL.
BUT MY FATHER'S FACE IS CARVED INTO MY MEMORY.
HIS ROMAN NOSE AND LOPSIDED FROWN. HIS HEAVY-LIDDED EYES, EXHAUSTED FROM A LIFETIME OF WORRY AND SUSPICION. HIS FRAGILE CHIN.
I SEE HIM EVERYWHERE I LOOK.
EXCEPT IN THE MIRROR.

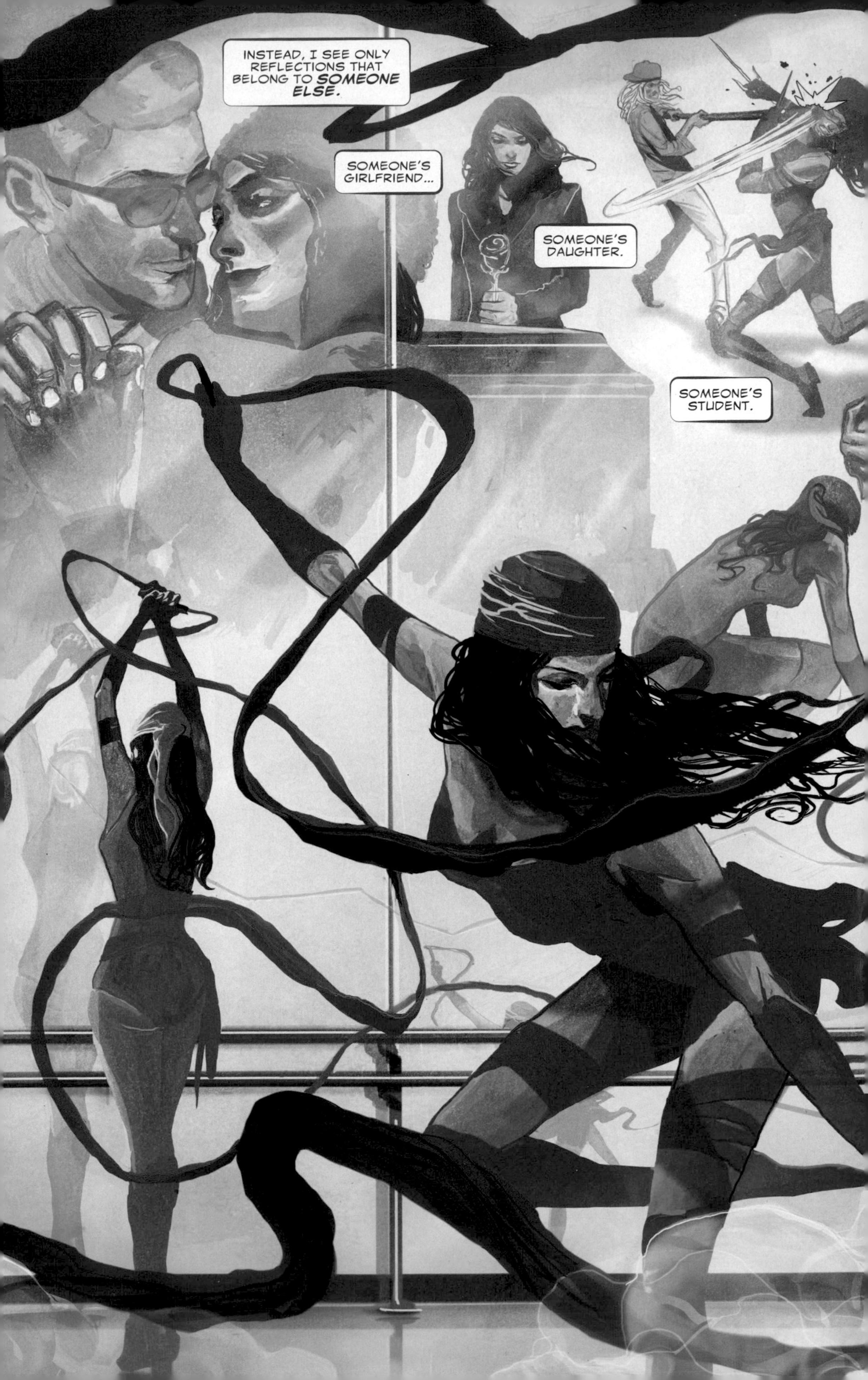

INSTEAD, I SEE ONLY REFLECTIONS THAT BELONG TO SOMEONE ELSE.
SOMEONE'S GIRLFRIEND...
SOMEONE'S DAUGHTER.
SOMEONE'S STUDENT.

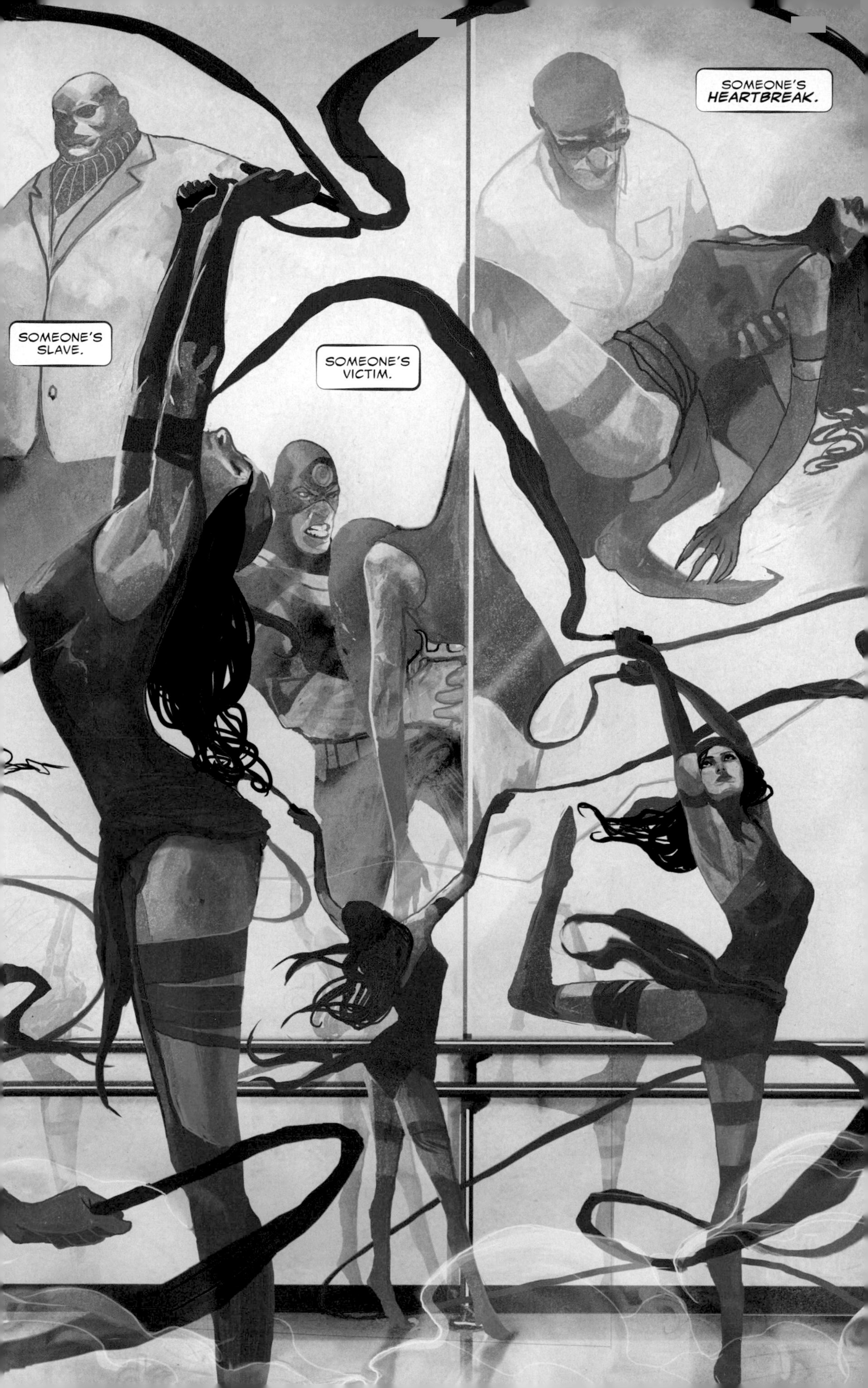
SOMEONE'S SLAVE.
SOMEONE'S VICTIM.
SOMEONE'S HEARTBREAK.

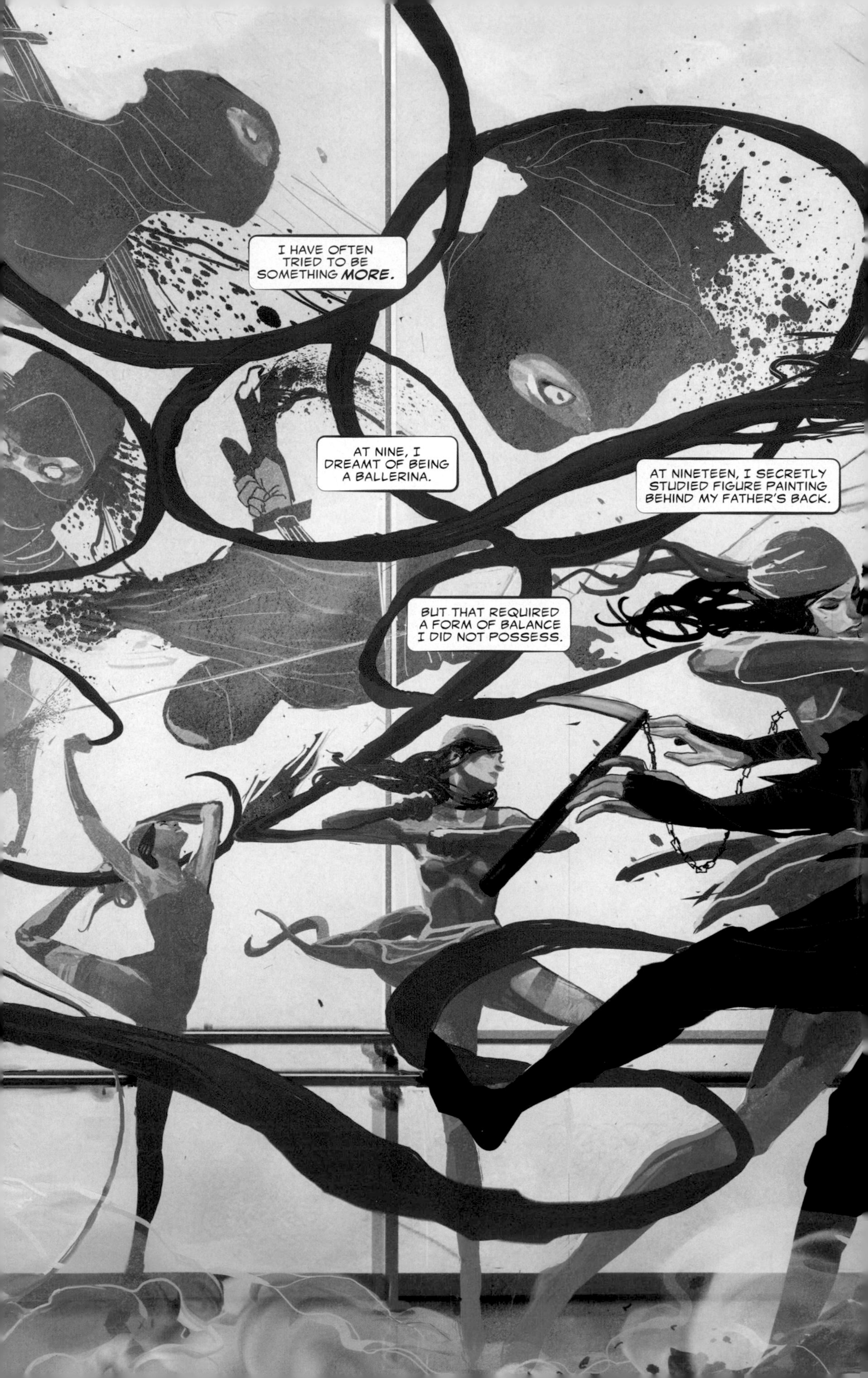
I HAVE OFTEN TRIED TO BE SOMETHING MORE.
AT NINE, I DREAMT OF BEING A BALLERINA.
BUT THAT REQUIRED A FORM OF BALANCE I DID NOT POSSESS.
AT NINETEEN, I SECRETLY STUDIED FIGURE PAINTING BEHIND MY FATHER'S BACK.

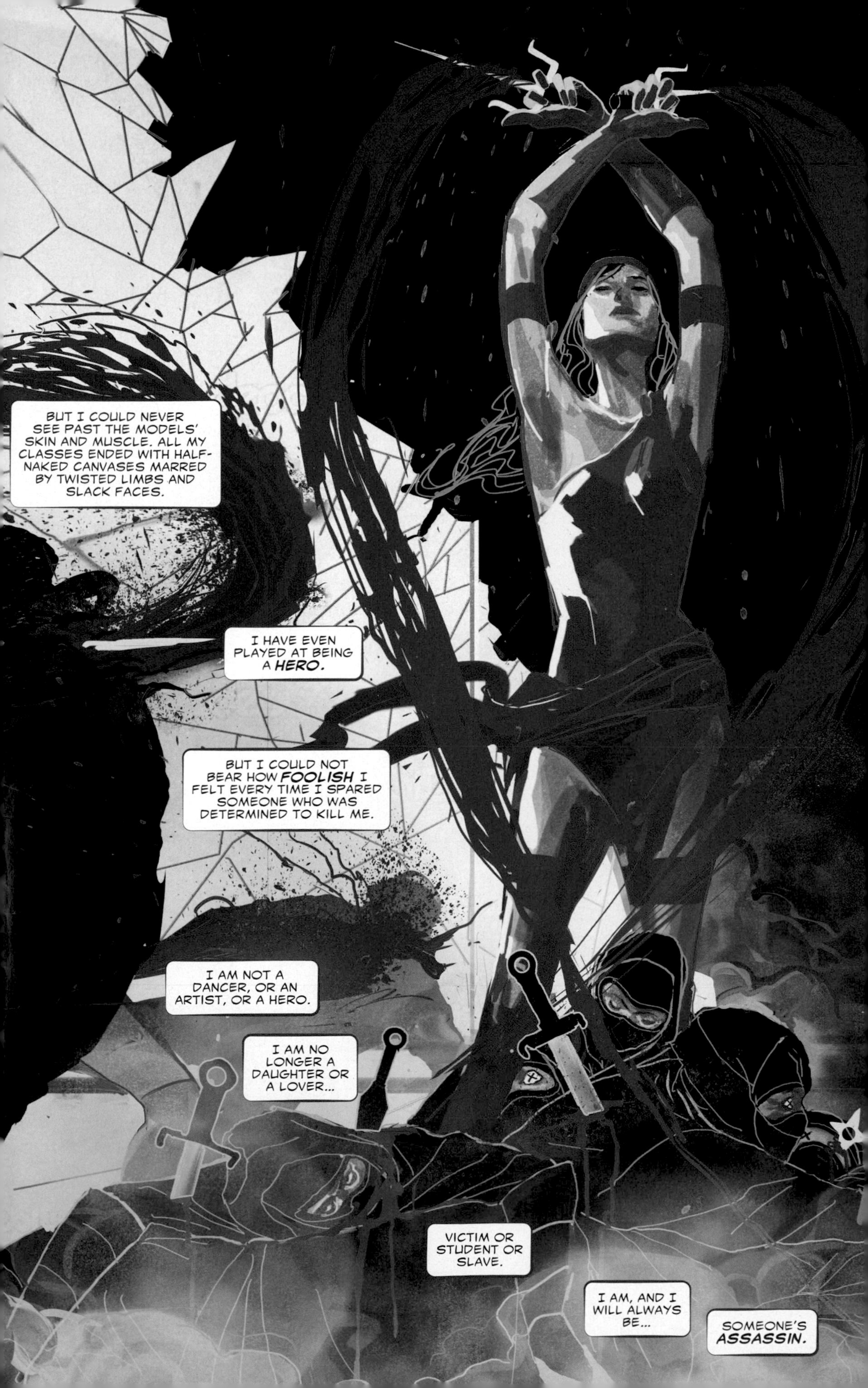
BUT I COULD NEVER SEE PAST THE MODELS' SKIN AND MUSCLE. ALL MY CLASSES ENDED WITH HALF-NAKED CANVASES MARRED BY TWISTED LIMBS AND SLACK FACES.
I HAVE EVEN PLAYED AT BEING A **HERO.**
BUT I COULD NOT BEAR HOW **FOOLISH** I FELT EVERY TIME I SPARED SOMEONE WHO WAS DETERMINED TO KILL ME.
I AM NOT A DANCER, OR AN ARTIST, OR A HERO.
I AM NO LONGER A DAUGHTER OR A LOVER...
VICTIM OR STUDENT OR SLAVE.
I AM, AND I WILL ALWAYS BE...
SOMEONE'S **ASSASSIN.**

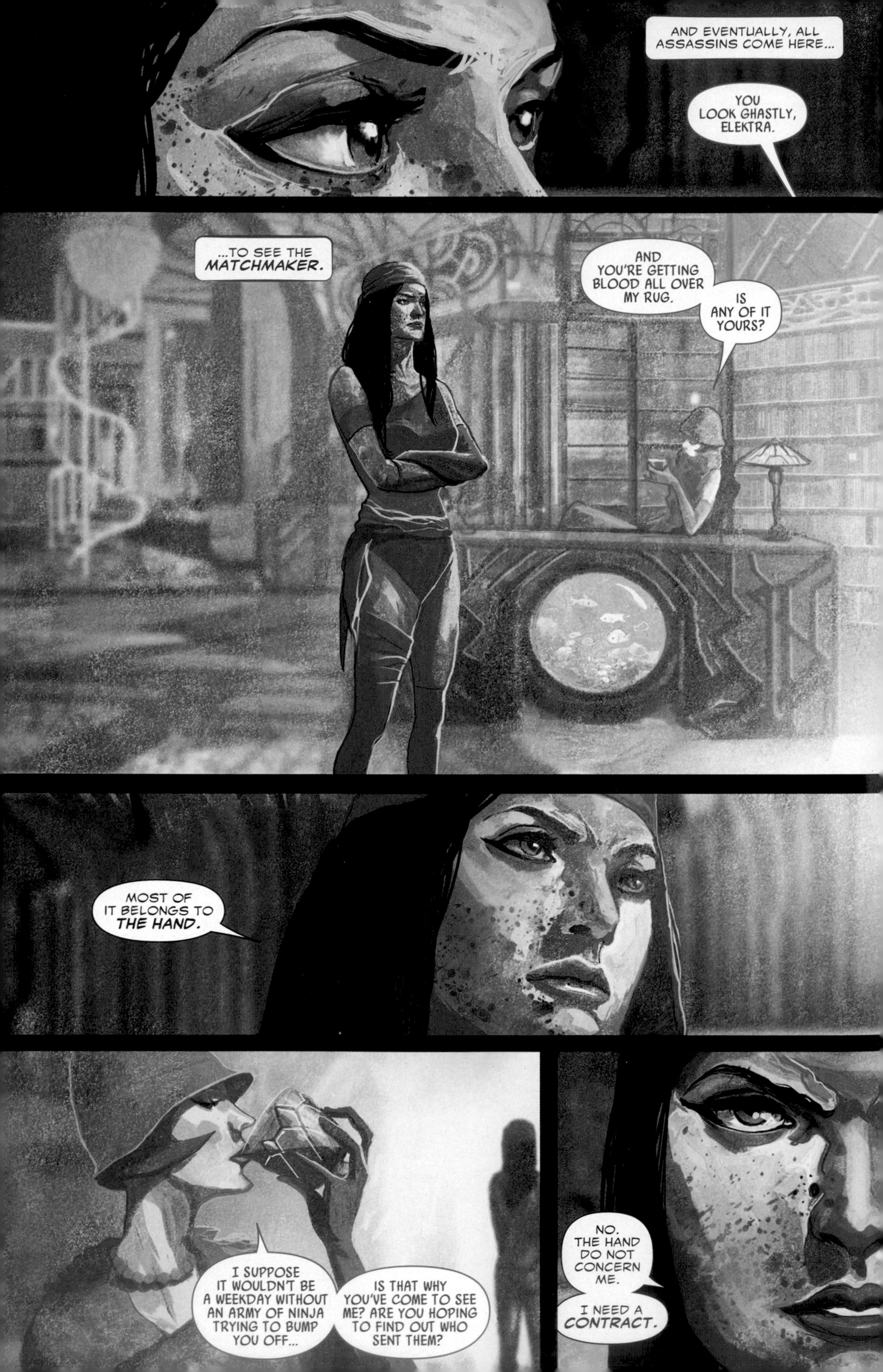
AND EVENTUALLY, ALL ASSASSINS COME HERE...
YOU LOOK GHASTLY, ELEKTRA.
...TO SEE THE MATCHMAKER.
AND YOU'RE GETTING BLOOD ALL OVER MY RUG.
IS ANY OF IT YOURS?
MOST OF IT BELONGS TO THE HAND.
I SUPPOSE IT WOULDN'T BE A WEEKDAY WITHOUT AN ARMY OF NINJA TRYING TO BUMP YOU OFF...
IS THAT WHY YOU'VE COME TO SEE ME? ARE YOU HOPING TO FIND OUT WHO SENT THEM?
NO. THE HAND DO NOT CONCERN ME.
I NEED A CONTRACT.

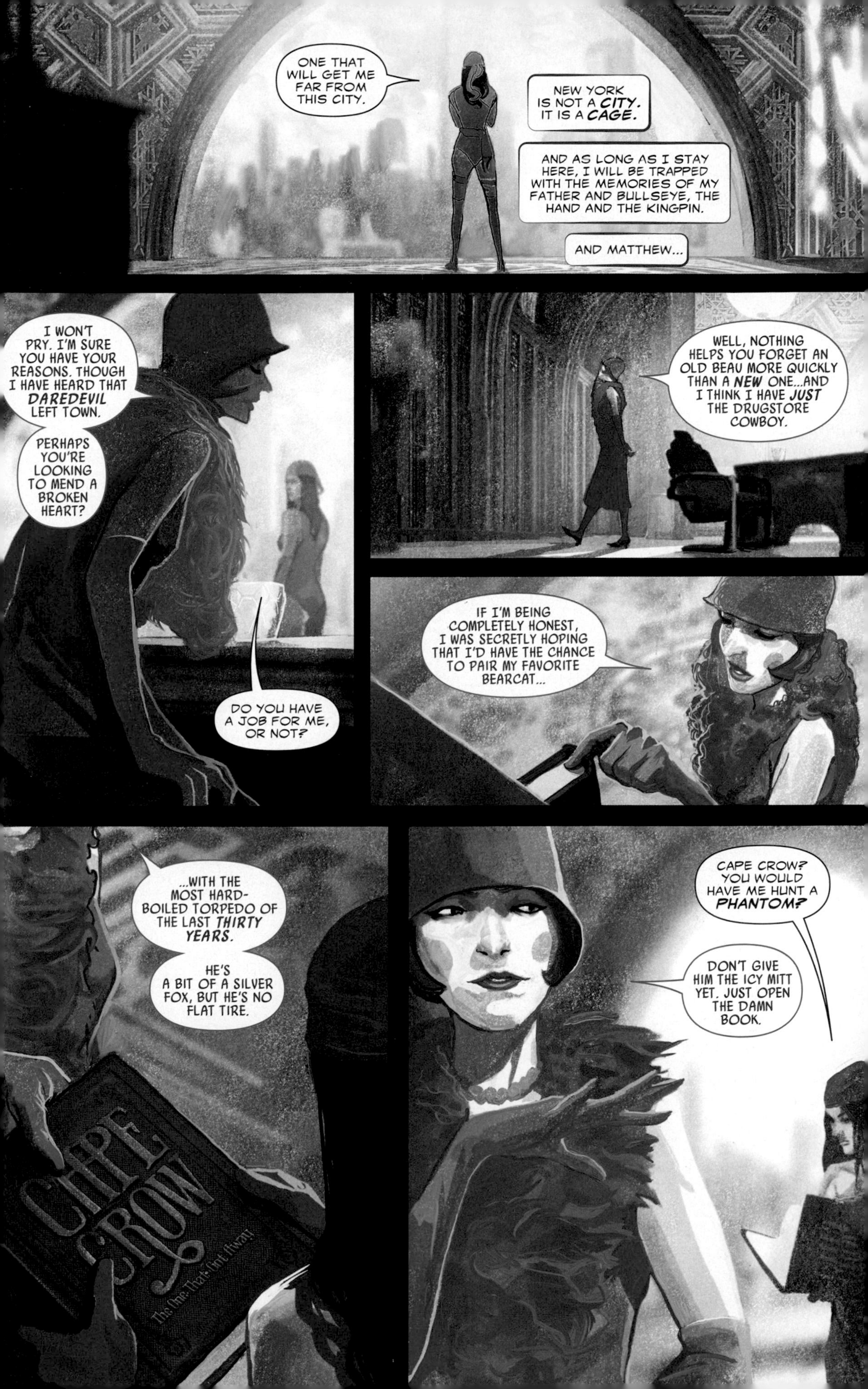
ONE THAT WILL GET ME FAR FROM THIS CITY.
NEW YORK IS NOT A CITY. IT IS A CAGE.
AND AS LONG AS I STAY HERE, I WILL BE TRAPPED WITH THE MEMORIES OF MY FATHER AND BULLSEYE, THE HAND AND THE KINGPIN.
AND MATTHEW...
I WON'T PRY. I'M SURE YOU HAVE YOUR REASONS. THOUGH I HAVE HEARD THAT DAREDEVIL LEFT TOWN.
PERHAPS YOU'RE LOOKING TO MEND A BROKEN HEART?
DO YOU HAVE A JOB FOR ME, OR NOT?
WELL, NOTHING HELPS YOU FORGET AN OLD BEAU MORE QUICKLY THAN A NEW ONE...AND I THINK I HAVE JUST THE DRUGSTORE COWBOY.
IF I'M BEING COMPLETELY HONEST, I WAS SECRETLY HOPING THAT I'D HAVE THE CHANCE TO PAIR MY FAVORITE BEARCAT...
...WITH THE MOST HARD-BOILED TORPEDO OF THE LAST THIRTY YEARS.
HE'S A BIT OF A SILVER FOX, BUT HE'S NO FLAT TIRE.
CAPE CROW
CAPE CROW? YOU WOULD HAVE ME HUNT A PHANTOM?
DON'T GIVE HIM THE ICY MITT YET. JUST OPEN THE DAMN BOOK.

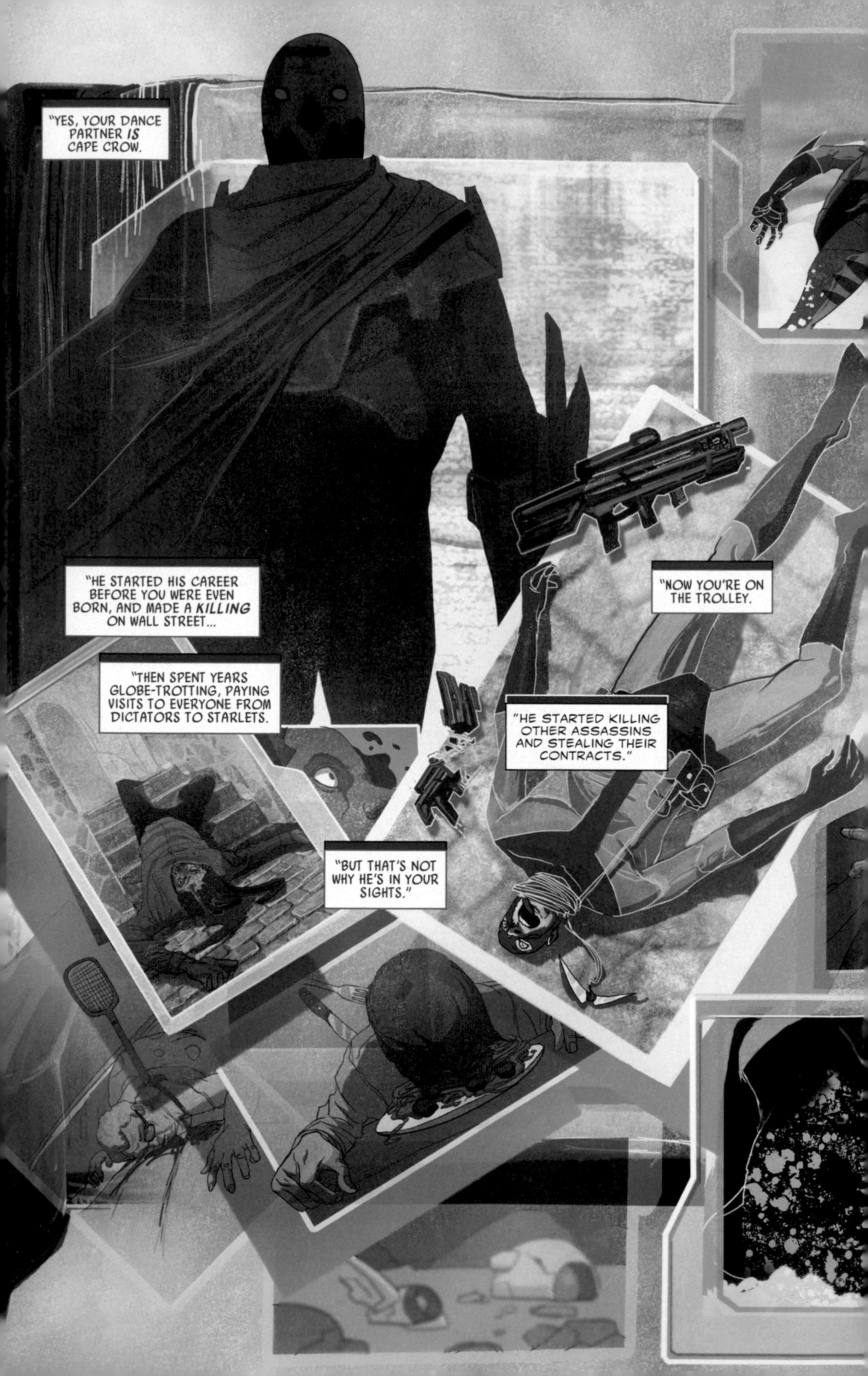
"YES, YOUR DANCE PARTNER *IS* CAPE CROW.
"HE STARTED HIS CAREER BEFORE YOU WERE EVEN BORN, AND MADE A *KILLING* ON WALL STREET...
"THEN SPENT YEARS GLOBE-TROTTING, PAYING VISITS TO EVERYONE FROM DICTATORS TO STARLETS.
"NOW YOU'RE ON THE TROLLEY.
"HE STARTED KILLING OTHER ASSASSINS AND STEALING THEIR CONTRACTS."
"BUT THAT'S NOT WHY HE'S IN YOUR SIGHTS."

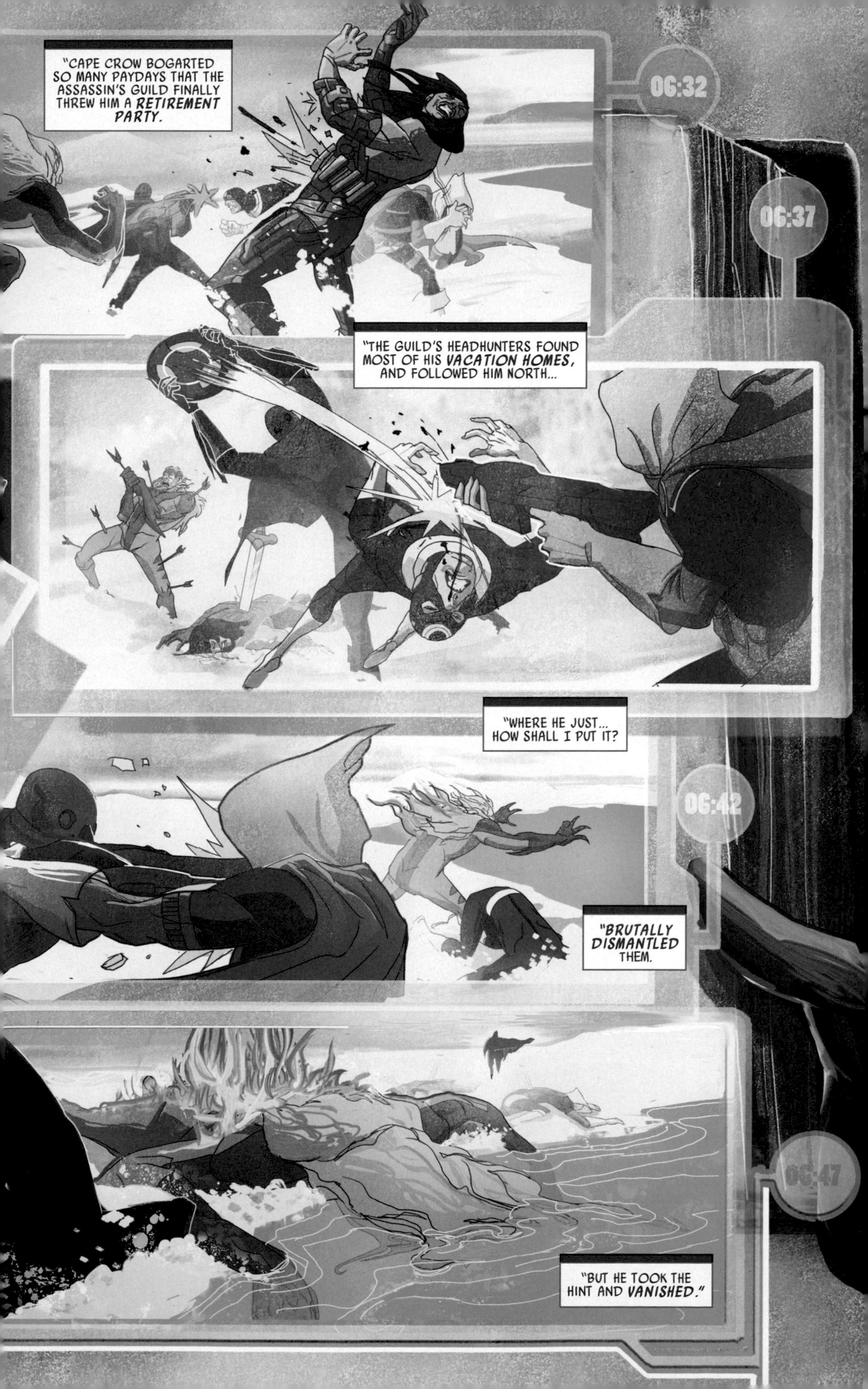
"CAPE CROW BOGARTED SO MANY PAYDAYS THAT THE ASSASSIN'S GUILD FINALLY THREW HIM A RETIREMENT PARTY.
06:32
06:37
"THE GUILD'S HEADHUNTERS FOUND MOST OF HIS VACATION HOMES, AND FOLLOWED HIM NORTH...
"WHERE HE JUST... HOW SHALL I PUT IT?
06:42
"BRUTALLY DISMANTLED THEM.
06:47
"BUT HE TOOK THE HINT AND VANISHED."

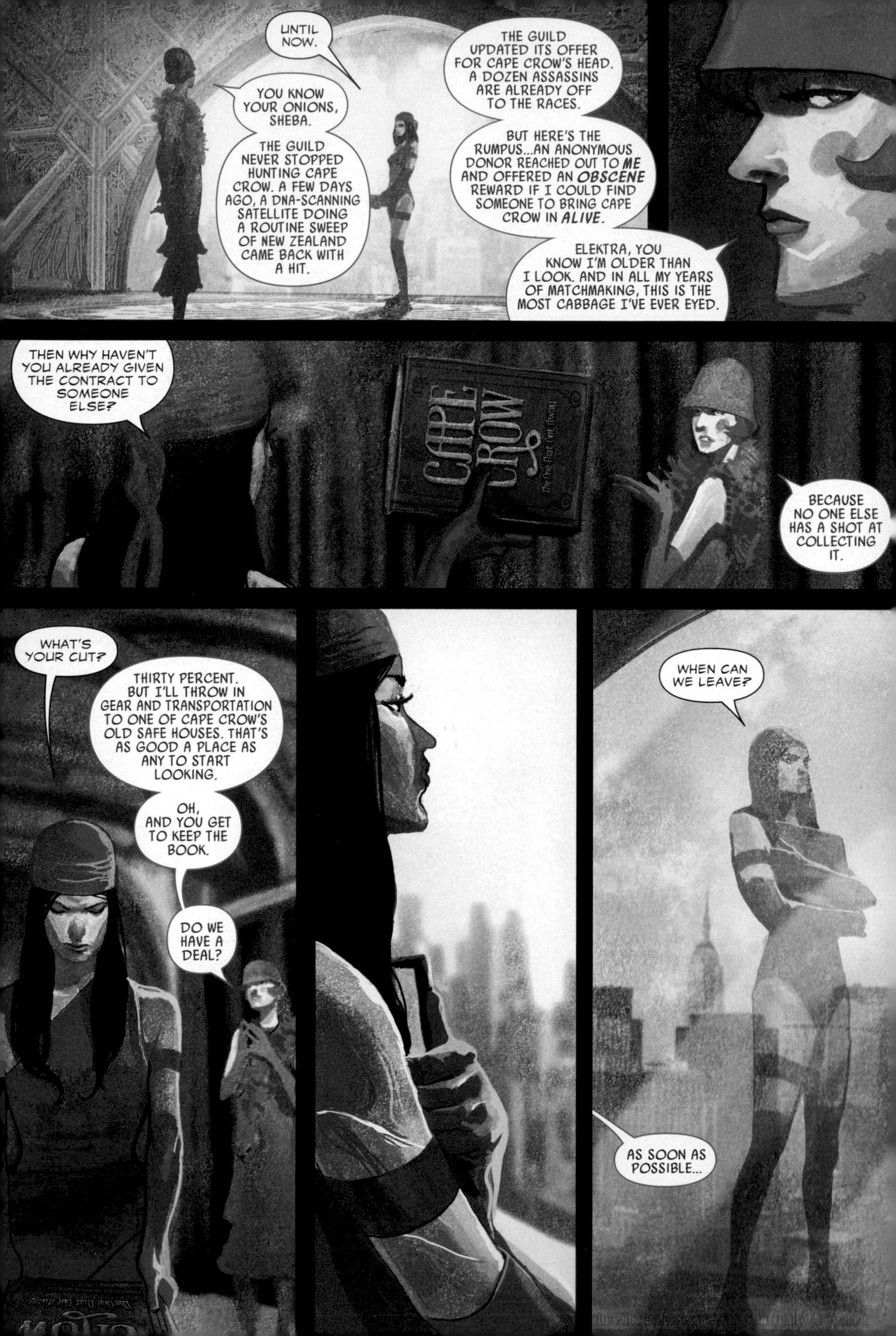
UNTIL NOW.
YOU KNOW YOUR ONIONS, SHEBA.
THE GUILD NEVER STOPPED HUNTING CAPE CROW. A FEW DAYS AGO, A DNA-SCANNING SATELLITE DOING A ROUTINE SWEEP OF NEW ZEALAND CAME BACK WITH A HIT.
THE GUILD UPDATED ITS OFFER FOR CAPE CROW'S HEAD. A DOZEN ASSASSINS ARE ALREADY OFF TO THE RACES.
BUT HERE'S THE RUMPUS...AN ANONYMOUS DONOR REACHED OUT TO *ME* AND OFFERED AN *OBSCENE* REWARD IF I COULD FIND SOMEONE TO BRING CAPE CROW IN *ALIVE*.
ELEKTRA, YOU KNOW I'M OLDER THAN I LOOK. AND IN ALL MY YEARS OF MATCHMAKING, THIS IS THE MOST CABBAGE I'VE EVER EYED.
THEN WHY HAVEN'T YOU ALREADY GIVEN THE CONTRACT TO SOMEONE ELSE?
CAPE CROW
BECAUSE NO ONE ELSE HAS A SHOT AT COLLECTING IT.
WHAT'S YOUR CUT?
THIRTY PERCENT. BUT I'LL THROW IN GEAR AND TRANSPORTATION TO ONE OF CAPE CROW'S OLD SAFE HOUSES. THAT'S AS GOOD A PLACE AS ANY TO START LOOKING.
OH, AND YOU GET TO KEEP THE BOOK.
DO WE HAVE A DEAL?
WHEN CAN WE LEAVE?
AS SOON AS POSSIBLE...

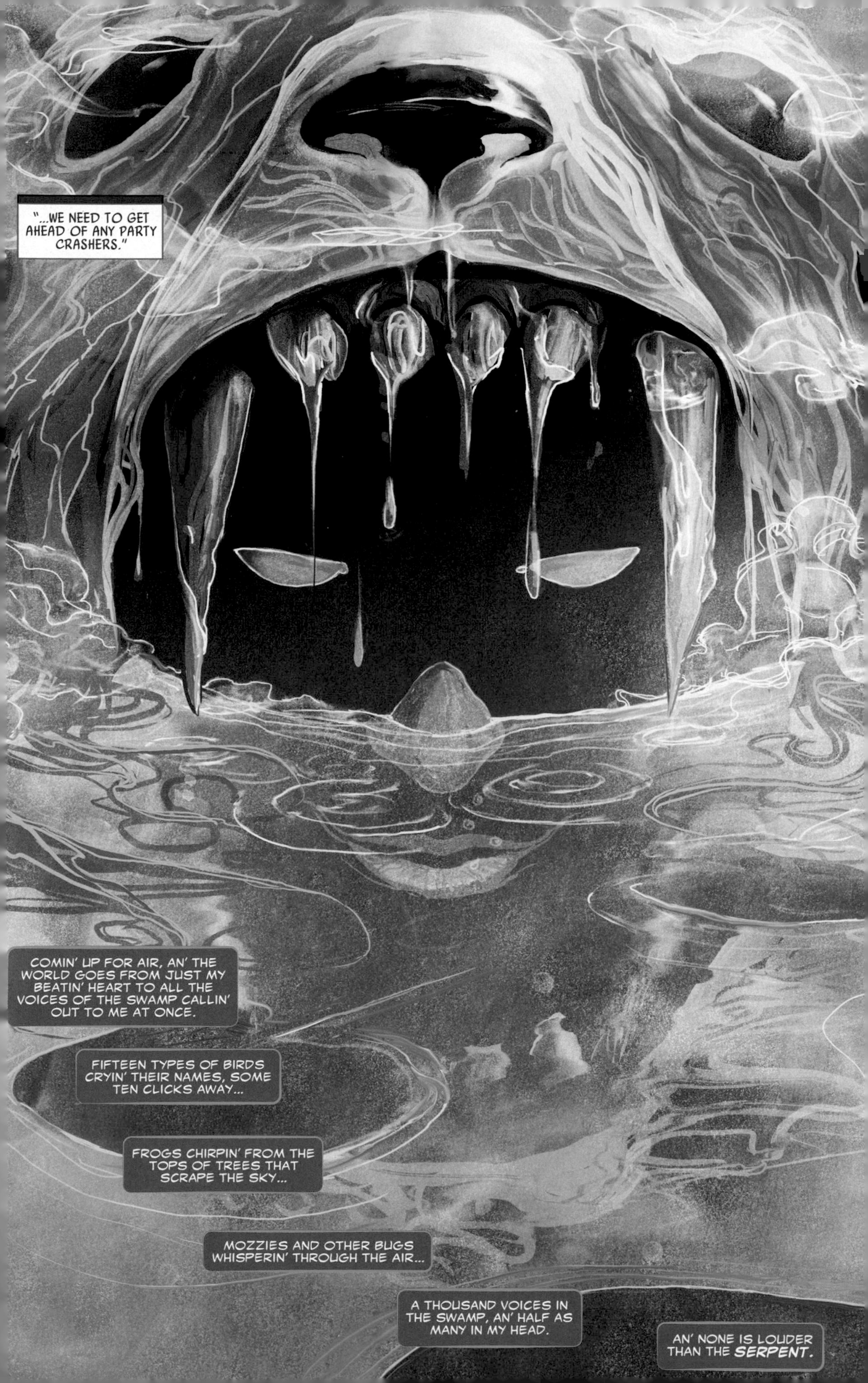
"...WE NEED TO GET AHEAD OF ANY PARTY CRASHERS."
COMIN' UP FOR AIR, AN' THE WORLD GOES FROM JUST MY BEATIN' HEART TO ALL THE VOICES OF THE SWAMP CALLIN' OUT TO ME AT ONCE.
FIFTEEN TYPES OF BIRDS CRYIN' THEIR NAMES, SOME TEN CLICKS AWAY...
FROGS CHIRPIN' FROM THE TOPS OF TREES THAT SCRAPE THE SKY...
MOZZIES AND OTHER BUGS WHISPERIN' THROUGH THE AIR...
A THOUSAND VOICES IN THE SWAMP, AN' HALF AS MANY IN MY HEAD.
AN' NONE IS LOUDER THAN THE ***SERPENT.***

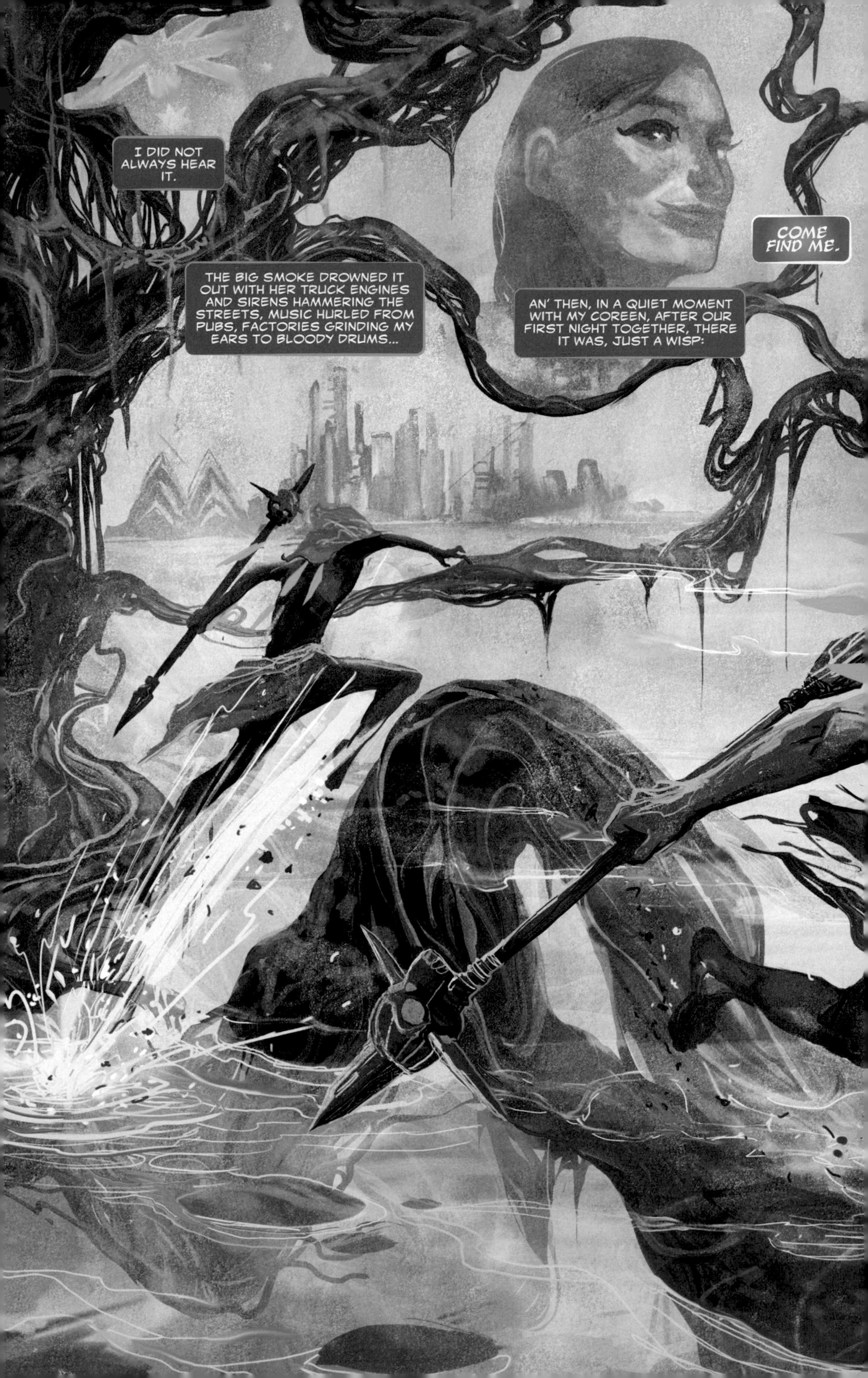
I DID NOT ALWAYS HEAR IT.
THE BIG SMOKE DROWNED IT OUT WITH HER TRUCK ENGINES AND SIRENS HAMMERING THE STREETS, MUSIC HURLED FROM PUBS, FACTORIES GRINDING MY EARS TO BLOODY DRUMS...
AN' THEN, IN A QUIET MOMENT WITH MY COREEN, AFTER OUR FIRST NIGHT TOGETHER, THERE IT WAS, JUST A WISP:
COME FIND ME.

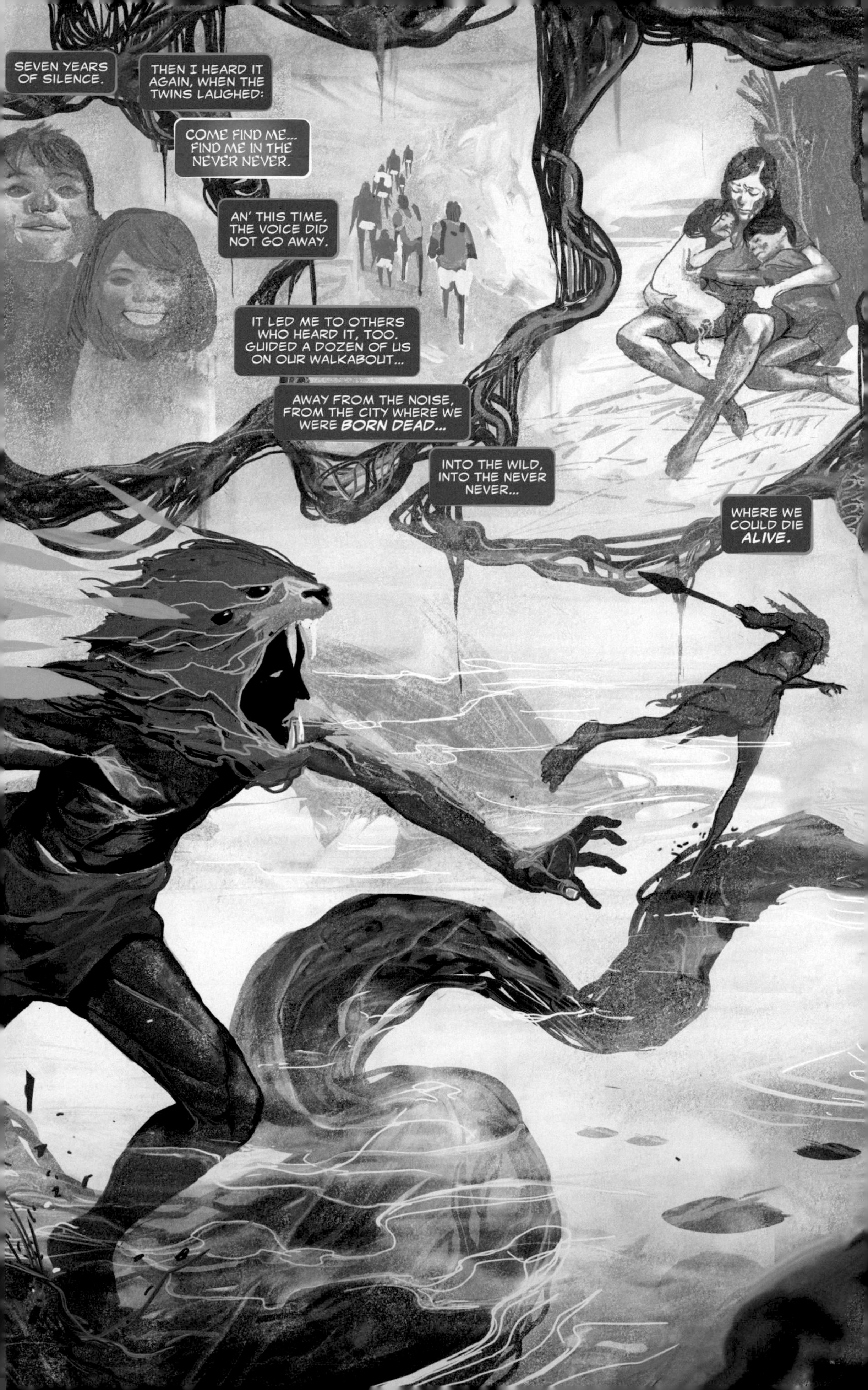
SEVEN YEARS OF SILENCE.
THEN I HEARD IT AGAIN, WHEN THE TWINS LAUGHED:
COME FIND ME... FIND ME IN THE NEVER NEVER.
AN' THIS TIME, THE VOICE DID NOT GO AWAY.
IT LED ME TO OTHERS WHO HEARD IT, TOO. GUIDED A DOZEN OF US ON OUR WALKABOUT...
AWAY FROM THE NOISE, FROM THE CITY WHERE WE WERE BORN DEAD...
INTO THE WILD, INTO THE NEVER NEVER...
WHERE WE COULD DIE ALIVE.

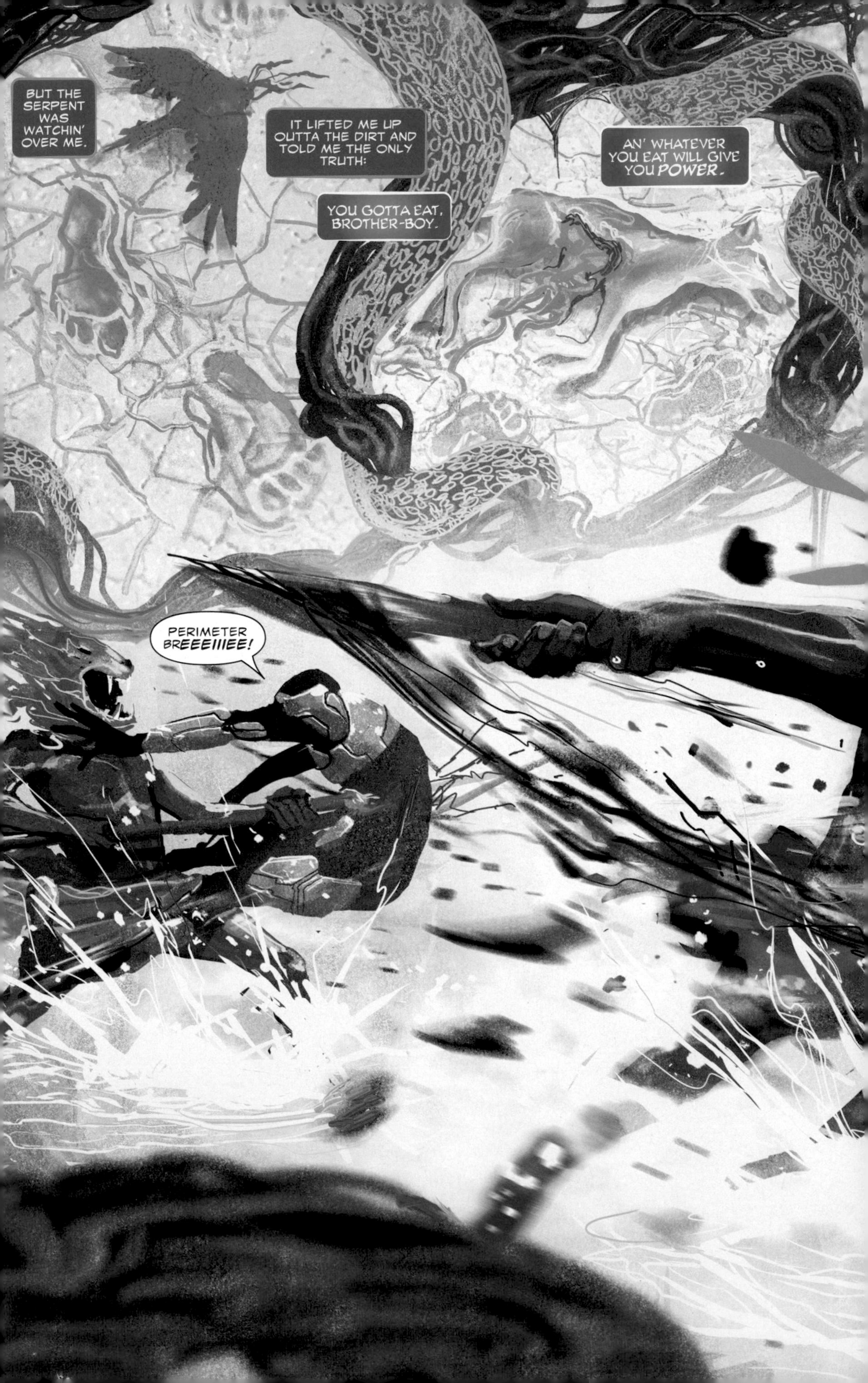
BUT THE SERPENT WAS WATCHIN' OVER ME.
IT LIFTED ME UP OUTTA THE DIRT AND TOLD ME THE ONLY TRUTH:
YOU GOTTA EAT, BROTHER-BOY.
AN' WHATEVER YOU EAT WILL GIVE YOU POWER.
PERIMETER BREEEIIIEE!

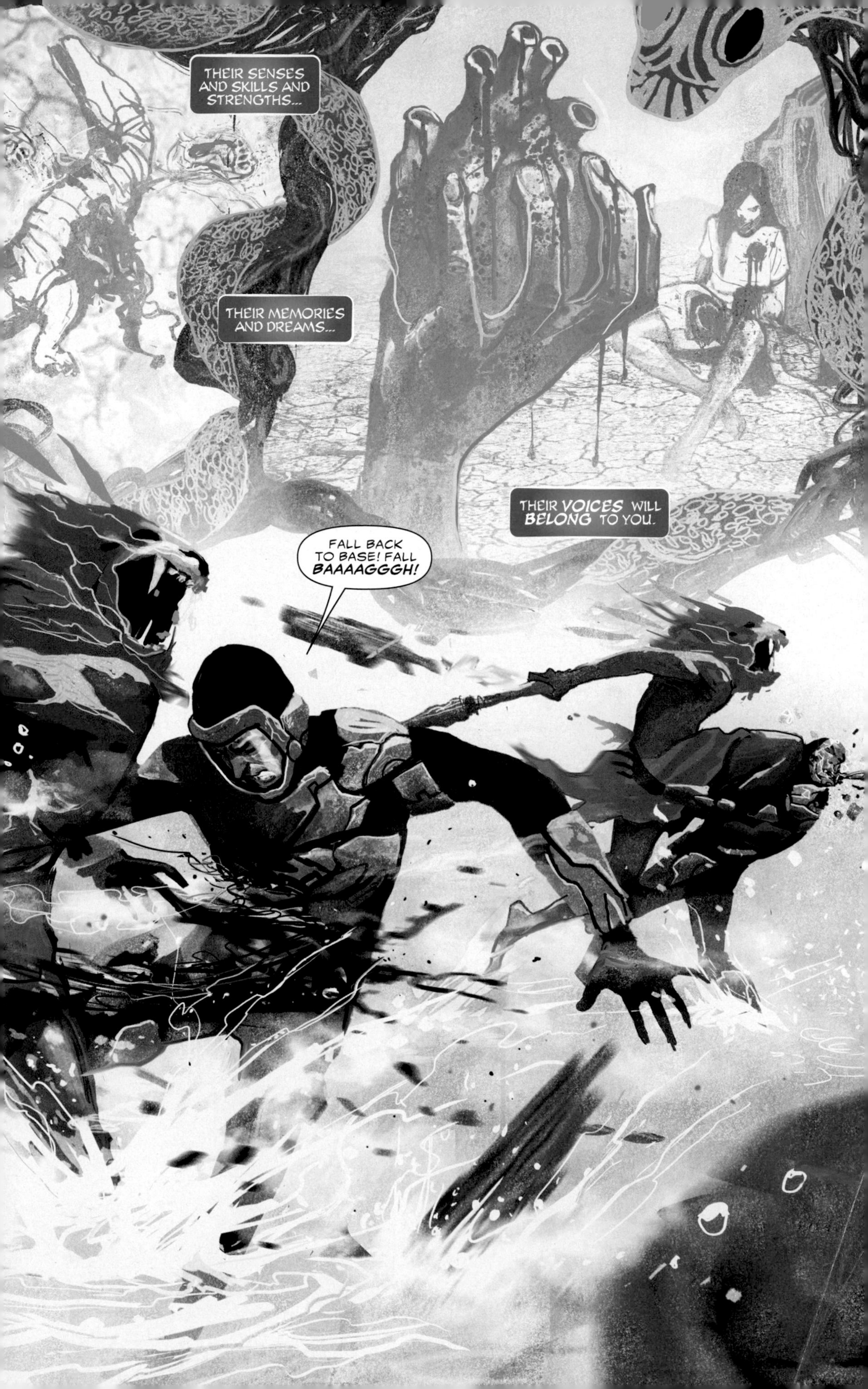
THEIR SENSES AND SKILLS AND STRENGTHS...
THEIR MEMORIES AND DREAMS...
THEIR VOICES WILL BELONG TO YOU.
FALL BACK TO BASE! FALL BAAAAGGGH!

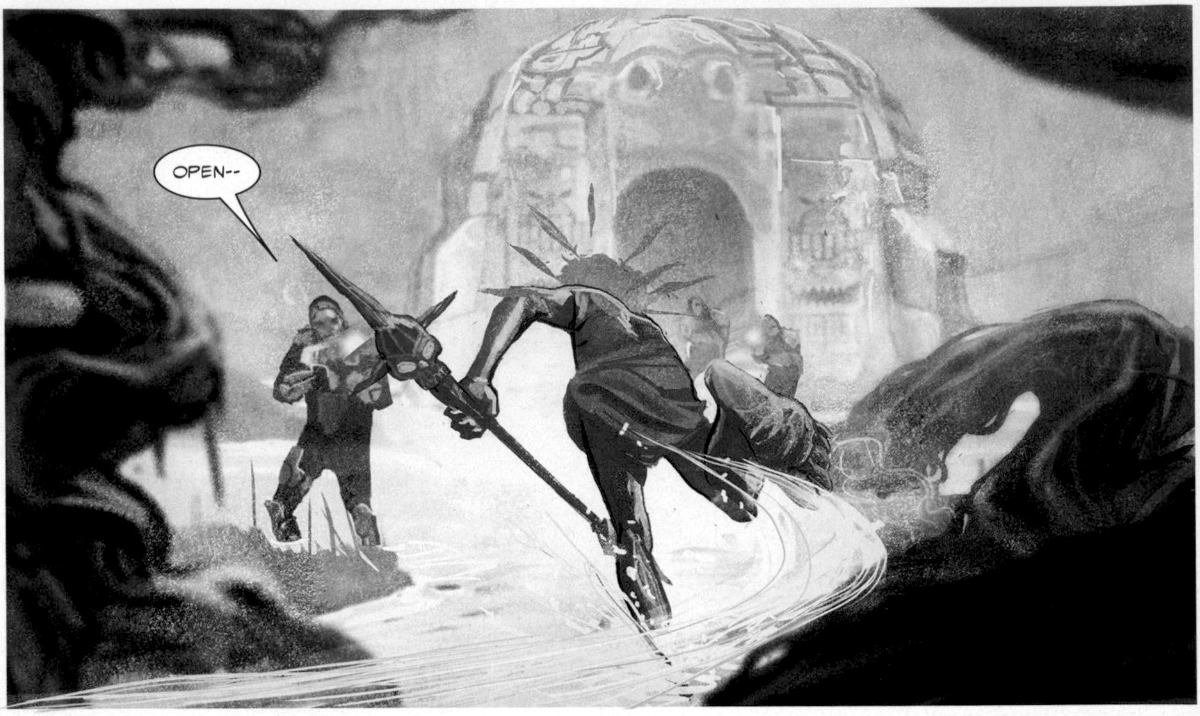
OPEN--
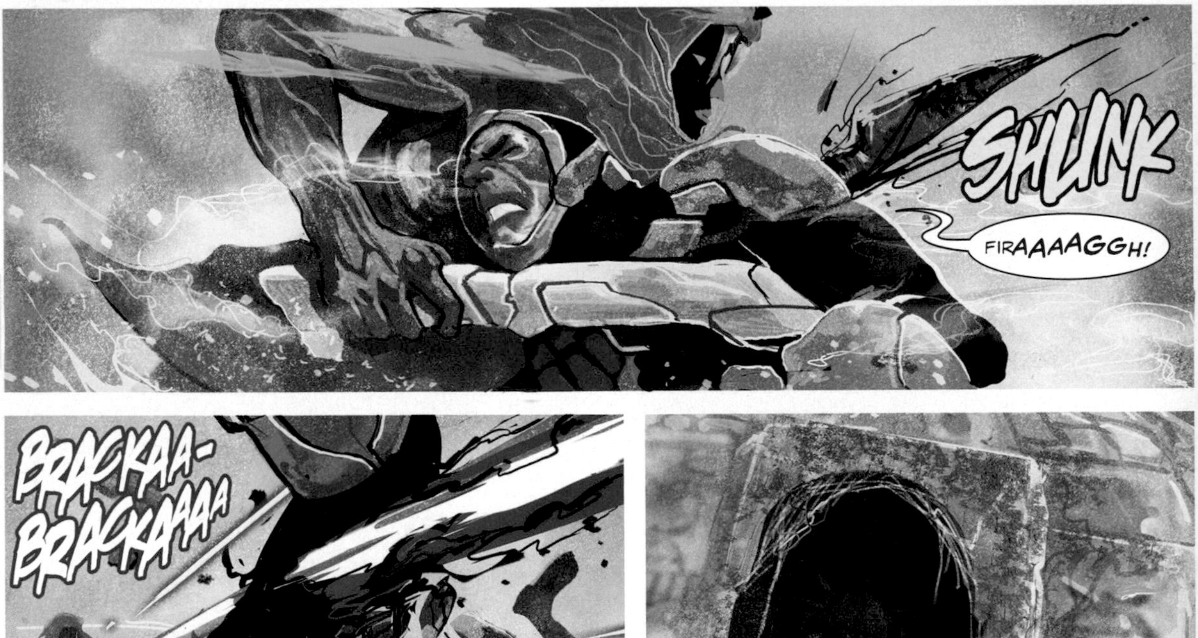
SHUNK
FIRAAAAGGH!
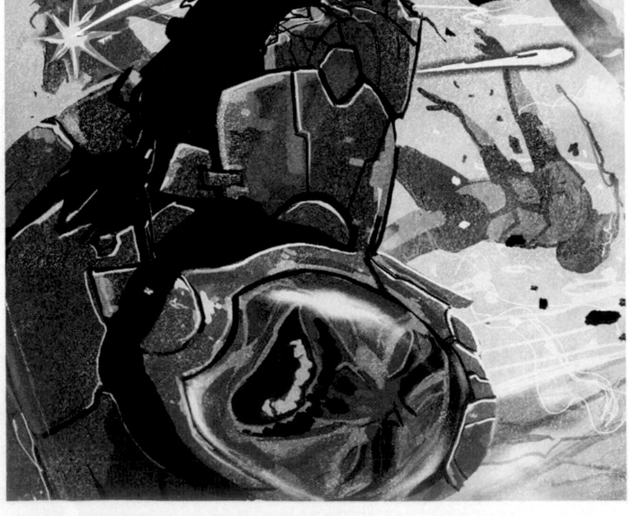
BRACKAA-
BRACKAAAA
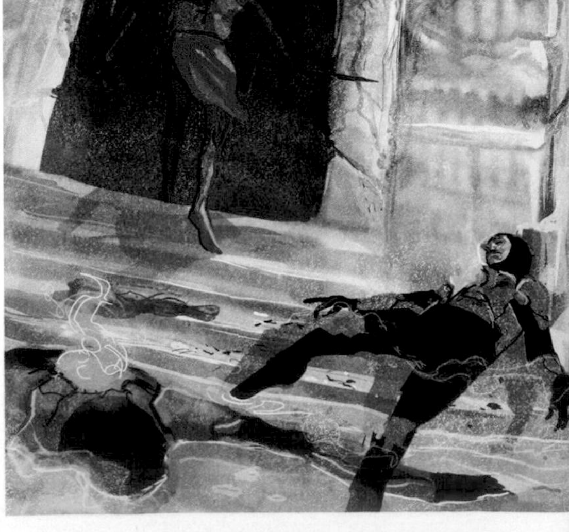

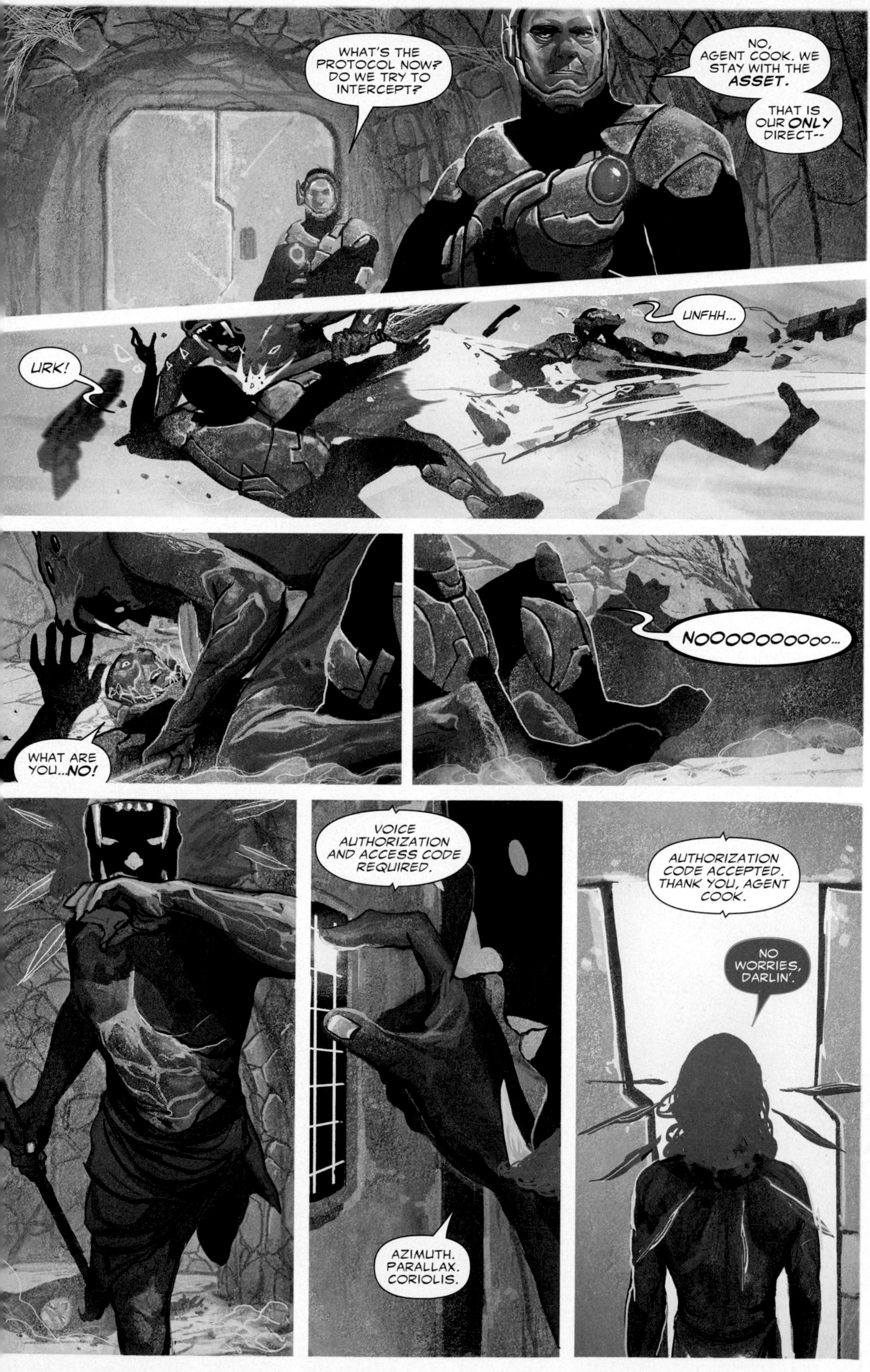
WHAT'S THE PROTOCOL NOW? DO WE TRY TO INTERCEPT?
NO, AGENT COOK. WE STAY WITH THE ASSET.
THAT IS OUR ONLY DIRECT--
URK!
UNFHH...
WHAT ARE YOU...NO!
NOOOOOOOOOO...
VOICE AUTHORIZATION AND ACCESS CODE REQUIRED.
AZIMUTH. PARALLAX. CORIOLIS.
AUTHORIZATION CODE ACCEPTED. THANK YOU, AGENT COOK.
NO WORRIES, DARLIN'.

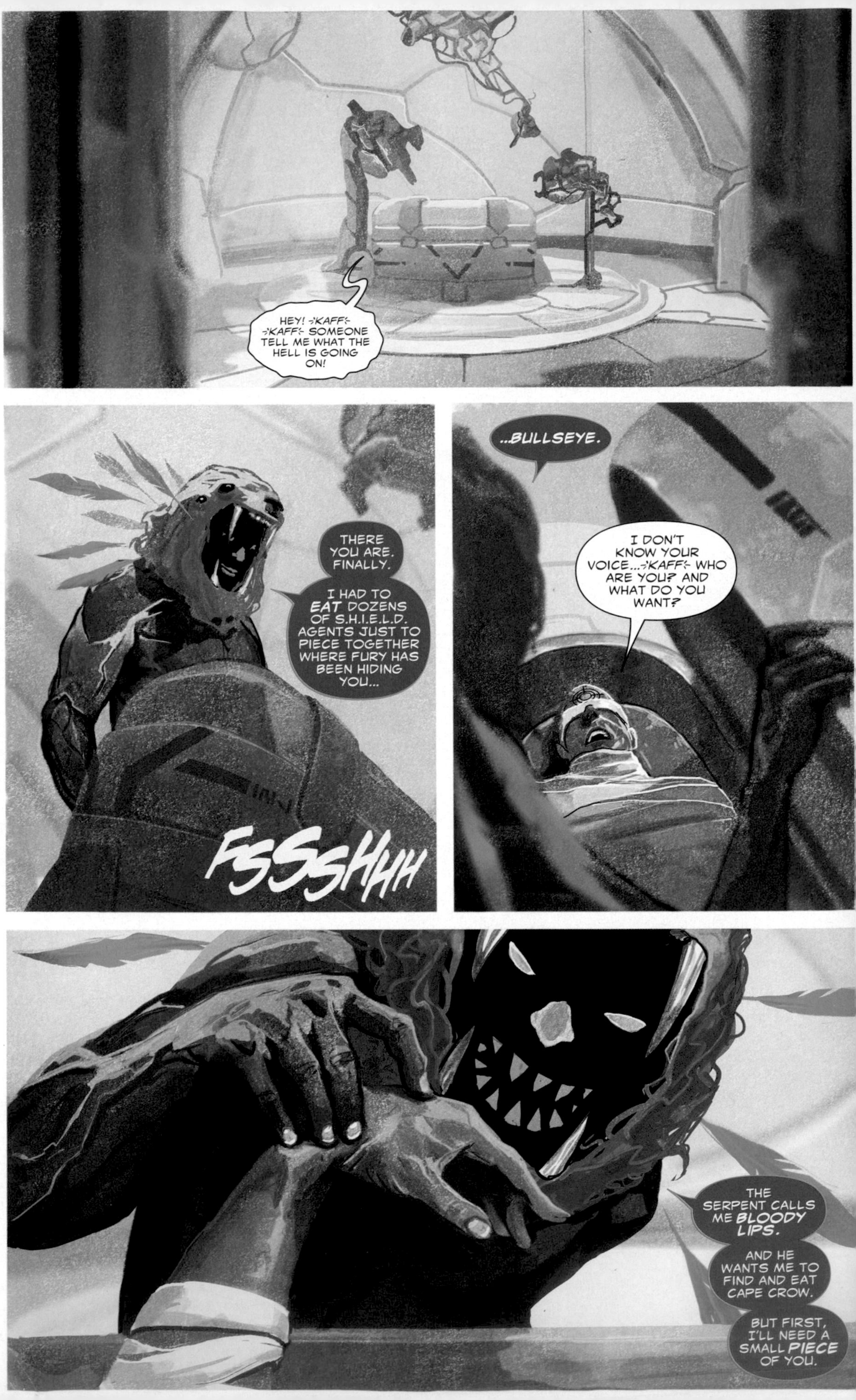
HEY! -KAFF- -KAFF- SOMEONE TELL ME WHAT THE HELL IS GOING ON!
THERE YOU ARE. FINALLY.
I HAD TO EAT DOZENS OF S.H.I.E.L.D. AGENTS JUST TO PIECE TOGETHER WHERE FURY HAS BEEN HIDING YOU...
FSSSHHH
...BULLSEYE.
I DON'T KNOW YOUR VOICE... -KAFF- WHO ARE YOU? AND WHAT DO YOU WANT?
THE SERPENT CALLS ME BLOODY LIPS.
AND HE WANTS ME TO FIND AND EAT CAPE CROW.
BUT FIRST, I'LL NEED A SMALL PIECE OF YOU.

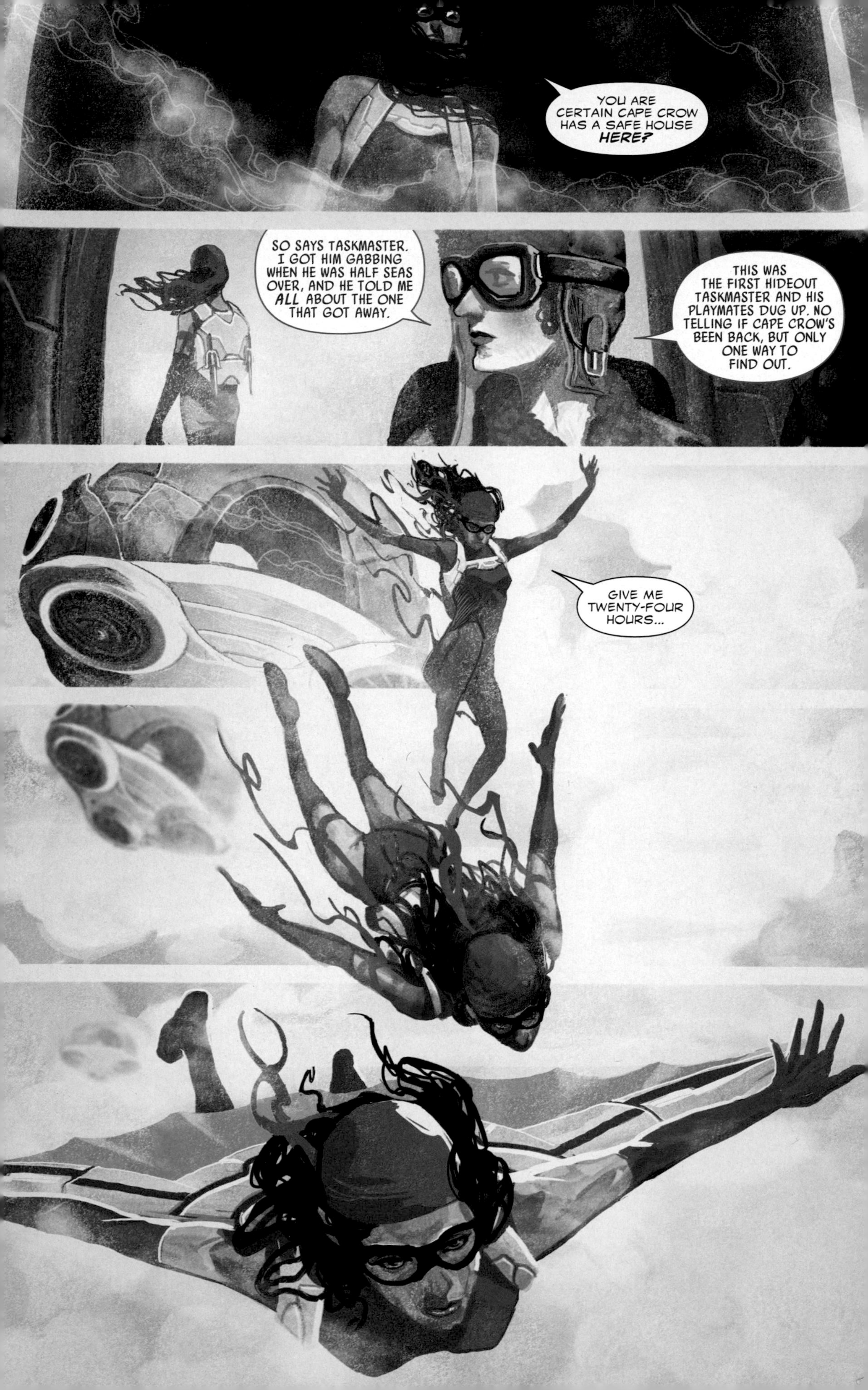
YOU ARE CERTAIN CAPE CROW HAS A SAFE HOUSE HERE?
SO SAYS TASKMASTER. I GOT HIM GABBING WHEN HE WAS HALF SEAS OVER, AND HE TOLD ME ALL ABOUT THE ONE THAT GOT AWAY.
THIS WAS THE FIRST HIDEOUT TASKMASTER AND HIS PLAYMATES DUG UP. NO TELLING IF CAPE CROW'S BEEN BACK, BUT ONLY ONE WAY TO FIND OUT.
GIVE ME TWENTY-FOUR HOURS...

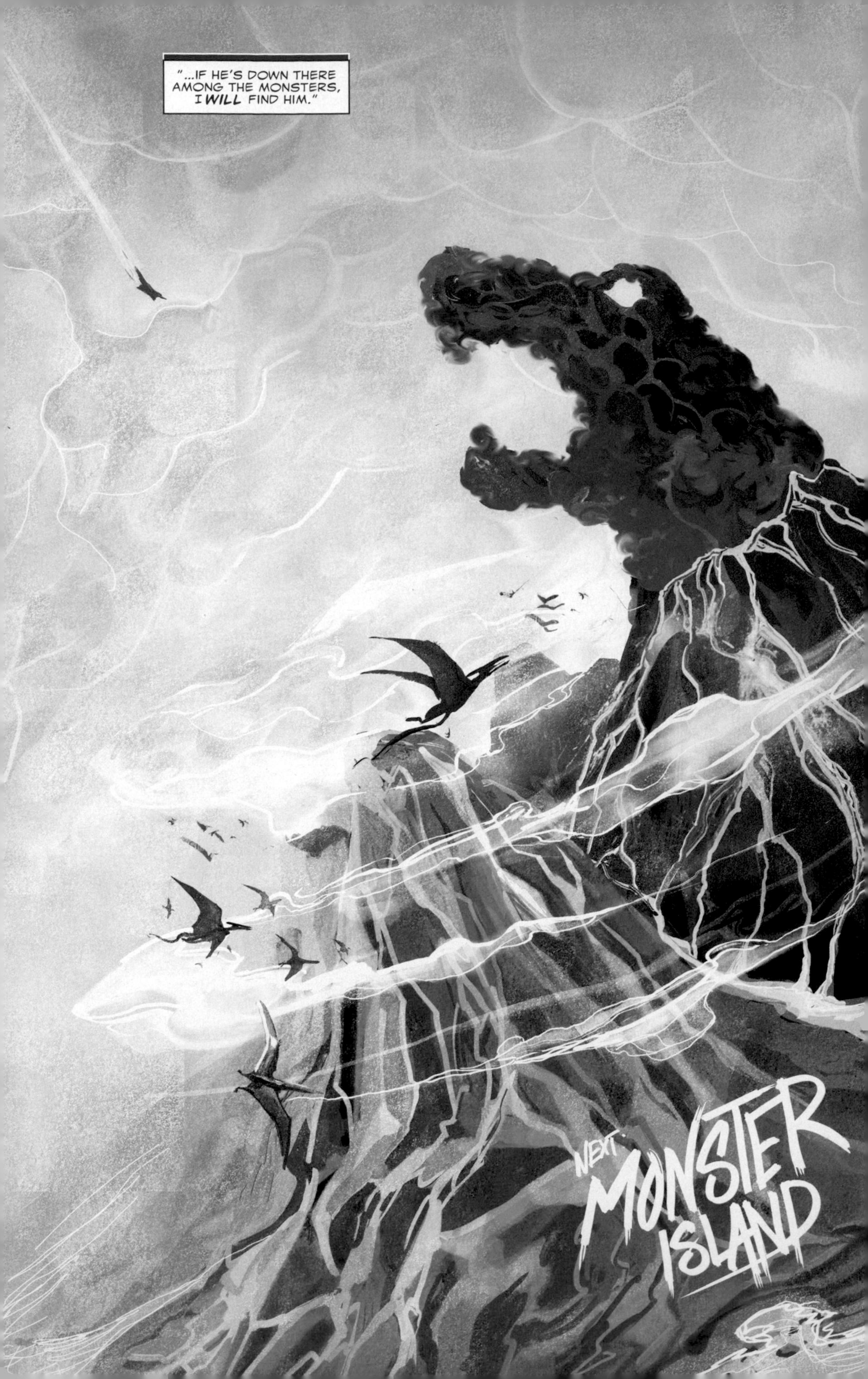
"...IF HE'S DOWN THERE AMONG THE MONSTERS, I **WILL** FIND HIM."
NEXT: MONSTER ISLAND

#1 VARIANT
BY PAOLO RIVERA

#1 VARIANT
BY SKOTTIE YOUNG

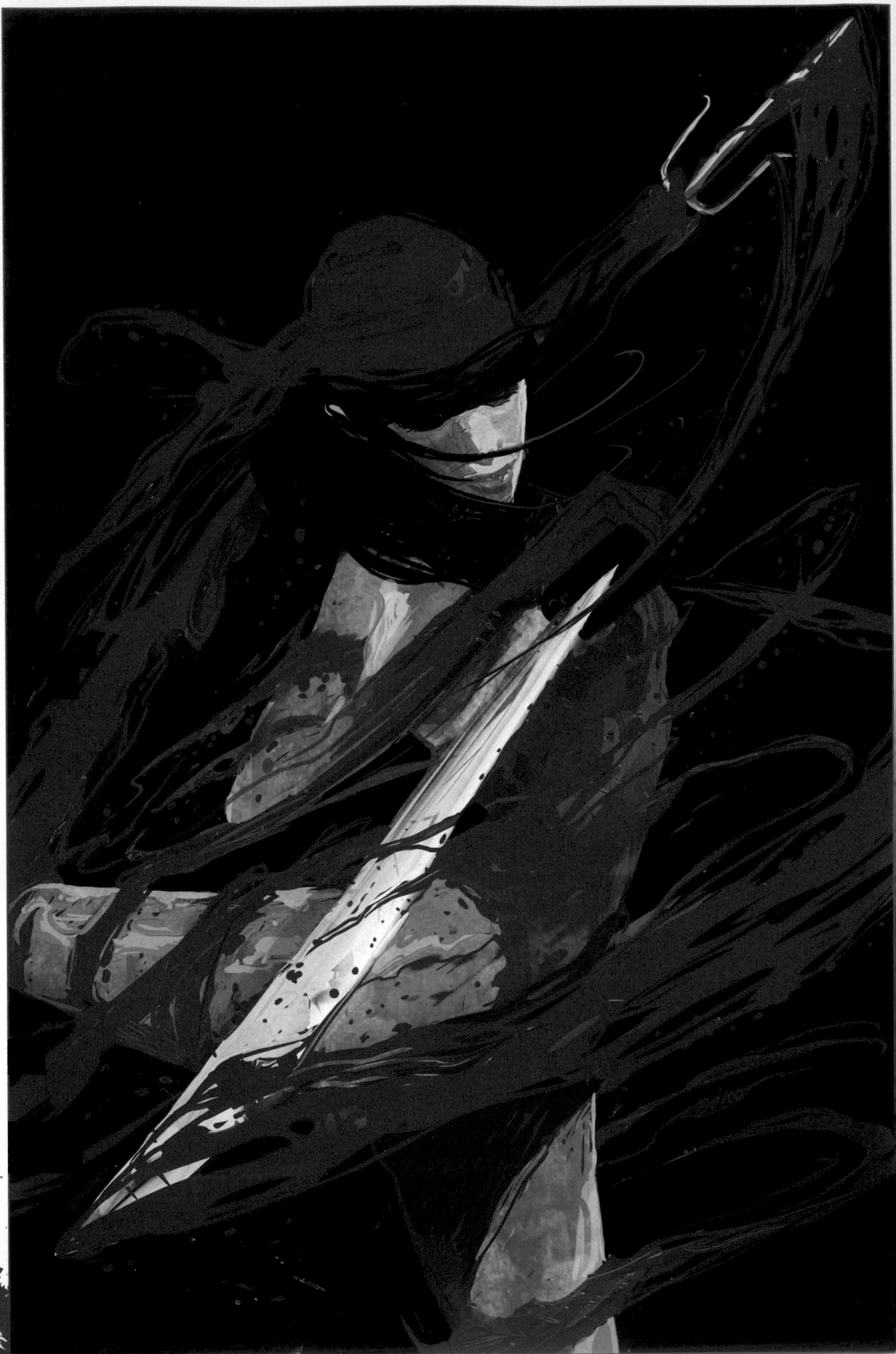

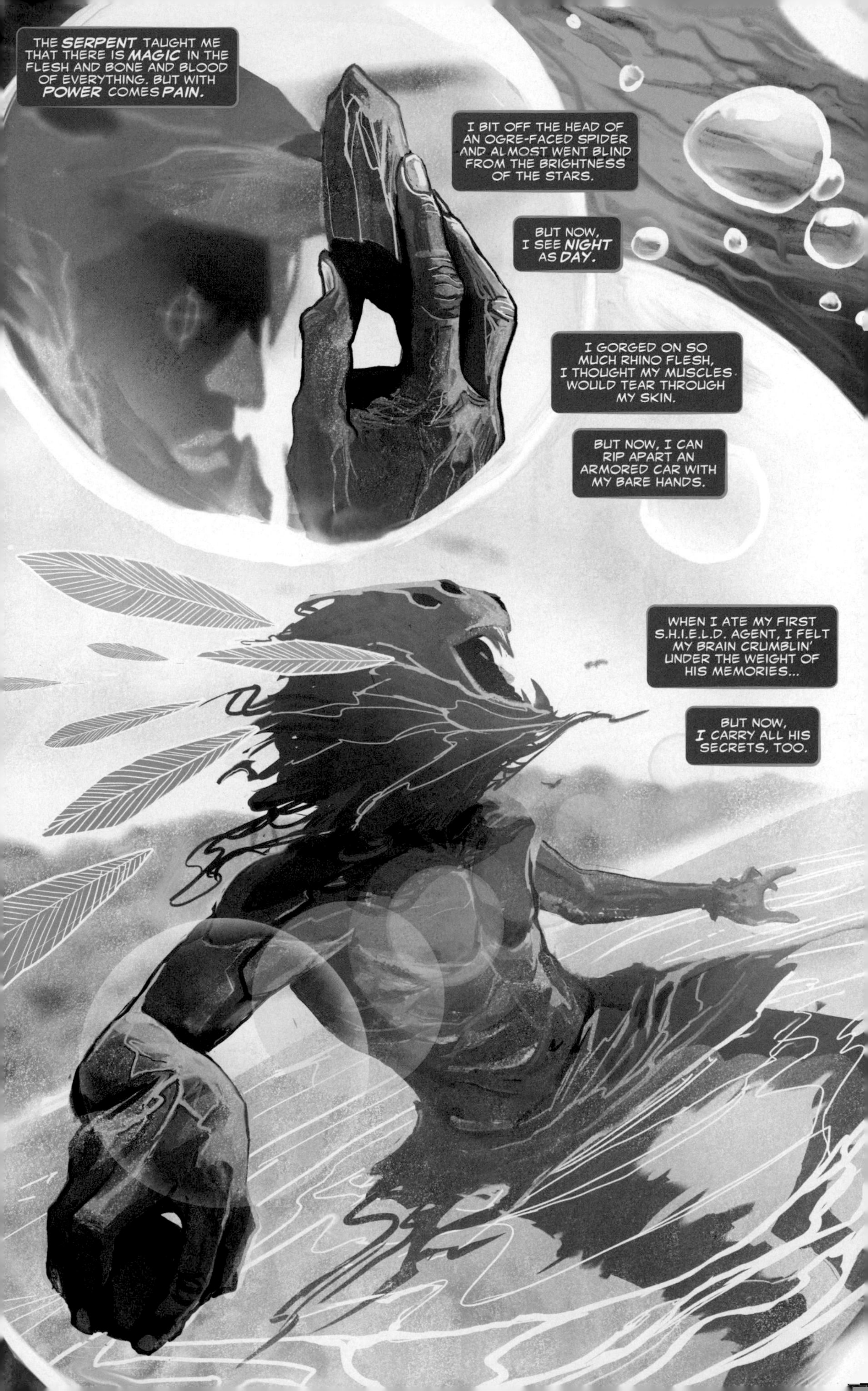
THE SERPENT TAUGHT ME THAT THERE IS MAGIC IN THE FLESH AND BONE AND BLOOD OF EVERYTHING. BUT WITH POWER COMES PAIN.
I BIT OFF THE HEAD OF AN OGRE-FACED SPIDER AND ALMOST WENT BLIND FROM THE BRIGHTNESS OF THE STARS.
BUT NOW, I SEE NIGHT AS DAY.
I GORGED ON SO MUCH RHINO FLESH, I THOUGHT MY MUSCLES WOULD TEAR THROUGH MY SKIN.
BUT NOW, I CAN RIP APART AN ARMORED CAR WITH MY BARE HANDS.
WHEN I ATE MY FIRST S.H.I.E.L.D. AGENT, I FELT MY BRAIN CRUMBLIN' UNDER THE WEIGHT OF HIS MEMORIES...
BUT NOW, I CARRY ALL HIS SECRETS, TOO.

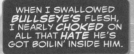

WHEN I SWALLOWED *BULLSEYE'S* FLESH, I NEARLY *CHOKED* ON ALL THAT *HATE* HE'S GOT BOILIN' INSIDE HIM.

BUT NOW? ANYTHIN' I TOUCH FEELS LIKE *A WEAPON.* I CAN SEE THE FLIGHT PATH OF EVERYTHIN' I THROW EVEN BEFORE I'VE THROWN IT.

MY HEAD IS A MASTER CLASS IN MURDER, WITH INSTANT REPLAYS OF A THOUSAND KILLS.

AND MOST IMPORTANT OF ALL, THERE IN THE WAY BACK OF BULLSEYE'S BRAIN, BURIED UNDER AN AVALANCHE OF *SHAME,* ARE THE MEMORIES OF THE ONE WHO GOT AWAY.

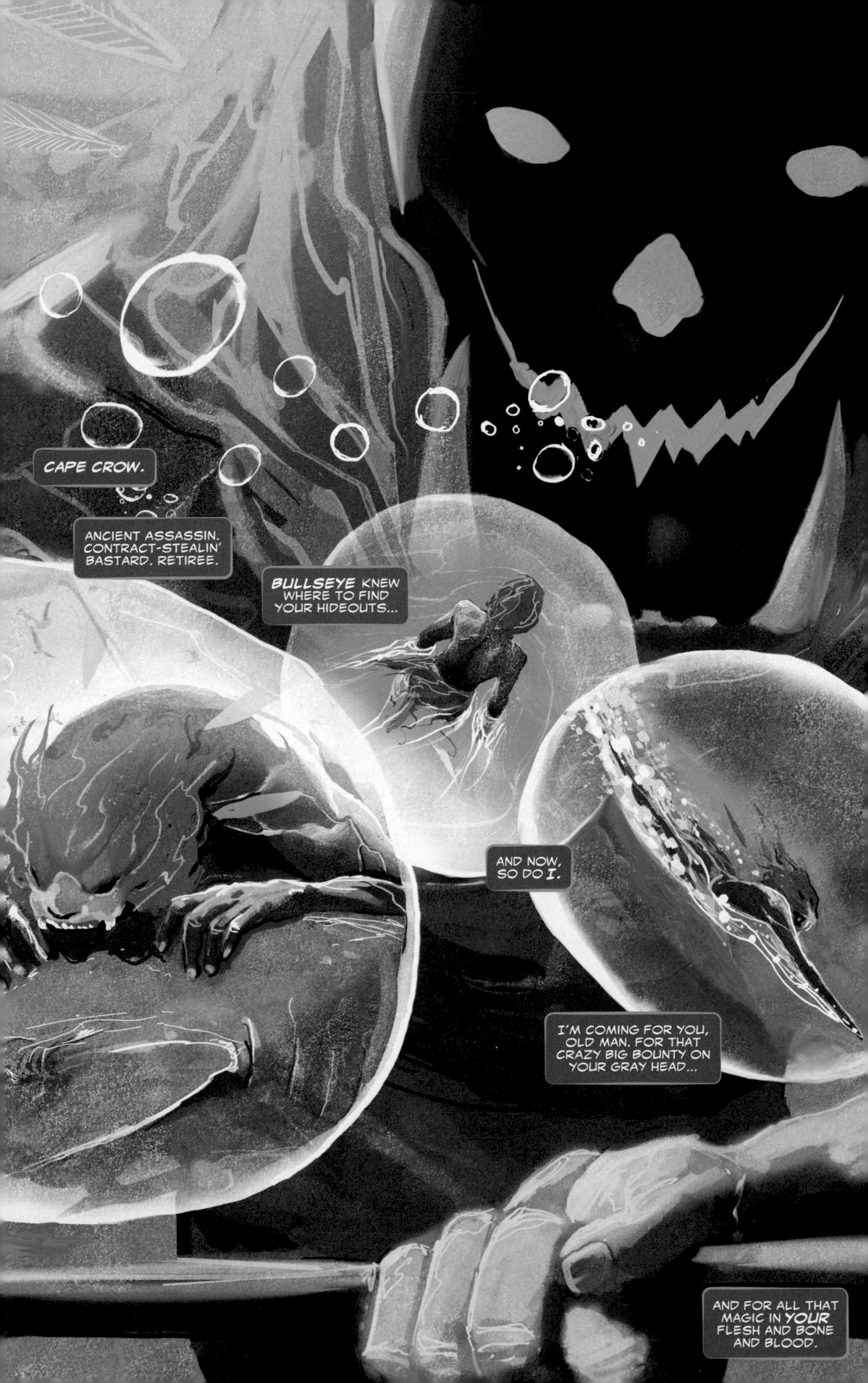
CAPE CROW.
ANCIENT ASSASSIN. CONTRACT-STEALIN' BASTARD. RETIREE.
BULLSEYE KNEW WHERE TO FIND YOUR HIDEOUTS...
AND NOW, SO DO I.
I'M COMING FOR YOU, OLD MAN. FOR THAT CRAZY BIG BOUNTY ON YOUR GRAY HEAD...
AND FOR ALL THAT MAGIC IN YOUR FLESH AND BONE AND BLOOD.

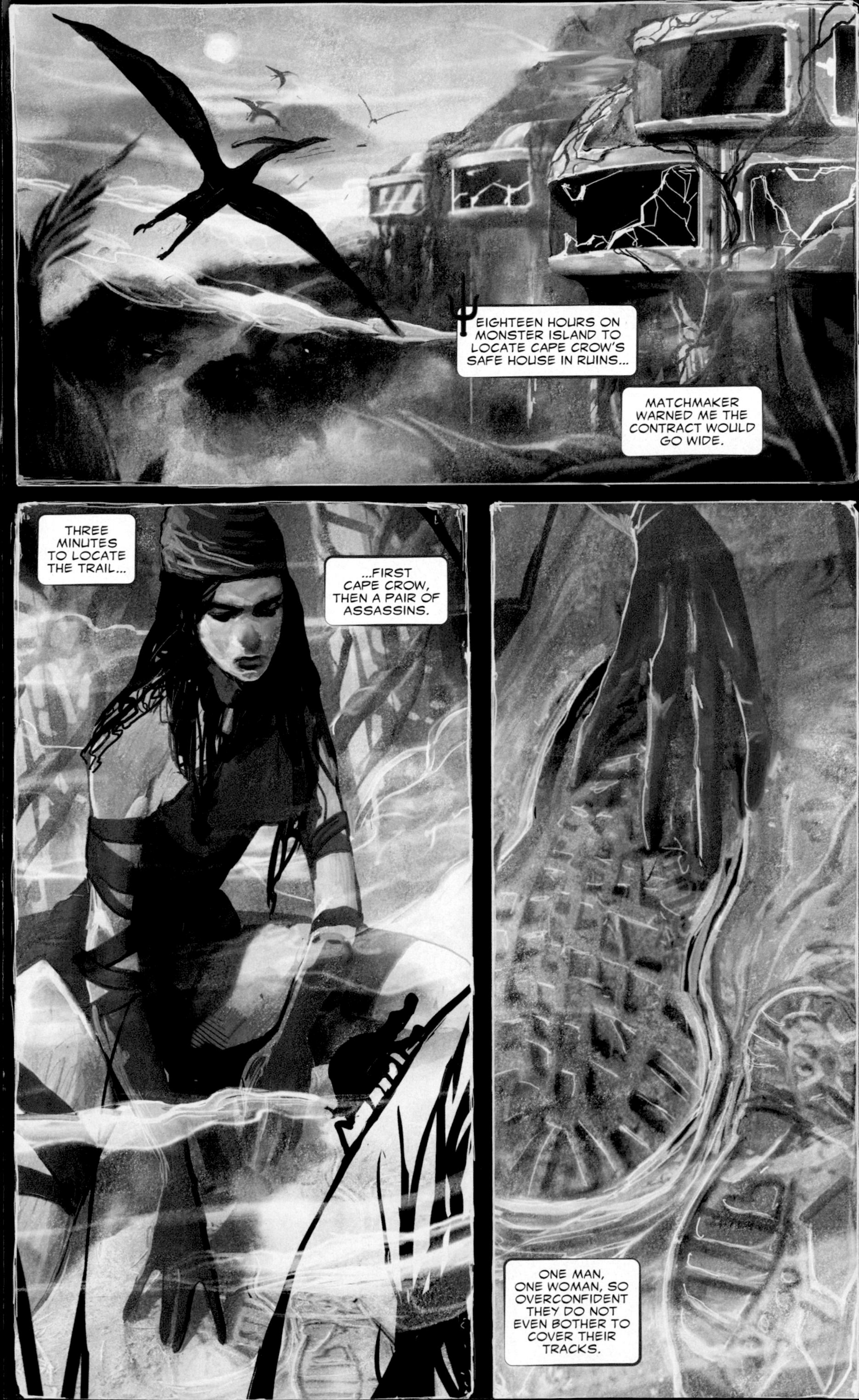
EIGHTEEN HOURS ON MONSTER ISLAND TO LOCATE CAPE CROW'S SAFE HOUSE IN RUINS...
MATCHMAKER WARNED ME THE CONTRACT WOULD GO WIDE.
THREE MINUTES TO LOCATE THE TRAIL...
...FIRST CAPE CROW, THEN A PAIR OF ASSASSINS.
ONE MAN, ONE WOMAN, SO OVERCONFIDENT THEY DO NOT EVEN BOTHER TO COVER THEIR TRACKS.

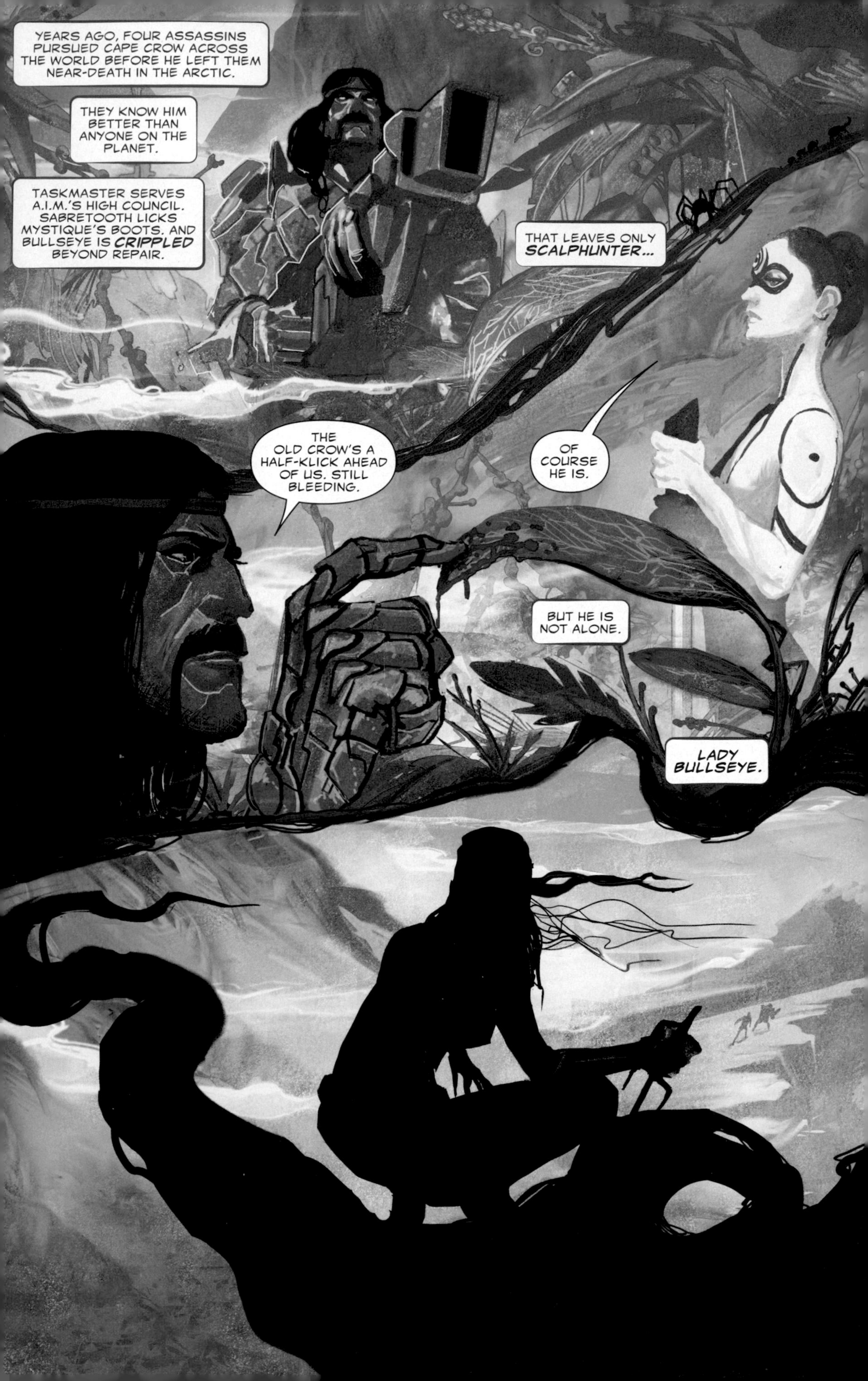
YEARS AGO, FOUR ASSASSINS PURSUED CAPE CROW ACROSS THE WORLD BEFORE HE LEFT THEM NEAR-DEATH IN THE ARCTIC.
THEY KNOW HIM BETTER THAN ANYONE ON THE PLANET.
TASKMASTER SERVES A.I.M.'S HIGH COUNCIL. SABRETOOTH LICKS MYSTIQUE'S BOOTS. AND BULLSEYE IS CRIPPLED BEYOND REPAIR.
THAT LEAVES ONLY SCALPHUNTER...
THE OLD CROW'S A HALF-KLICK AHEAD OF US. STILL BLEEDING.
OF COURSE HE IS.
BUT HE IS NOT ALONE.
LADY BULLSEYE.

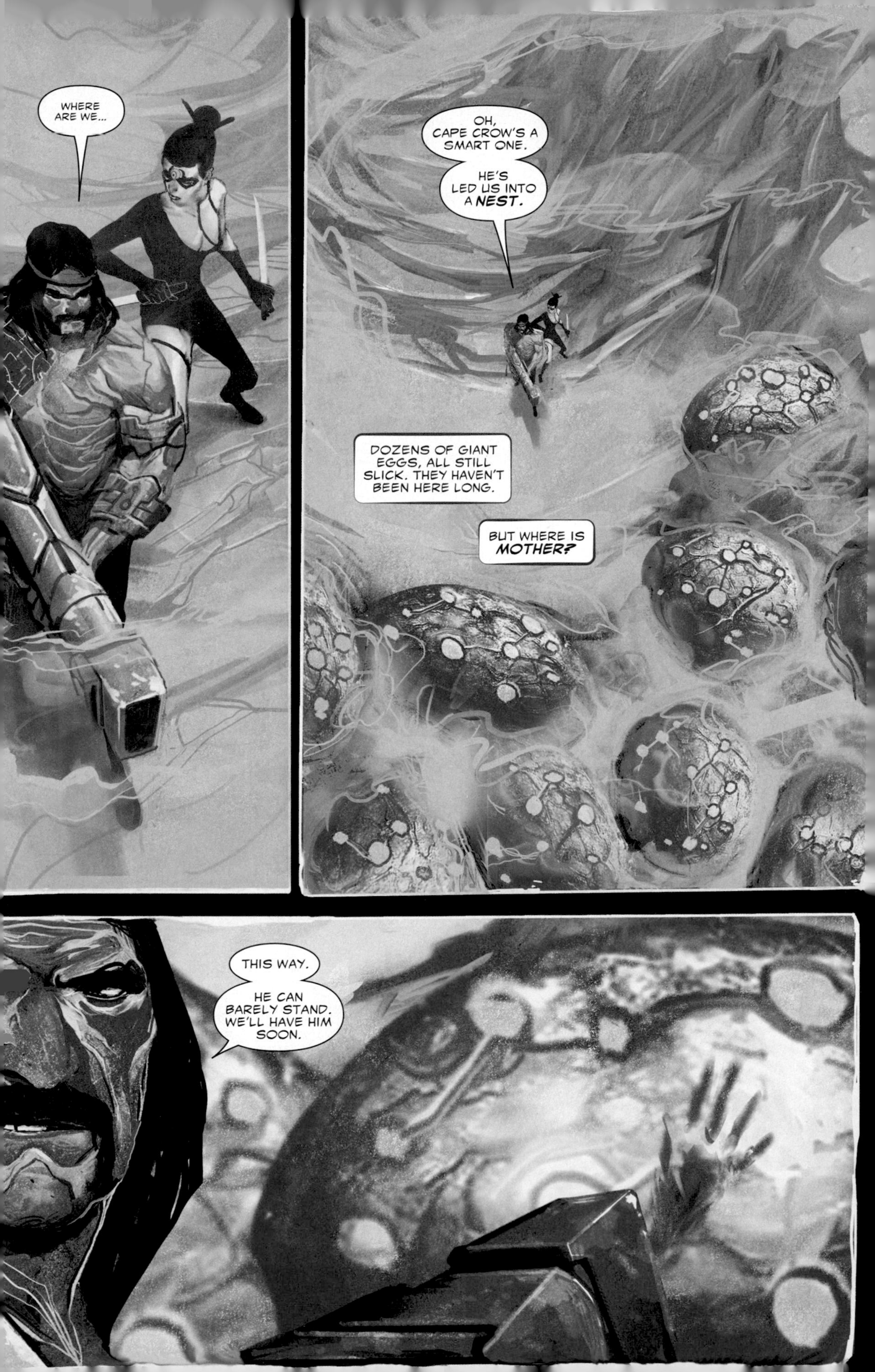
WHERE ARE WE...
OH, CAPE CROW'S A SMART ONE.
HE'S LED US INTO A NEST.
DOZENS OF GIANT EGGS, ALL STILL SLICK. THEY HAVEN'T BEEN HERE LONG.
BUT WHERE IS MOTHER?
THIS WAY.
HE CAN BARELY STAND. WE'LL HAVE HIM SOON.

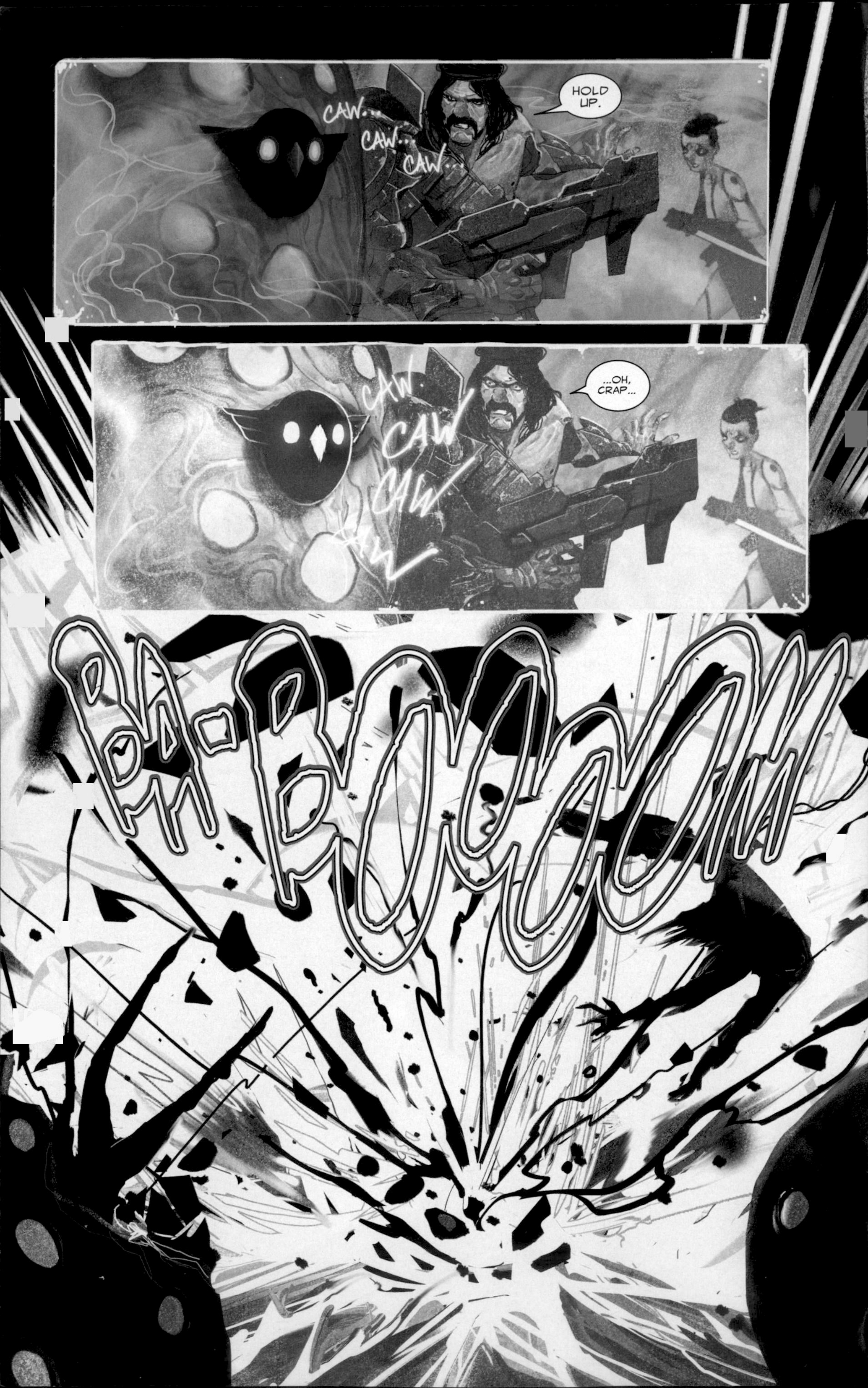
CAW... CAW... CAW...
HOLD UP.
CAW CAW CAW CAW
...OH, CRAP...
BA-BOOOOOM

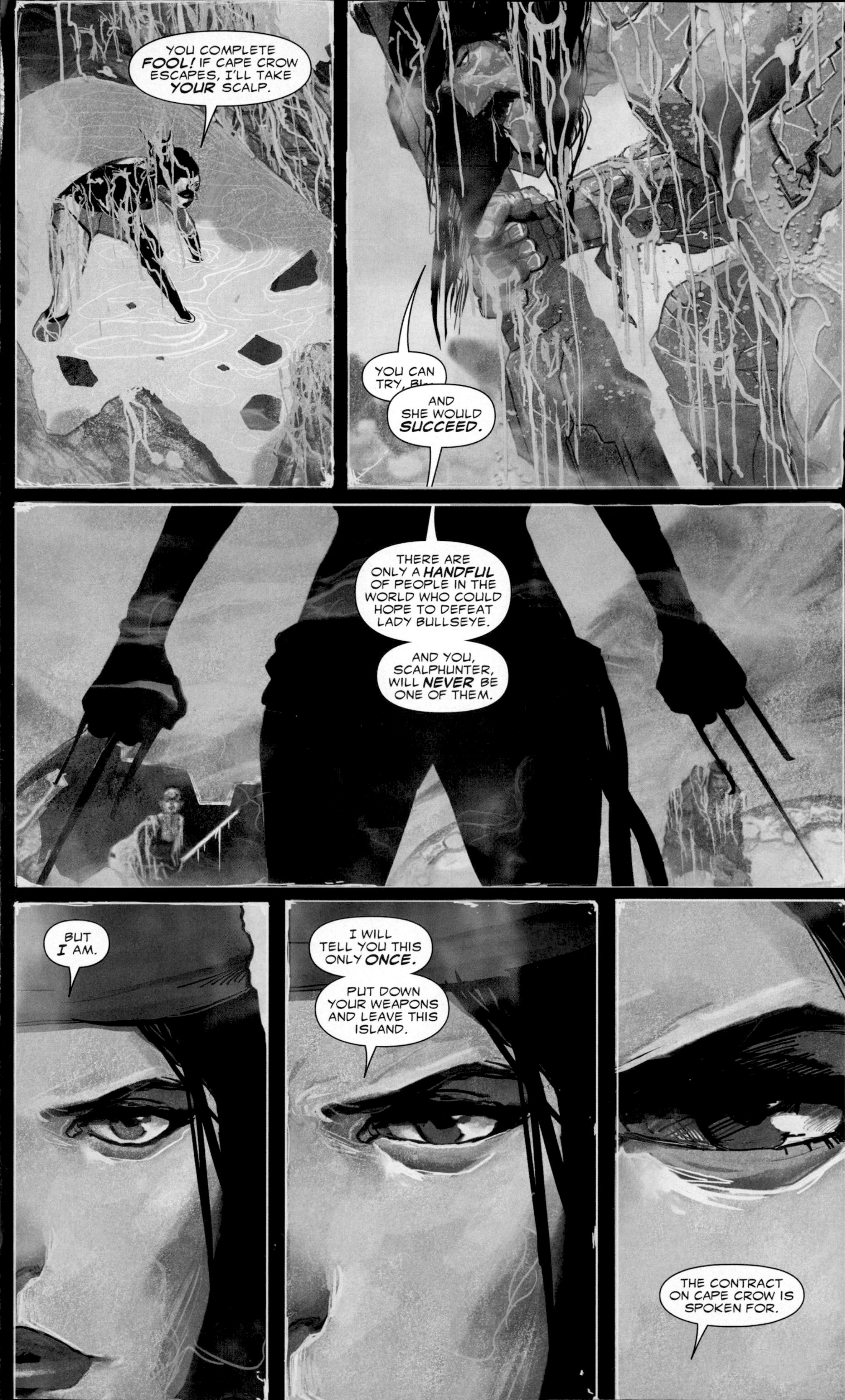
YOU COMPLETE FOOL! IF CAPE CROW ESCAPES, I'LL TAKE YOUR SCALP.
YOU CAN TRY, BL-
AND SHE WOULD SUCCEED.
THERE ARE ONLY A HANDFUL OF PEOPLE IN THE WORLD WHO COULD HOPE TO DEFEAT LADY BULLSEYE.
AND YOU, SCALPHUNTER, WILL NEVER BE ONE OF THEM.
BUT I AM.
I WILL TELL YOU THIS ONLY ONCE.
PUT DOWN YOUR WEAPONS AND LEAVE THIS ISLAND.
THE CONTRACT ON CAPE CROW IS SPOKEN FOR.

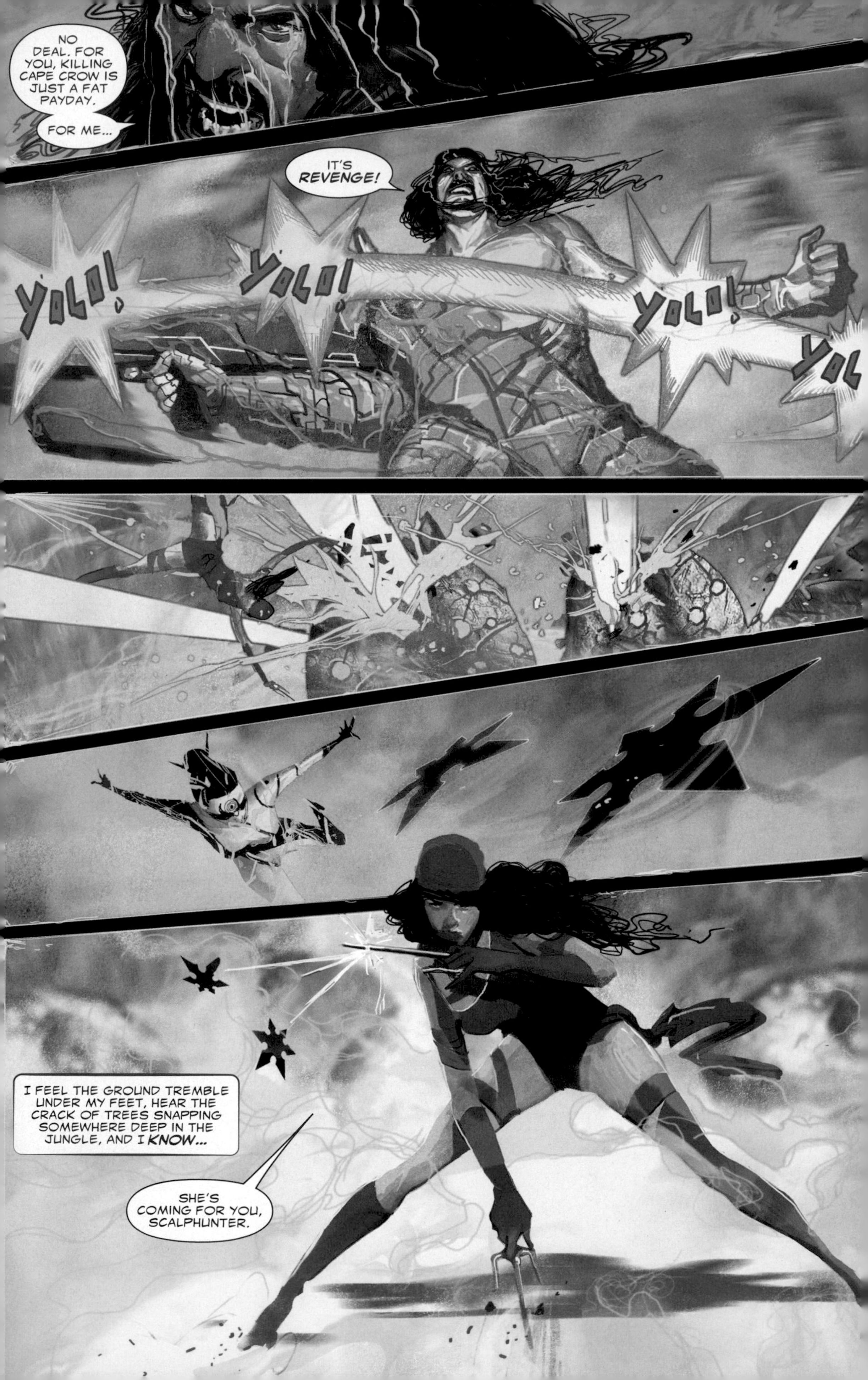
NO DEAL. FOR YOU, KILLING CAPE CROW IS JUST A FAT PAYDAY.
FOR ME...
IT'S REVENGE!
YOLO!
YOLO!
YOLO!
YOL
I FEEL THE GROUND TREMBLE UNDER MY FEET, HEAR THE CRACK OF TREES SNAPPING SOMEWHERE DEEP IN THE JUNGLE, AND I KNOW...
SHE'S COMING FOR YOU, SCALPHUNTER.

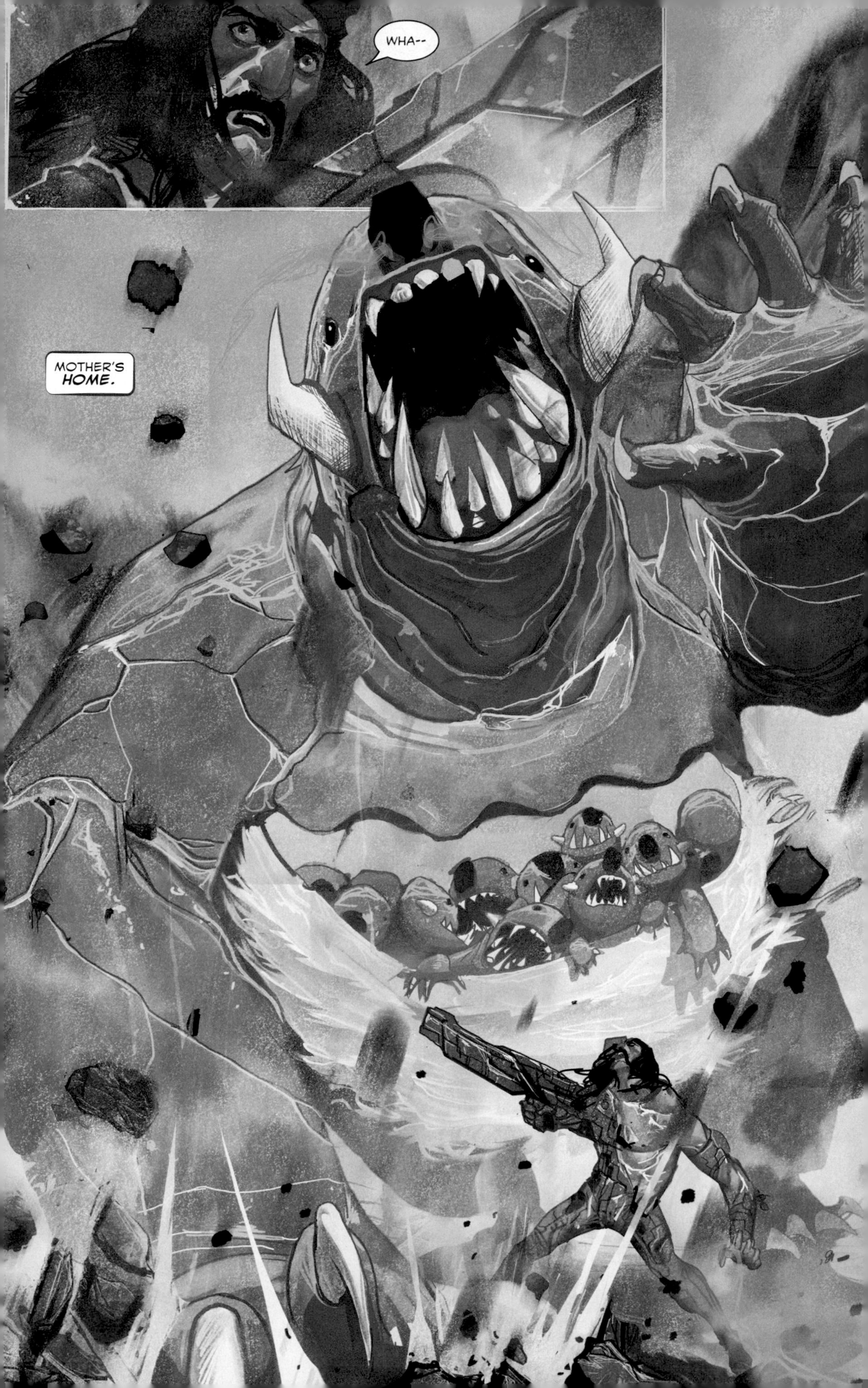
WHA--
MOTHER'S HOME.

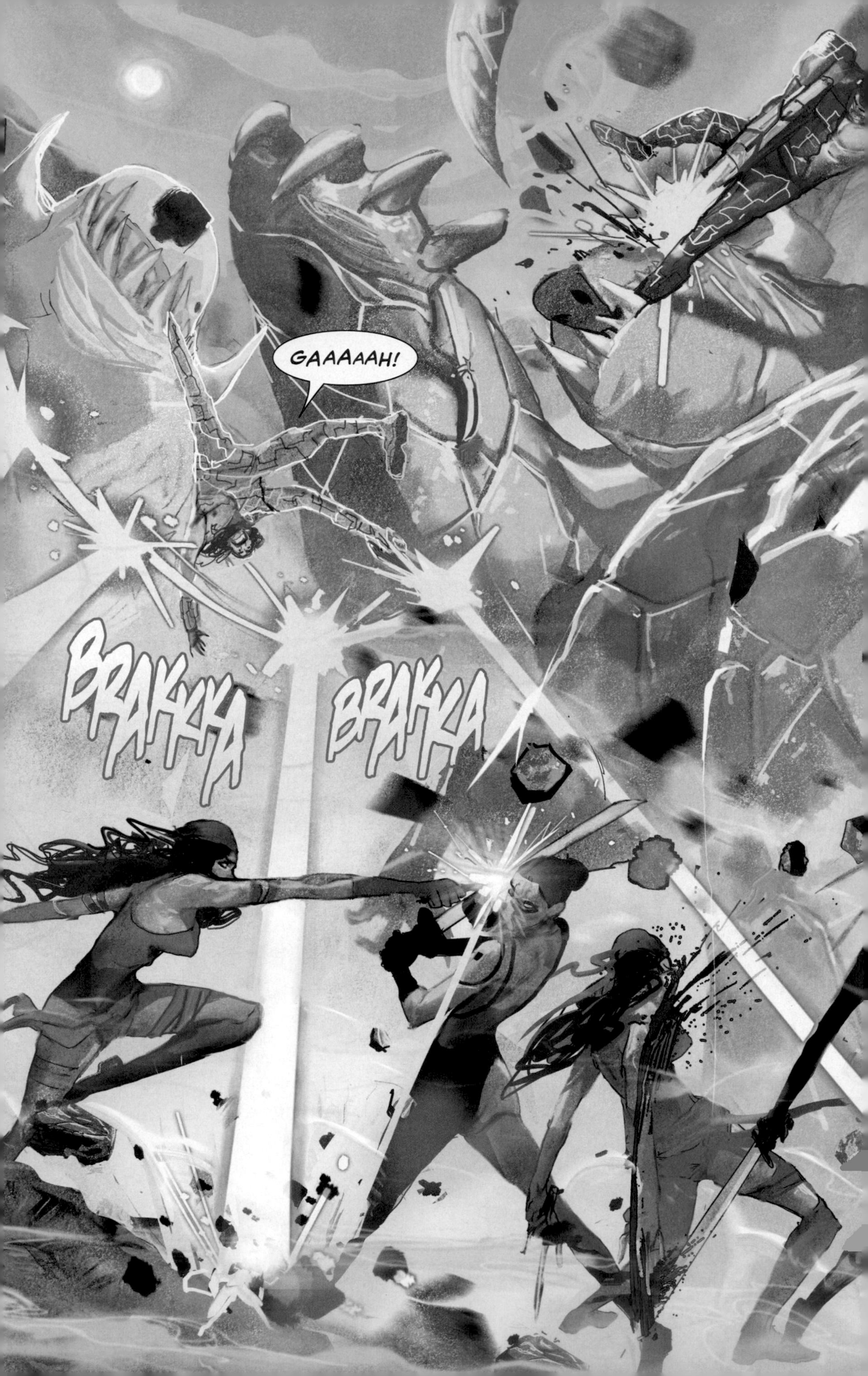
GAAAAAH!
BRAKKA
BRAKKA

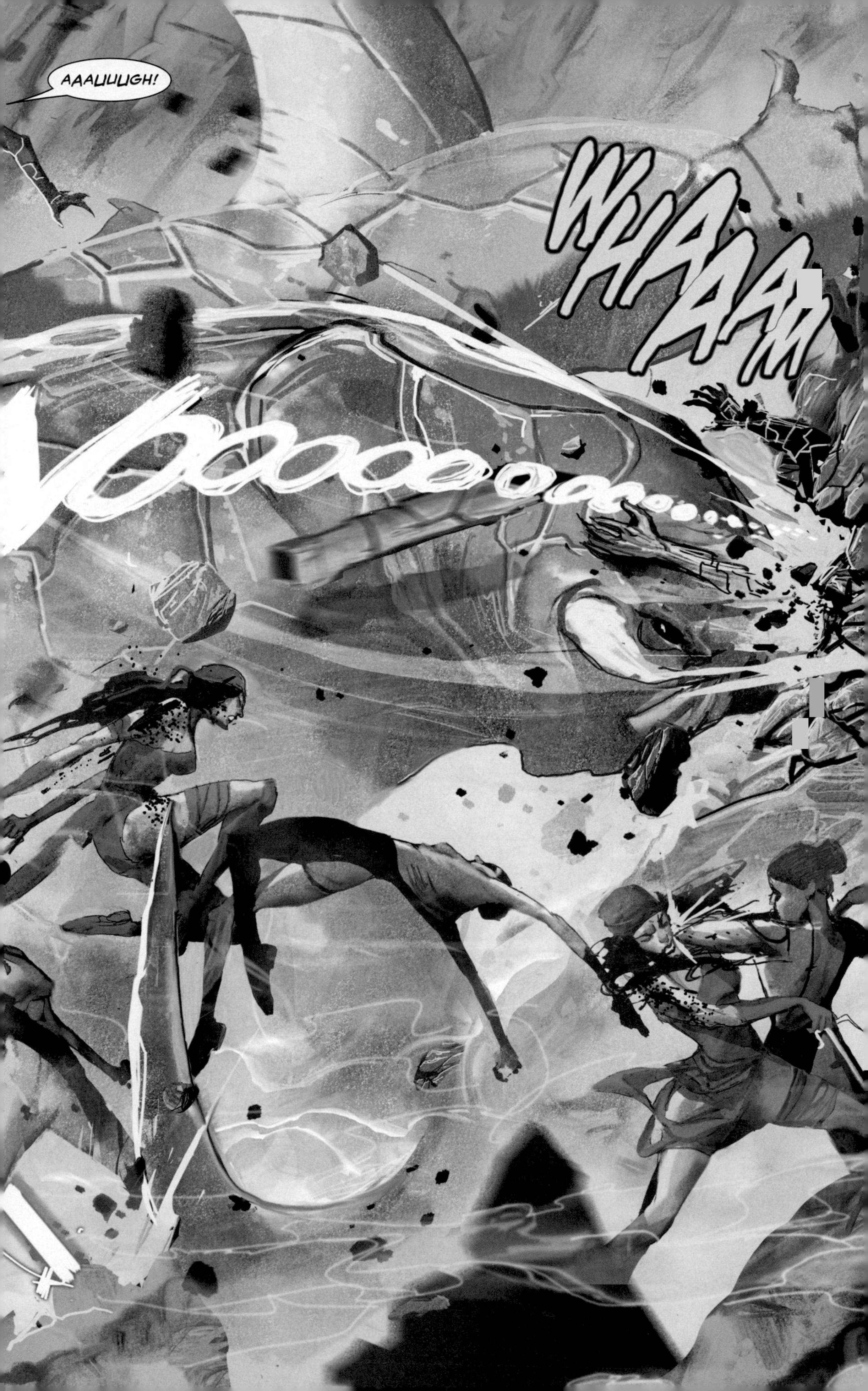
AAAUUUGH!
WHAAAM

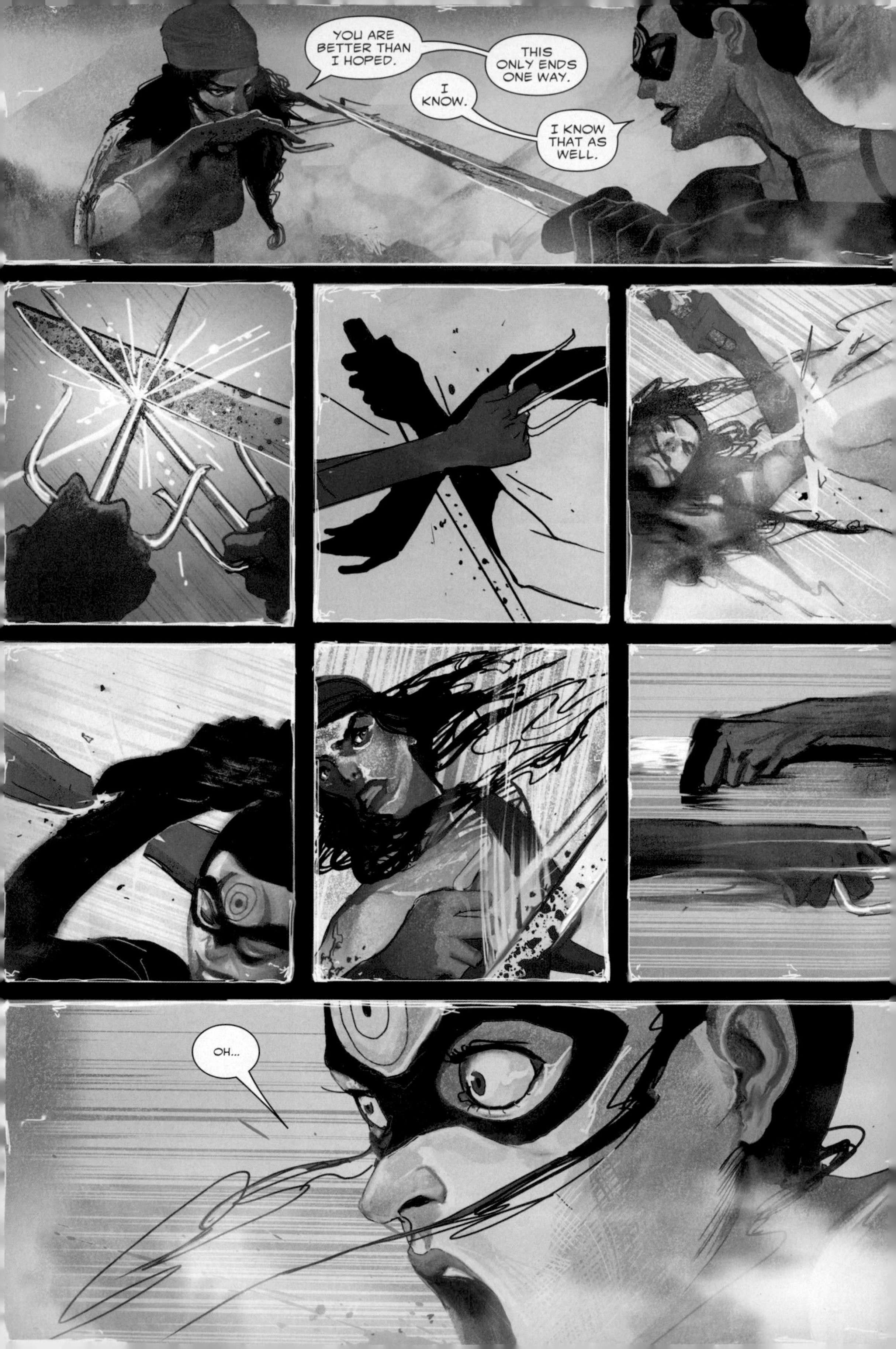
YOU ARE BETTER THAN I HOPED.
THIS ONLY ENDS ONE WAY.
I KNOW.
I KNOW THAT AS WELL.
OH...

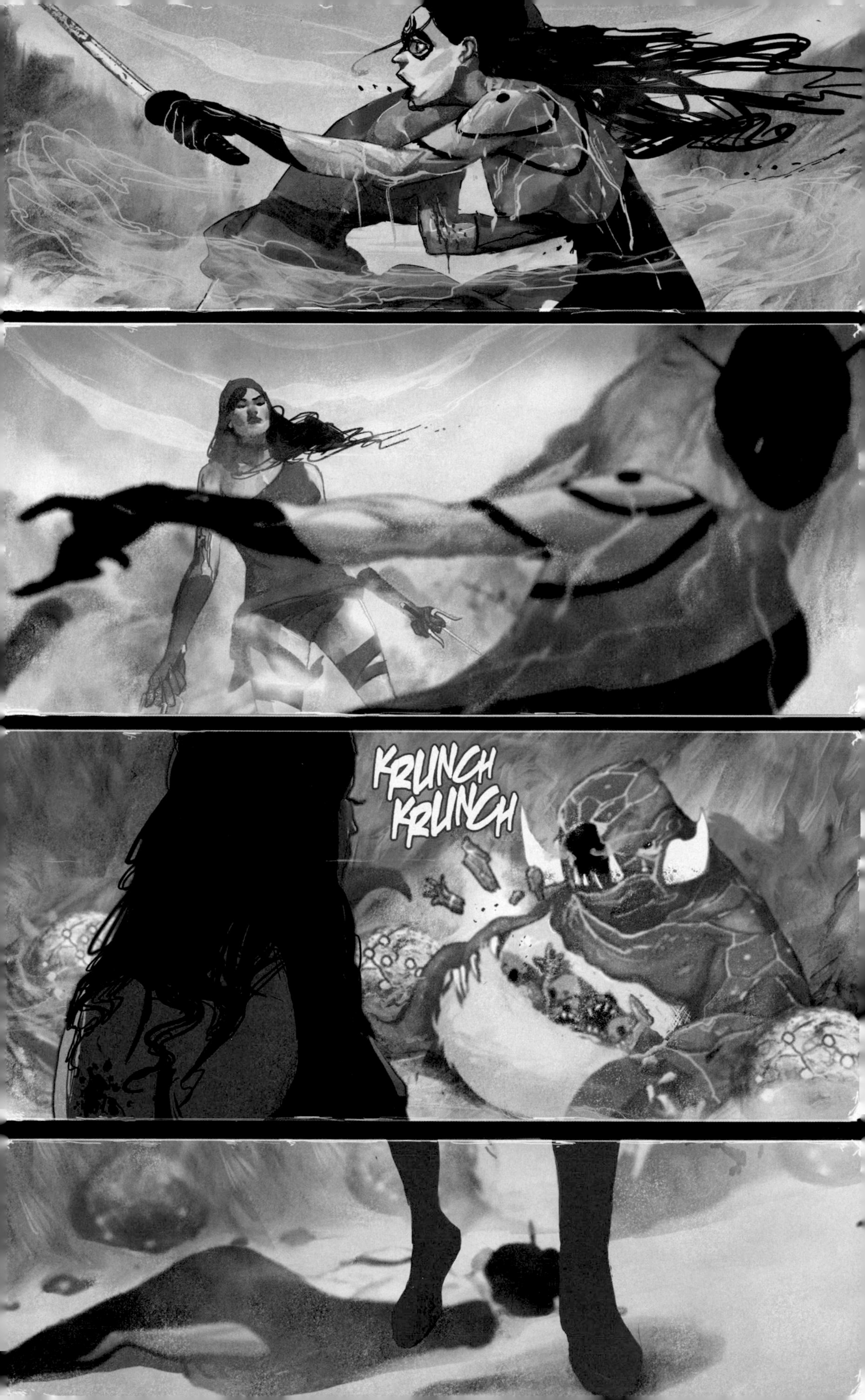
KRUNCH
KRUNCH

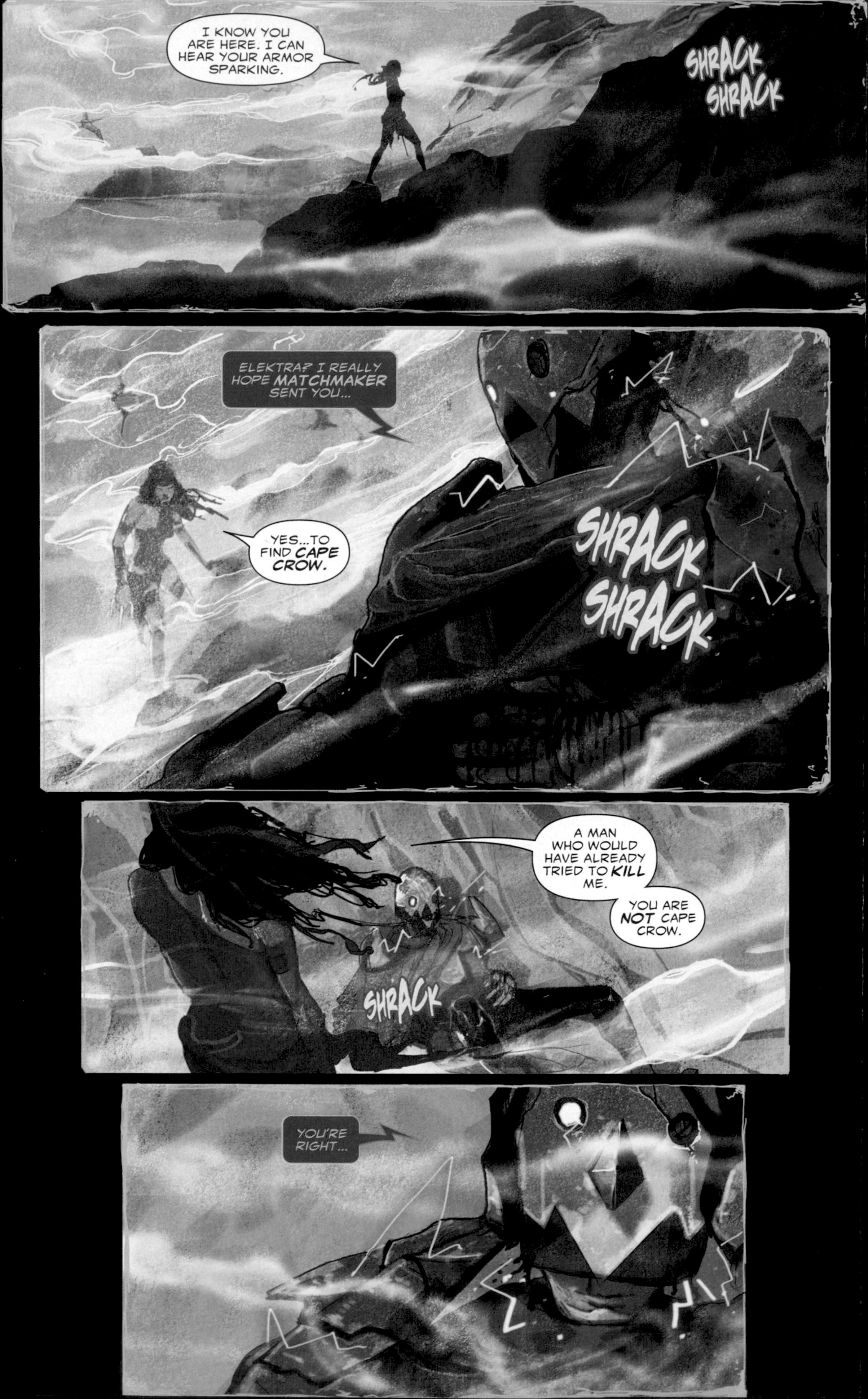
I KNOW YOU ARE HERE. I CAN HEAR YOUR ARMOR SPARKING.
SHRACK SHRACK
ELEKTRA? I REALLY HOPE MATCHMAKER SENT YOU...
YES...TO FIND CAPE CROW.
SHRACK SHRACK
A MAN WHO WOULD HAVE ALREADY TRIED TO KILL ME.
YOU ARE NOT CAPE CROW.
SHRACK
YOU'RE RIGHT...

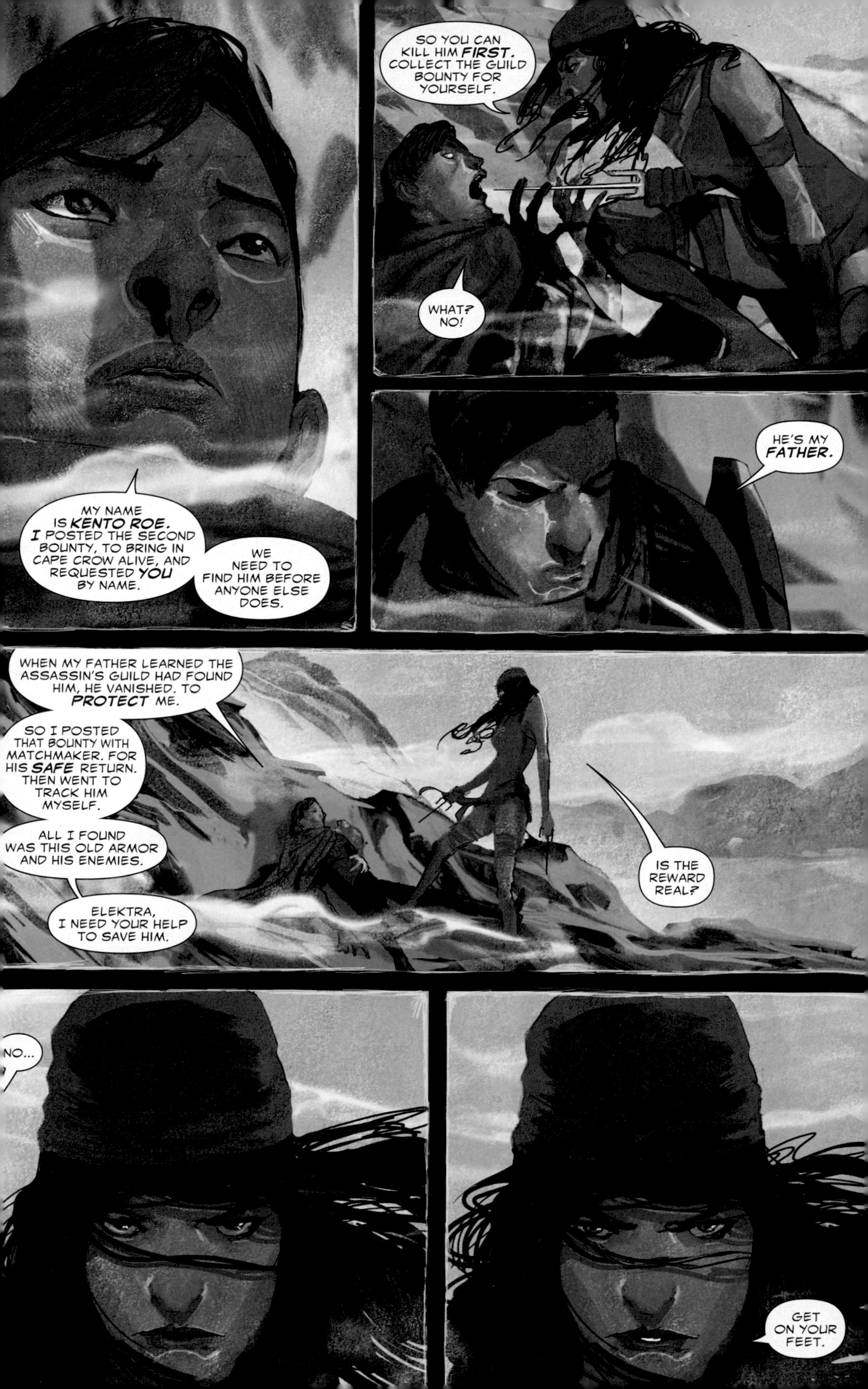
MY NAME IS KENTO ROE. I POSTED THE SECOND BOUNTY, TO BRING IN CAPE CROW ALIVE, AND REQUESTED YOU BY NAME.
WE NEED TO FIND HIM BEFORE ANYONE ELSE DOES.
SO YOU CAN KILL HIM FIRST. COLLECT THE GUILD BOUNTY FOR YOURSELF.
WHAT? NO!
HE'S MY FATHER.
WHEN MY FATHER LEARNED THE ASSASSIN'S GUILD HAD FOUND HIM, HE VANISHED. TO PROTECT ME.
SO I POSTED THAT BOUNTY WITH MATCHMAKER. FOR HIS SAFE RETURN. THEN WENT TO TRACK HIM MYSELF.
ALL I FOUND WAS THIS OLD ARMOR AND HIS ENEMIES.
ELEKTRA, I NEED YOUR HELP TO SAVE HIM.
IS THE REWARD REAL?
NO...
GET ON YOUR FEET.

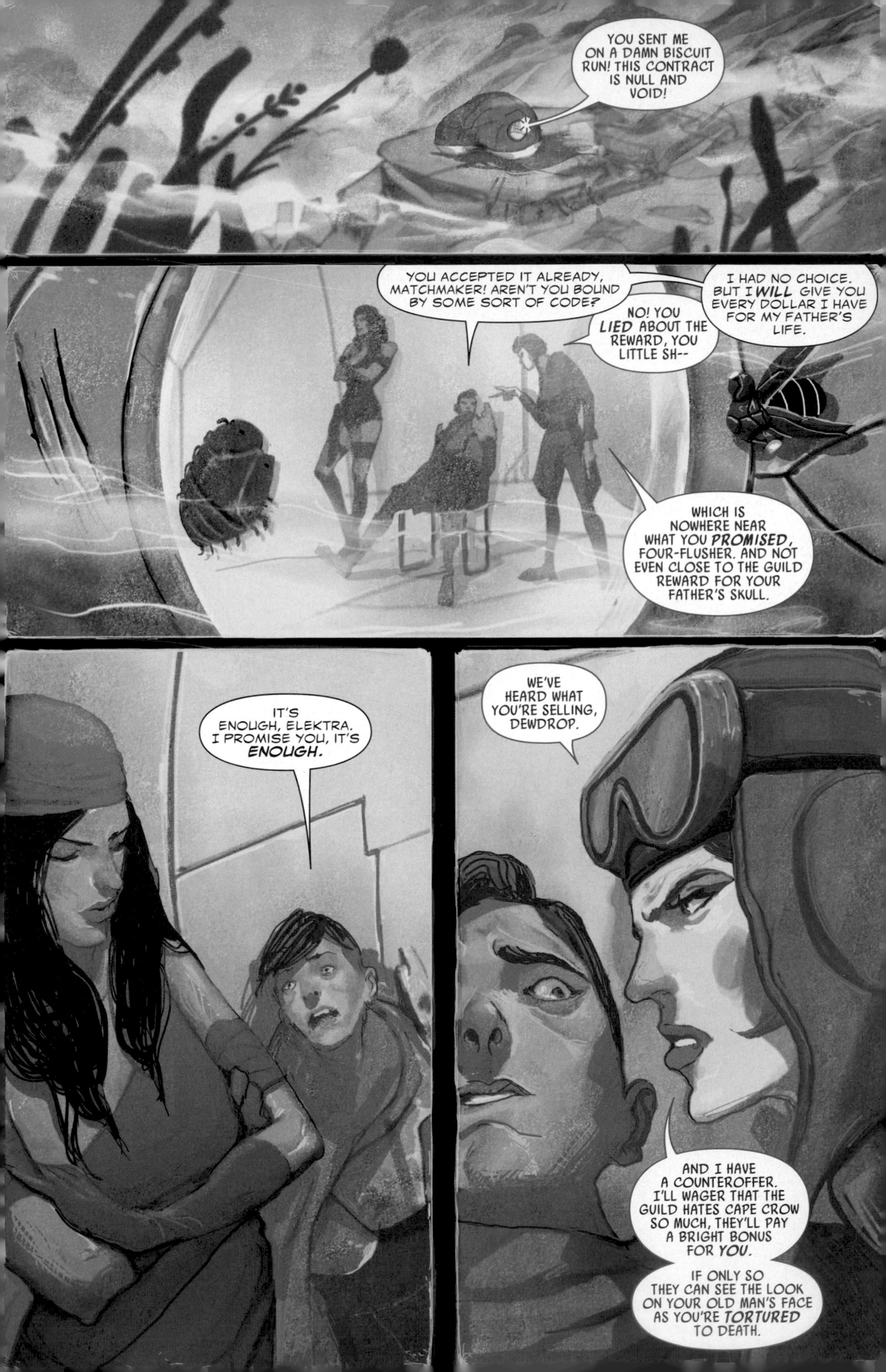
YOU SENT ME ON A DAMN BISCUIT RUN! THIS CONTRACT IS NULL AND VOID!
YOU ACCEPTED IT ALREADY, MATCHMAKER! AREN'T YOU BOUND BY SOME SORT OF CODE?
NO! YOU LIED ABOUT THE REWARD, YOU LITTLE SH--
I HAD NO CHOICE. BUT I WILL GIVE YOU EVERY DOLLAR I HAVE FOR MY FATHER'S LIFE.
WHICH IS NOWHERE NEAR WHAT YOU PROMISED, FOUR-FLUSHER. AND NOT EVEN CLOSE TO THE GUILD REWARD FOR YOUR FATHER'S SKULL.
IT'S ENOUGH, ELEKTRA. I PROMISE YOU, IT'S ENOUGH.
WE'VE HEARD WHAT YOU'RE SELLING, DEWDROP.
AND I HAVE A COUNTEROFFER. I'LL WAGER THAT THE GUILD HATES CAPE CROW SO MUCH, THEY'LL PAY A BRIGHT BONUS FOR YOU.
IF ONLY SO THEY CAN SEE THE LOOK ON YOUR OLD MAN'S FACE AS YOU'RE TORTURED TO DEATH.

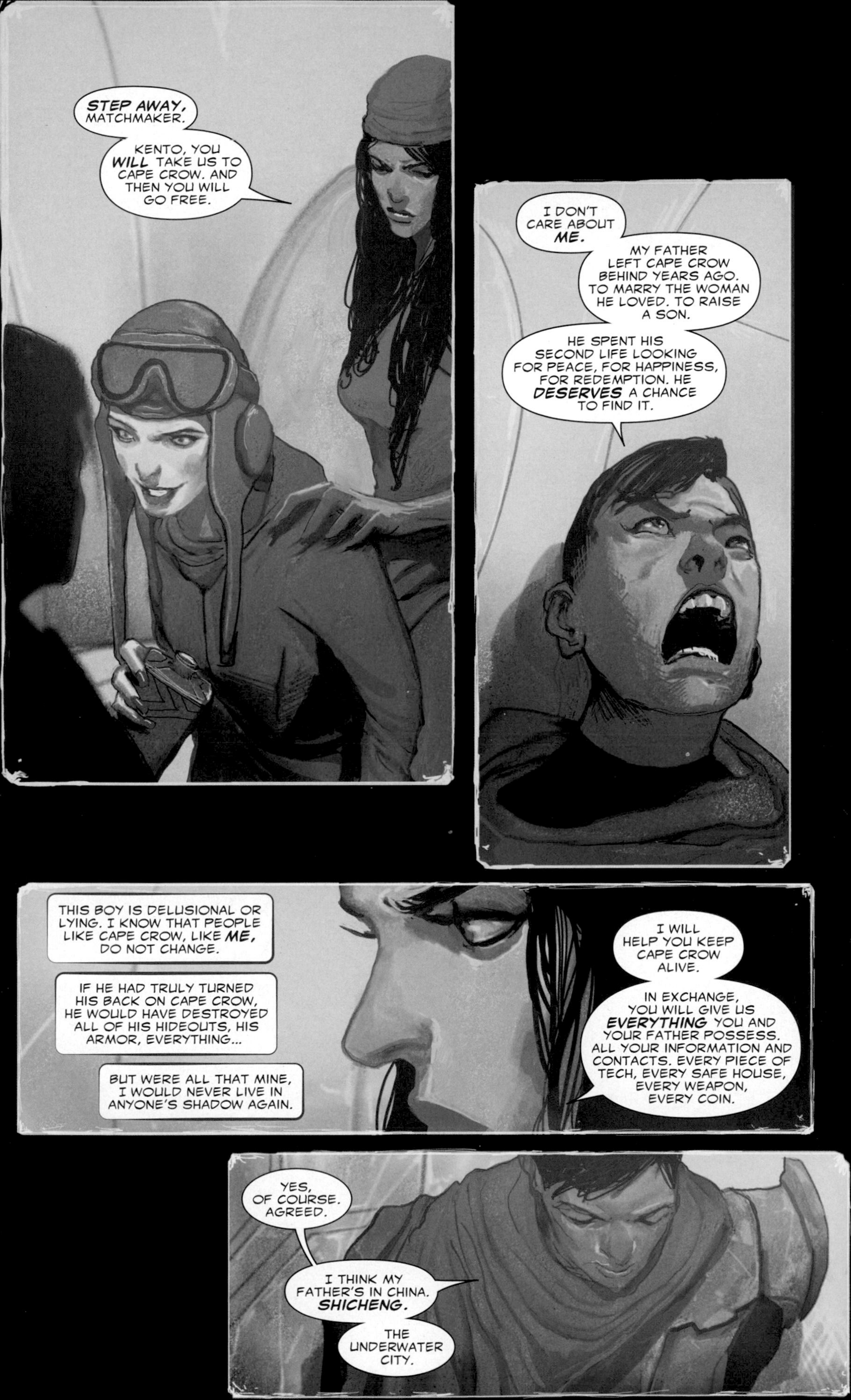
STEP AWAY, MATCHMAKER.
KENTO, YOU WILL TAKE US TO CAPE CROW. AND THEN YOU WILL GO FREE.
I DON'T CARE ABOUT ME.
MY FATHER LEFT CAPE CROW BEHIND YEARS AGO. TO MARRY THE WOMAN HE LOVED. TO RAISE A SON.
HE SPENT HIS SECOND LIFE LOOKING FOR PEACE, FOR HAPPINESS, FOR REDEMPTION. HE DESERVES A CHANCE TO FIND IT.
THIS BOY IS DELUSIONAL OR LYING. I KNOW THAT PEOPLE LIKE CAPE CROW, LIKE ME, DO NOT CHANGE.
IF HE HAD TRULY TURNED HIS BACK ON CAPE CROW, HE WOULD HAVE DESTROYED ALL OF HIS HIDEOUTS, HIS ARMOR, EVERYTHING...
BUT WERE ALL THAT MINE, I WOULD NEVER LIVE IN ANYONE'S SHADOW AGAIN.
I WILL HELP YOU KEEP CAPE CROW ALIVE.
IN EXCHANGE, YOU WILL GIVE US EVERYTHING YOU AND YOUR FATHER POSSESS. ALL YOUR INFORMATION AND CONTACTS. EVERY PIECE OF TECH, EVERY SAFE HOUSE, EVERY WEAPON, EVERY COIN.
YES, OF COURSE. AGREED.
I THINK MY FATHER'S IN CHINA. SHICHENG.
THE UNDERWATER CITY.

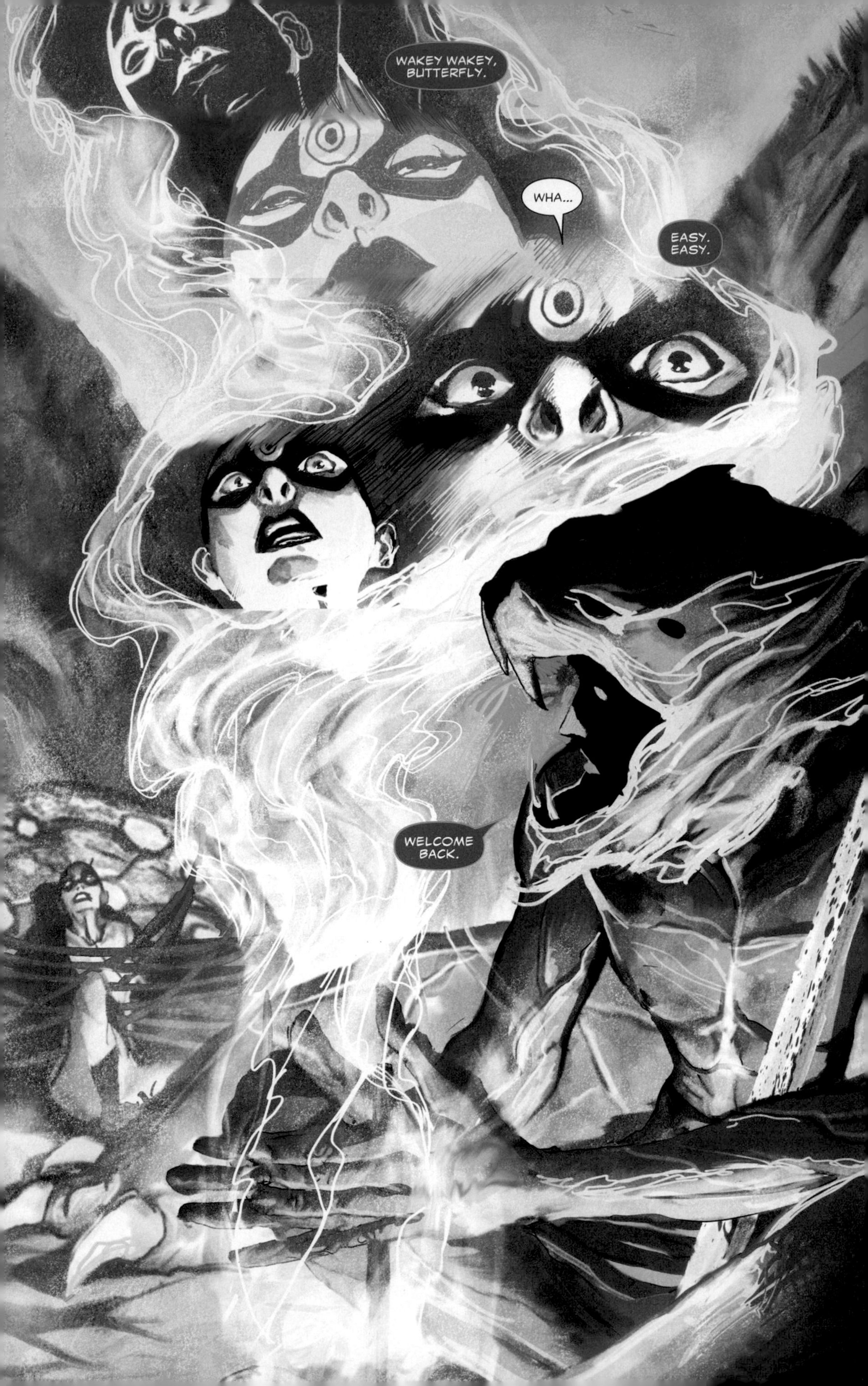
WAKEY WAKEY, BUTTERFLY.
WHA...
EASY. EASY.
WELCOME BACK.

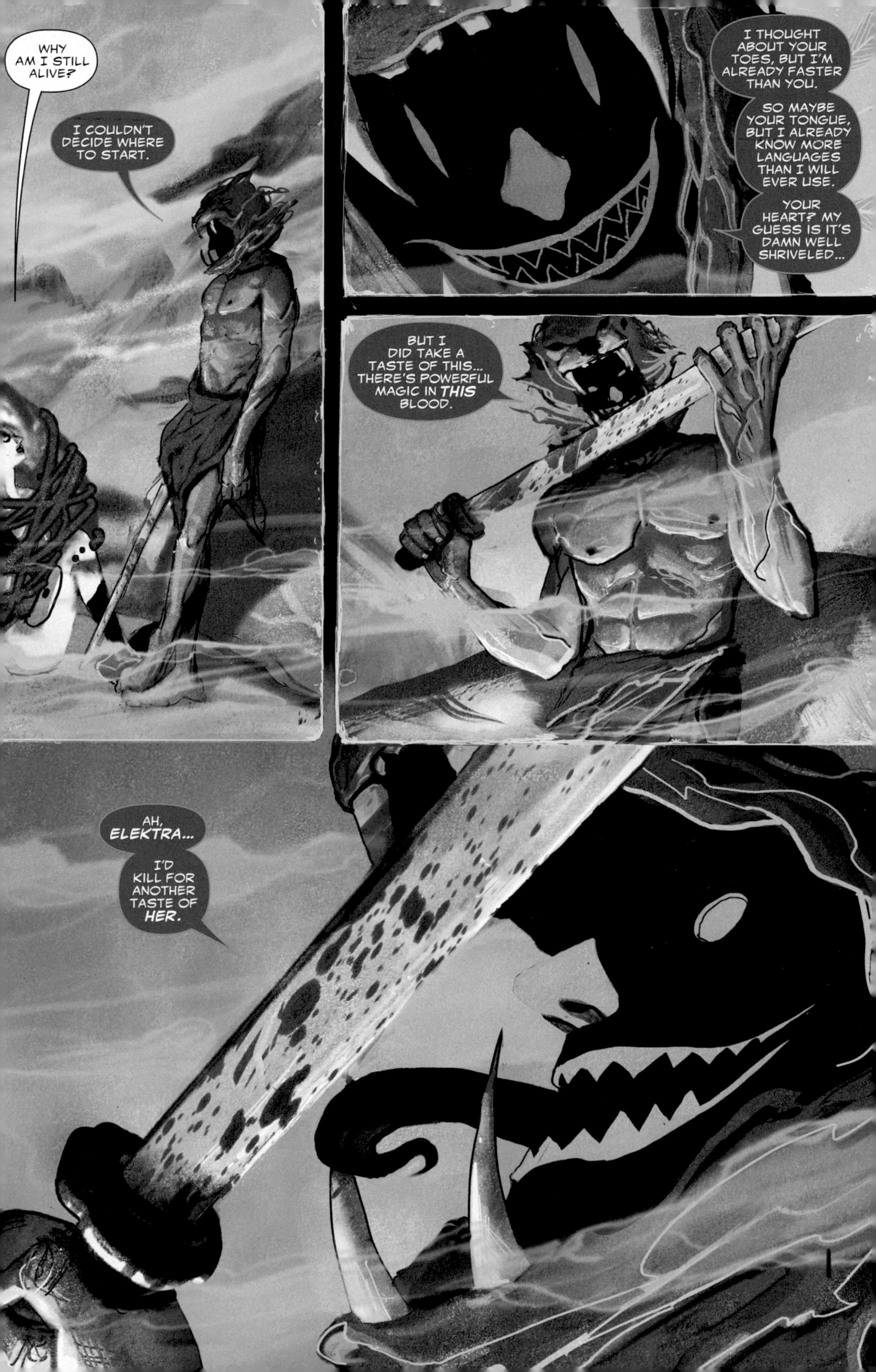
WHY AM I STILL ALIVE?
I COULDN'T DECIDE WHERE TO START.
I THOUGHT ABOUT YOUR TOES, BUT I'M ALREADY FASTER THAN YOU.
SO MAYBE YOUR TONGUE, BUT I ALREADY KNOW MORE LANGUAGES THAN I WILL EVER USE.
YOUR HEART? MY GUESS IS IT'S DAMN WELL SHRIVELED...
BUT I DID TAKE A TASTE OF THIS... THERE'S POWERFUL MAGIC IN THIS BLOOD.
AH, ELEKTRA...
I'D KILL FOR ANOTHER TASTE OF HER.

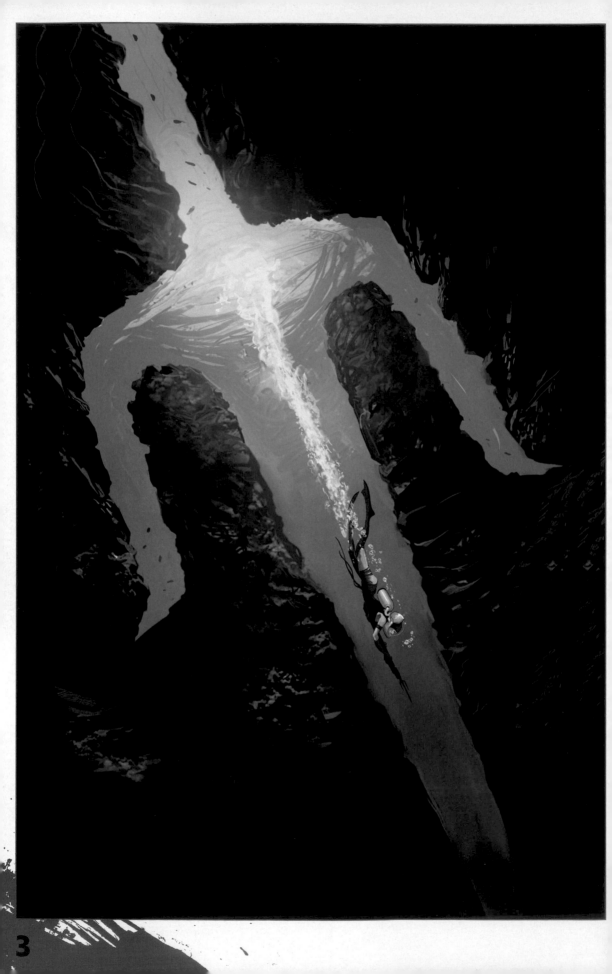

3

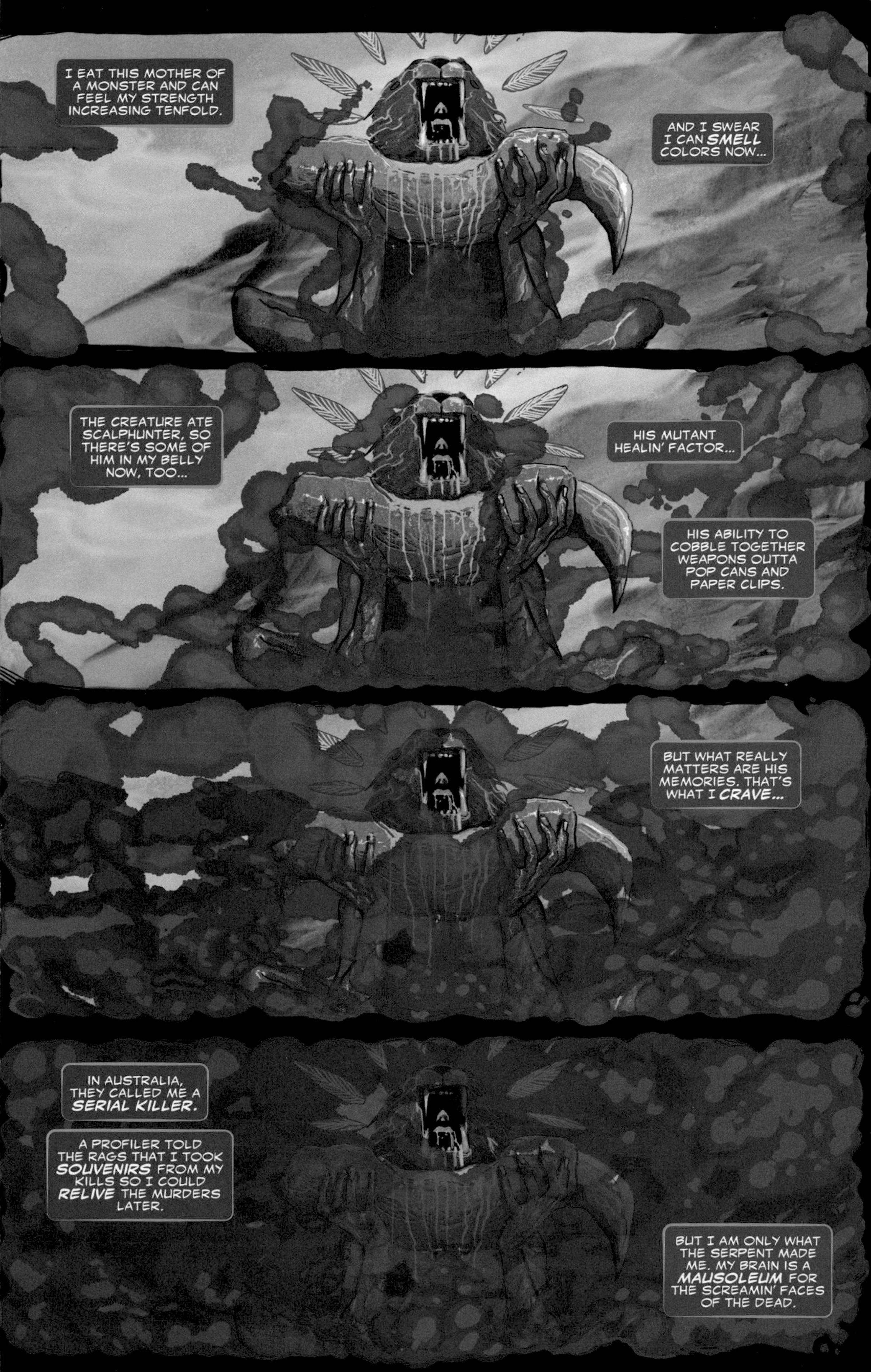
I EAT THIS MOTHER OF A MONSTER AND CAN FEEL MY STRENGTH INCREASING TENFOLD.
AND I SWEAR I CAN SMELL COLORS NOW...
THE CREATURE ATE SCALPHUNTER, SO THERE'S SOME OF HIM IN MY BELLY NOW, TOO...
HIS MUTANT HEALIN' FACTOR...
HIS ABILITY TO COBBLE TOGETHER WEAPONS OUTTA POP CANS AND PAPER CLIPS.
BUT WHAT REALLY MATTERS ARE HIS MEMORIES. THAT'S WHAT I CRAVE...
IN AUSTRALIA, THEY CALLED ME A SERIAL KILLER.
A PROFILER TOLD THE RAGS THAT I TOOK SOUVENIRS FROM MY KILLS SO I COULD RELIVE THE MURDERS LATER.
BUT I AM ONLY WHAT THE SERPENT MADE ME. MY BRAIN IS A MAUSOLEUM FOR THE SCREAMIN' FACES OF THE DEAD.

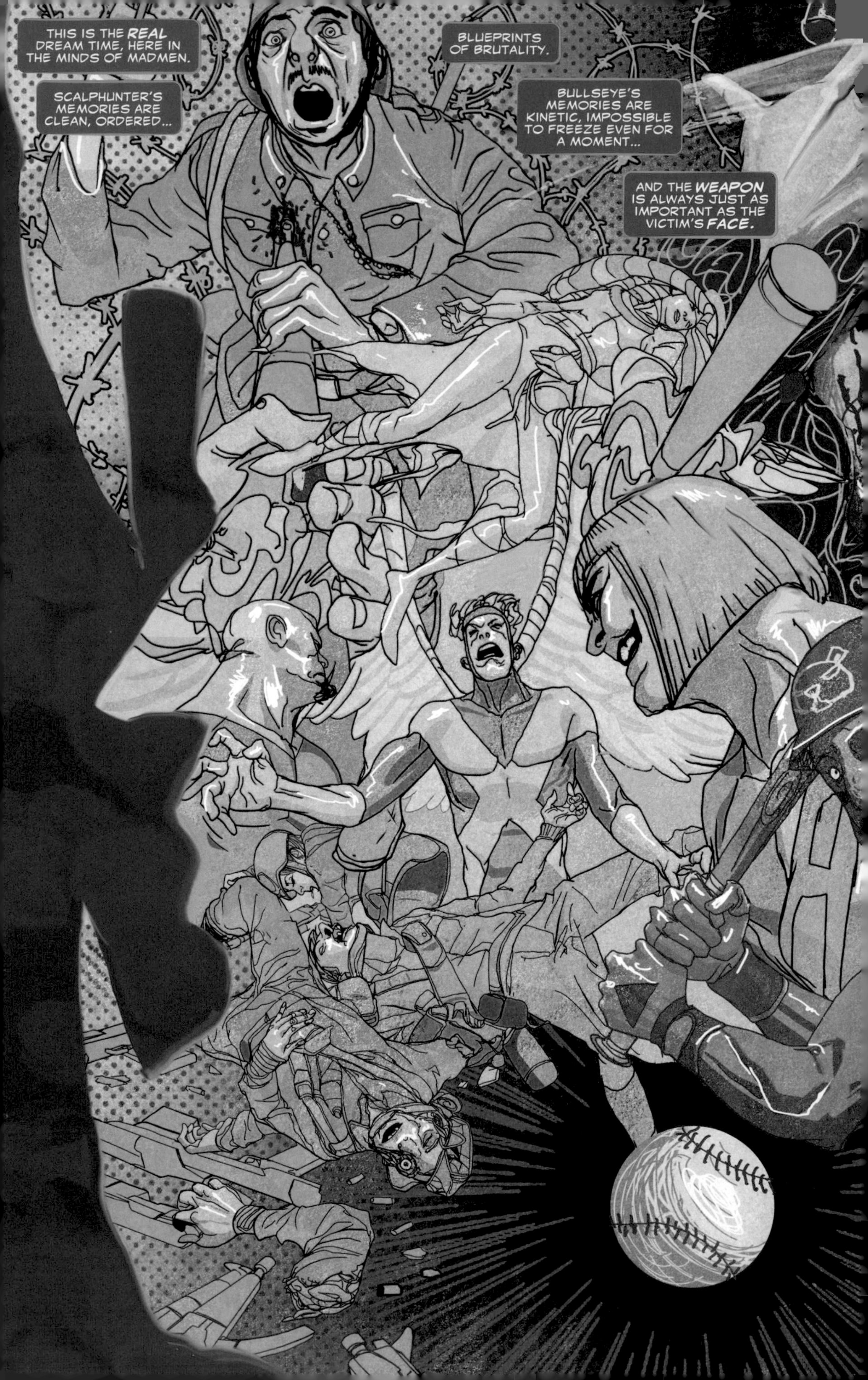
THIS IS THE REAL DREAM TIME, HERE IN THE MINDS OF MADMEN.
SCALPHUNTER'S MEMORIES ARE CLEAN, ORDERED...
BLUEPRINTS OF BRUTALITY.
BULLSEYE'S MEMORIES ARE KINETIC, IMPOSSIBLE TO FREEZE EVEN FOR A MOMENT...
AND THE WEAPON IS ALWAYS JUST AS IMPORTANT AS THE VICTIM'S FACE.

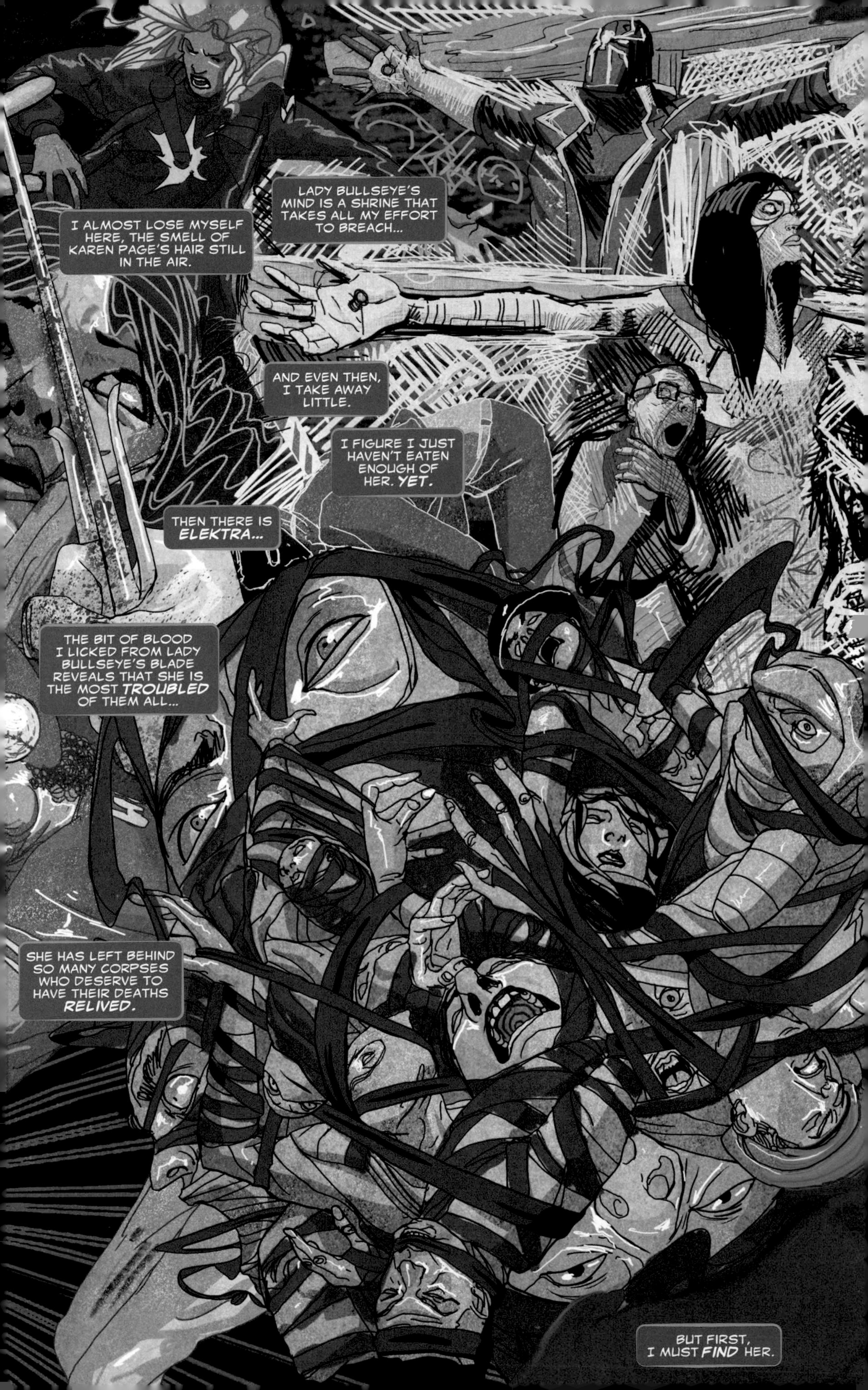
LADY BULLSEYE'S MIND IS A SHRINE THAT TAKES ALL MY EFFORT TO BREACH...
I ALMOST LOSE MYSELF HERE, THE SMELL OF KAREN PAGE'S HAIR STILL IN THE AIR.
AND EVEN THEN, I TAKE AWAY LITTLE.
I FIGURE I JUST HAVEN'T EATEN ENOUGH OF HER. ***YET.***
THEN THERE IS ***ELEKTRA...***
THE BIT OF BLOOD I LICKED FROM LADY BULLSEYE'S BLADE REVEALS THAT SHE IS THE MOST ***TROUBLED*** OF THEM ALL...
SHE HAS LEFT BEHIND SO MANY CORPSES WHO DESERVE TO HAVE THEIR DEATHS ***RELIVED.***
BUT FIRST, I MUST ***FIND*** HER.

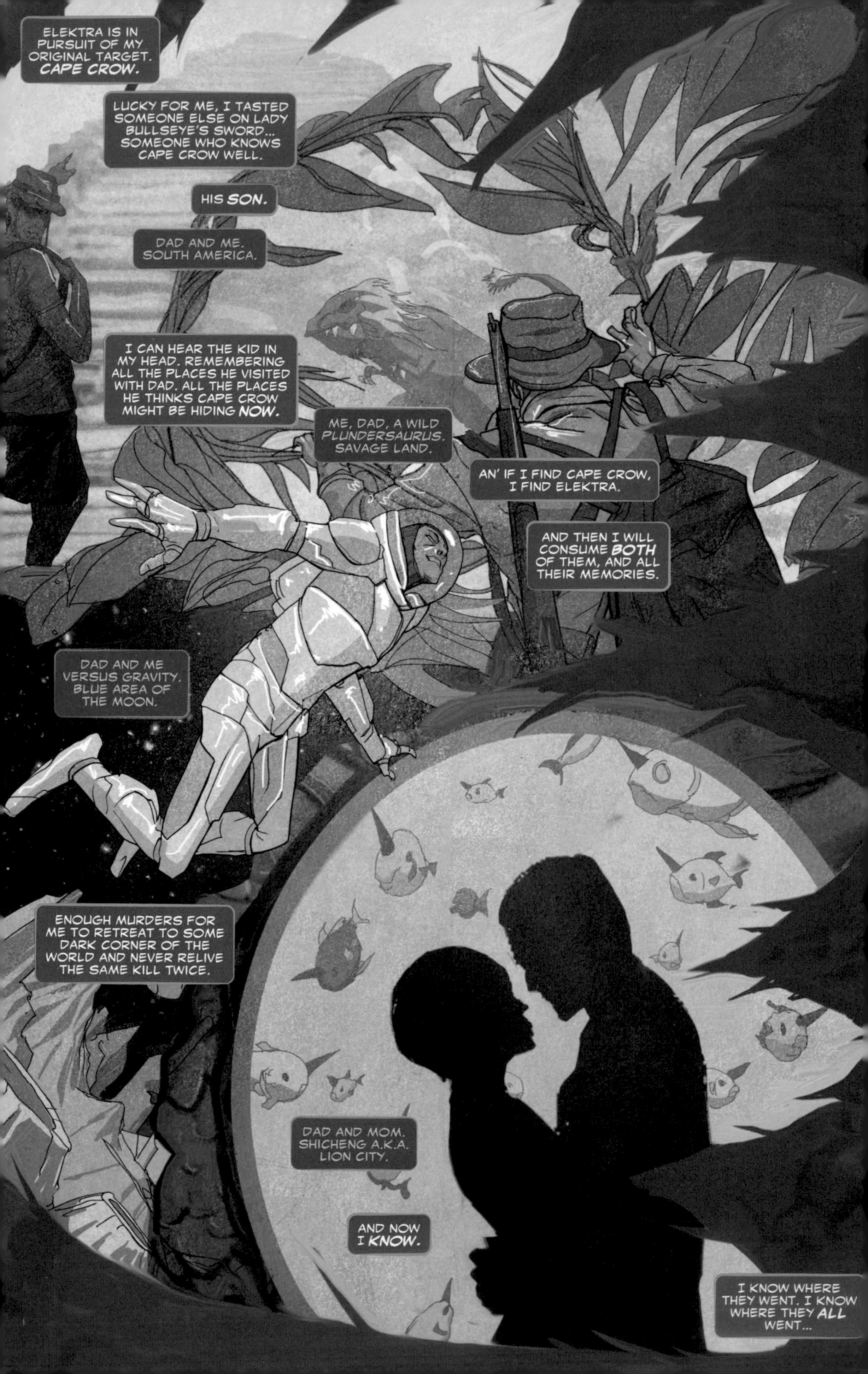
ELEKTRA IS IN PURSUIT OF MY ORIGINAL TARGET. CAPE CROW.
LUCKY FOR ME, I TASTED SOMEONE ELSE ON LADY BULLSEYE'S SWORD... SOMEONE WHO KNOWS CAPE CROW WELL.
HIS SON.
DAD AND ME. SOUTH AMERICA.
I CAN HEAR THE KID IN MY HEAD. REMEMBERING ALL THE PLACES HE VISITED WITH DAD. ALL THE PLACES HE THINKS CAPE CROW MIGHT BE HIDING NOW.
ME, DAD, A WILD PLUNDERSAURUS. SAVAGE LAND.
AN' IF I FIND CAPE CROW, I FIND ELEKTRA.
AND THEN I WILL CONSUME BOTH OF THEM, AND ALL THEIR MEMORIES.
DAD AND ME VERSUS GRAVITY. BLUE AREA OF THE MOON.
ENOUGH MURDERS FOR ME TO RETREAT TO SOME DARK CORNER OF THE WORLD AND NEVER RELIVE THE SAME KILL TWICE.
DAD AND MOM. SHICHENG A.K.A. LION CITY.
AND NOW I KNOW.
I KNOW WHERE THEY WENT. I KNOW WHERE THEY ALL WENT...

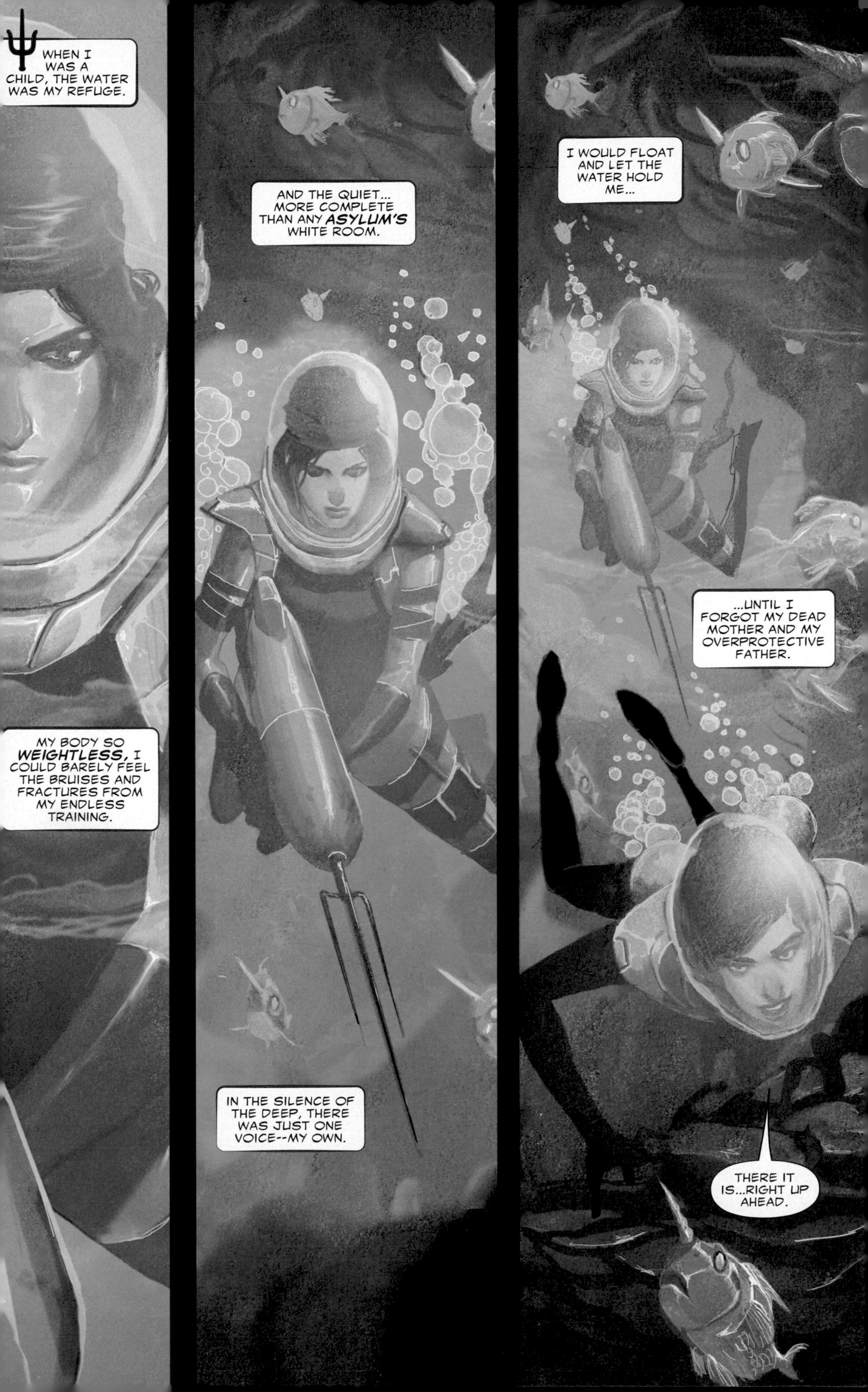
WHEN I WAS A CHILD, THE WATER WAS MY REFUGE.
MY BODY SO WEIGHTLESS, I COULD BARELY FEEL THE BRUISES AND FRACTURES FROM MY ENDLESS TRAINING.
AND THE QUIET... MORE COMPLETE THAN ANY ASYLUM'S WHITE ROOM.
IN THE SILENCE OF THE DEEP, THERE WAS JUST ONE VOICE--MY OWN.
I WOULD FLOAT AND LET THE WATER HOLD ME...
...UNTIL I FORGOT MY DEAD MOTHER AND MY OVERPROTECTIVE FATHER.
THERE IT IS...RIGHT UP AHEAD.

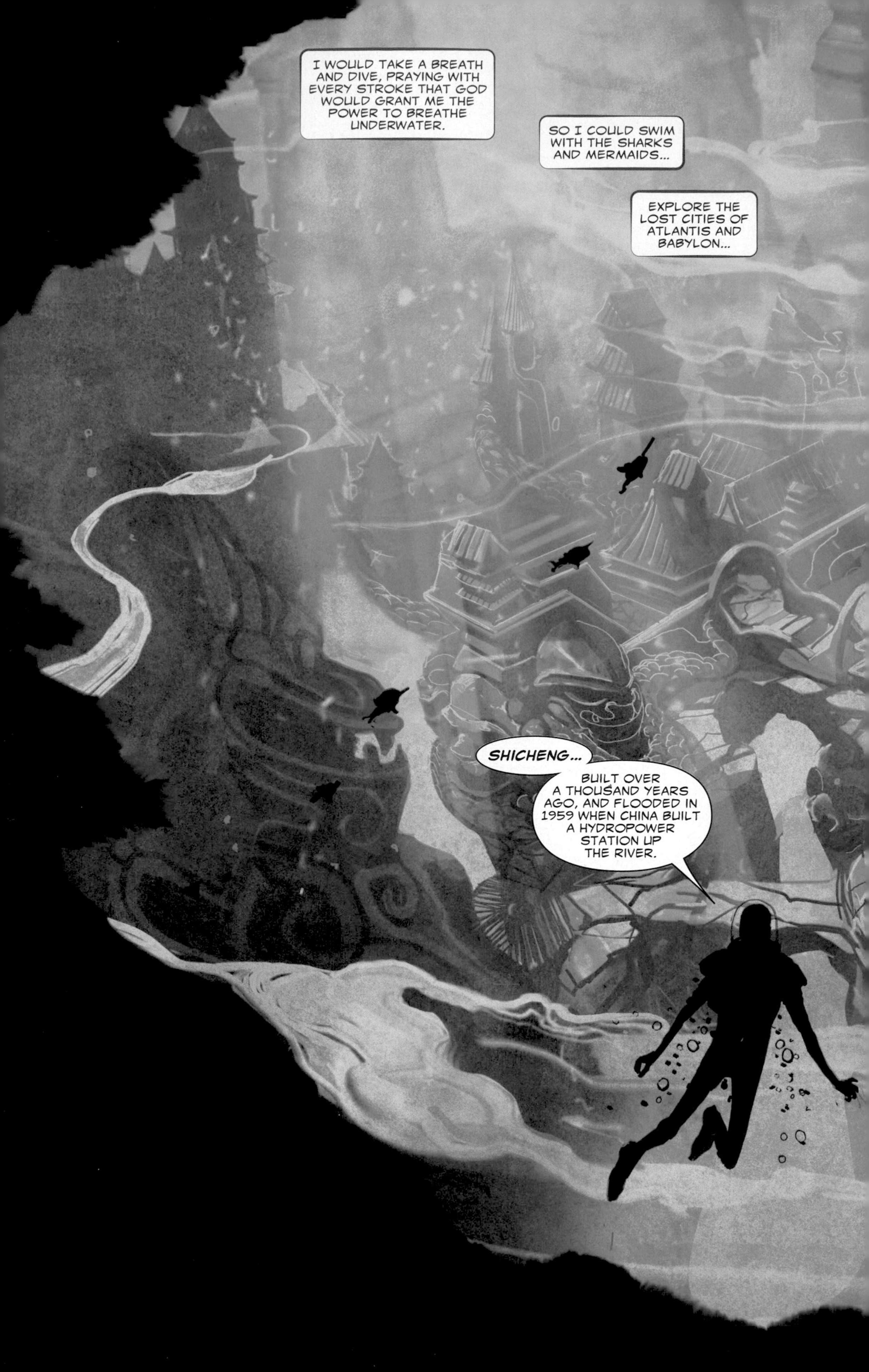
I WOULD TAKE A BREATH AND DIVE, PRAYING WITH EVERY STROKE THAT GOD WOULD GRANT ME THE POWER TO BREATHE UNDERWATER.
SO I COULD SWIM WITH THE SHARKS AND MERMAIDS...
EXPLORE THE LOST CITIES OF ATLANTIS AND BABYLON...
SHICHENG...
BUILT OVER A THOUSAND YEARS AGO, AND FLOODED IN 1959 WHEN CHINA BUILT A HYDROPOWER STATION UP THE RIVER.

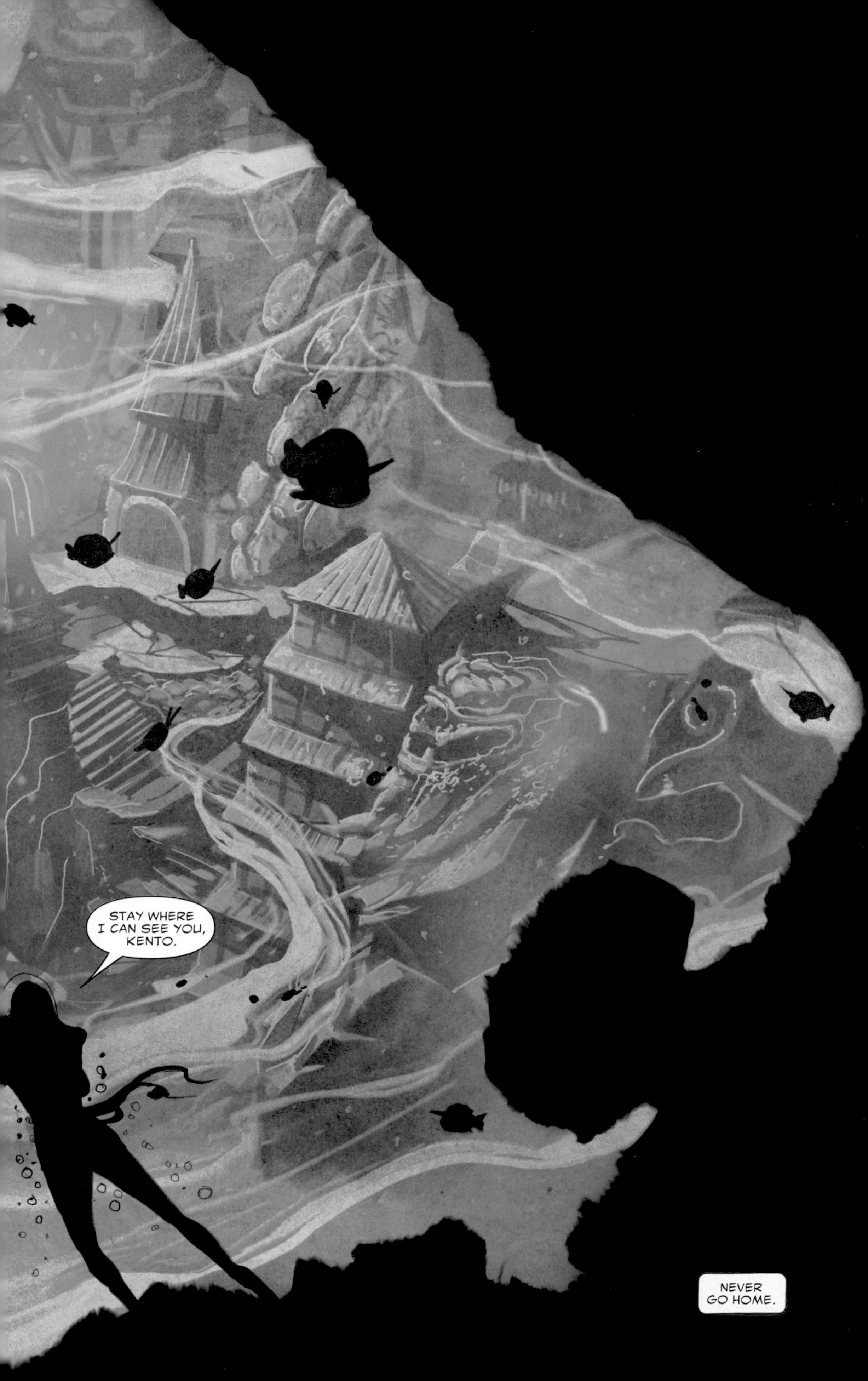
STAY WHERE I CAN SEE YOU, KENTO.
NEVER GO HOME.

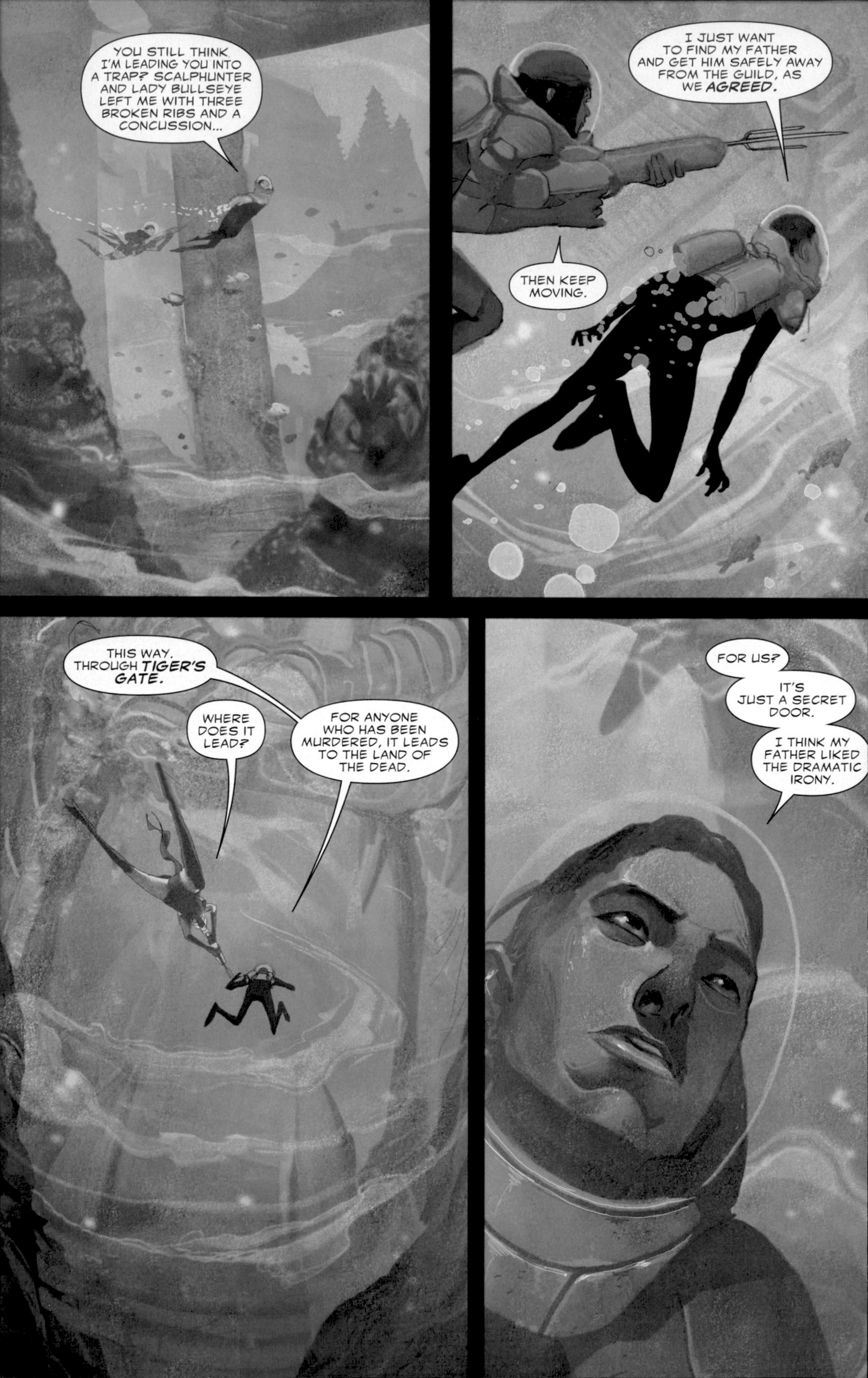
YOU STILL THINK I'M LEADING YOU INTO A TRAP? SCALPHUNTER AND LADY BULLSEYE LEFT ME WITH THREE BROKEN RIBS AND A CONCUSSION...
I JUST WANT TO FIND MY FATHER AND GET HIM SAFELY AWAY FROM THE GUILD, AS WE AGREED.
THEN KEEP MOVING.
THIS WAY. THROUGH TIGER'S GATE.
WHERE DOES IT LEAD?
FOR ANYONE WHO HAS BEEN MURDERED, IT LEADS TO THE LAND OF THE DEAD.
FOR US?
IT'S JUST A SECRET DOOR.
I THINK MY FATHER LIKED THE DRAMATIC IRONY.

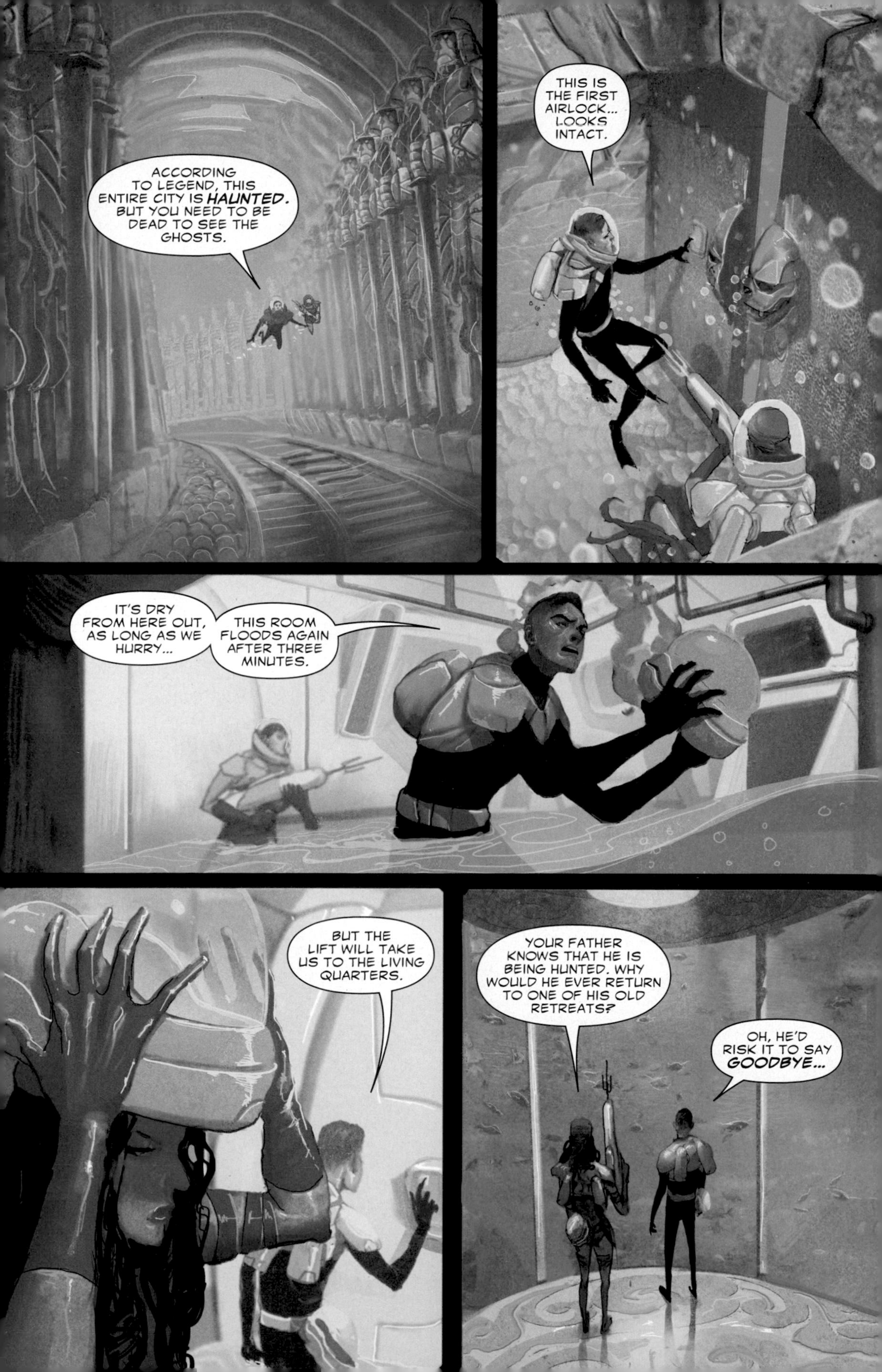
ACCORDING TO LEGEND, THIS ENTIRE CITY IS **HAUNTED.** BUT YOU NEED TO BE DEAD TO SEE THE GHOSTS.
THIS IS THE FIRST AIRLOCK... LOOKS INTACT.
IT'S DRY FROM HERE OUT, AS LONG AS WE HURRY...
THIS ROOM FLOODS AGAIN AFTER THREE MINUTES.
BUT THE LIFT WILL TAKE US TO THE LIVING QUARTERS.
YOUR FATHER KNOWS THAT HE IS BEING HUNTED. WHY WOULD HE EVER RETURN TO ONE OF HIS OLD RETREATS?
OH, HE'D RISK IT TO SAY **GOODBYE...**

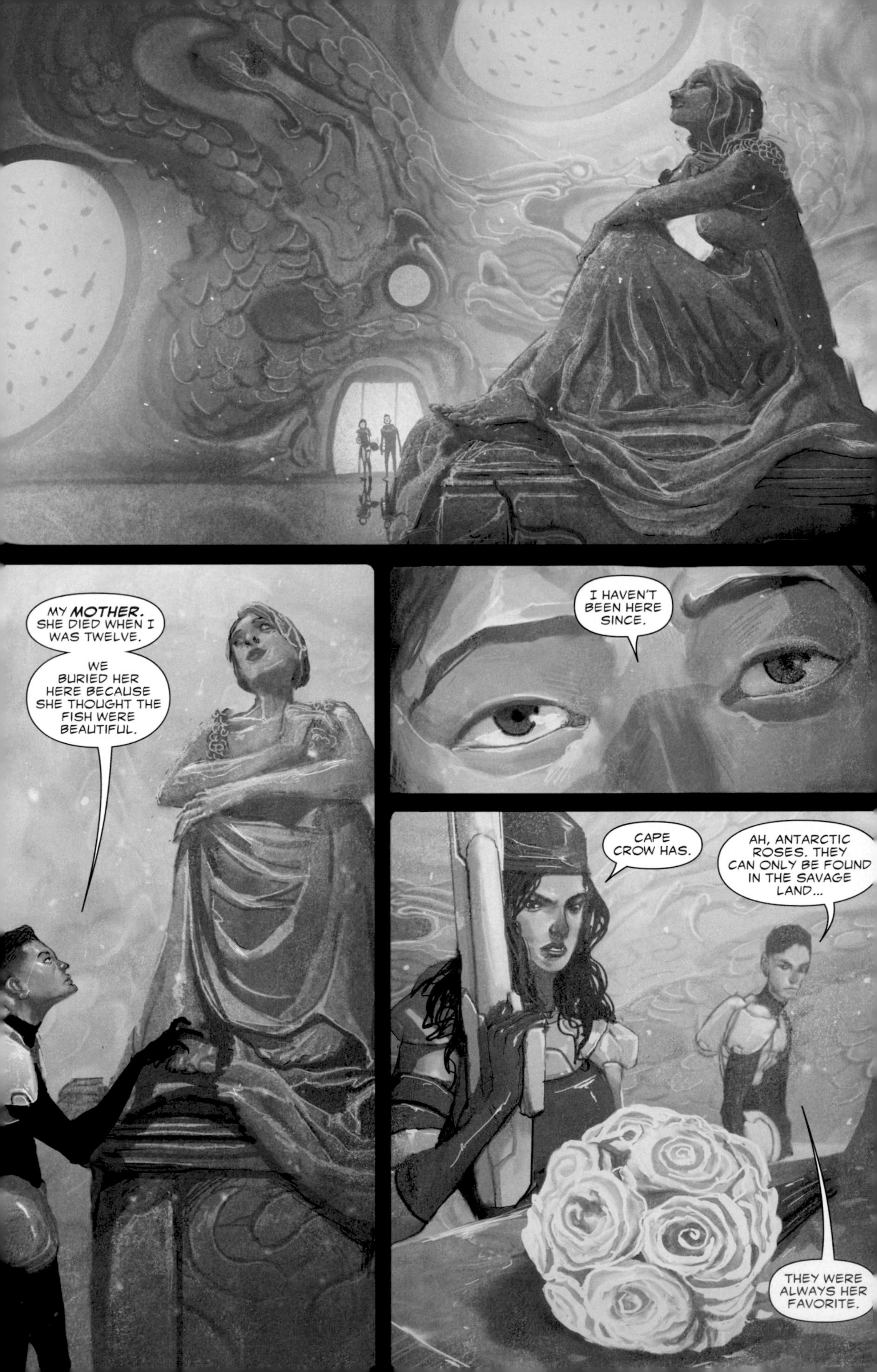

MY **MOTHER.** SHE DIED WHEN I WAS TWELVE.
WE BURIED HER HERE BECAUSE SHE THOUGHT THE FISH WERE BEAUTIFUL.
I HAVEN'T BEEN HERE SINCE.
CAPE CROW HAS.
AH, ANTARCTIC ROSES. THEY CAN ONLY BE FOUND IN THE SAVAGE LAND...
THEY WERE ALWAYS HER FAVORITE.

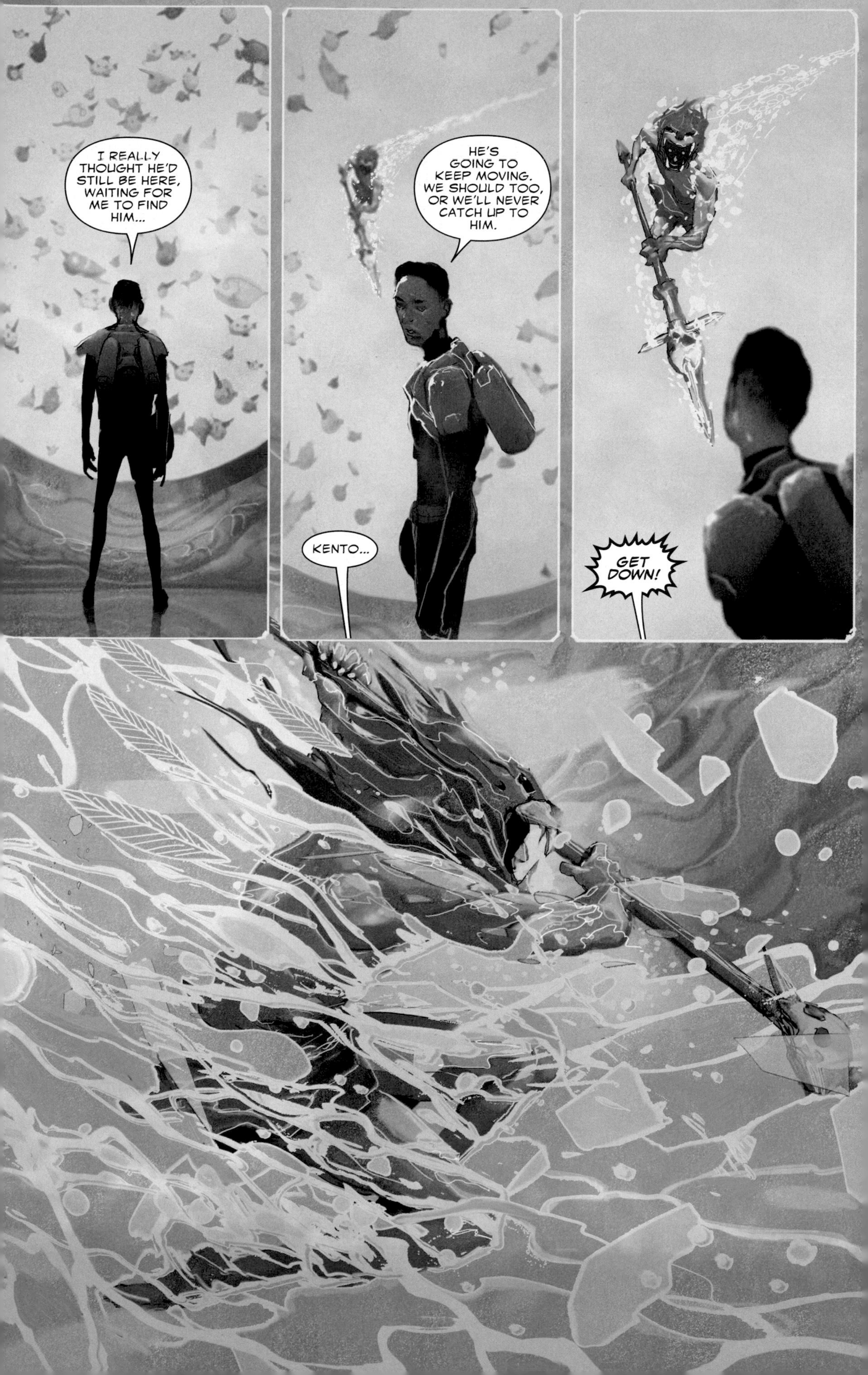
I REALLY THOUGHT HE'D STILL BE HERE, WAITING FOR ME TO FIND HIM...
HE'S GOING TO KEEP MOVING. WE SHOULD TOO, OR WE'LL NEVER CATCH UP TO HIM.
KENTO...
GET DOWN!

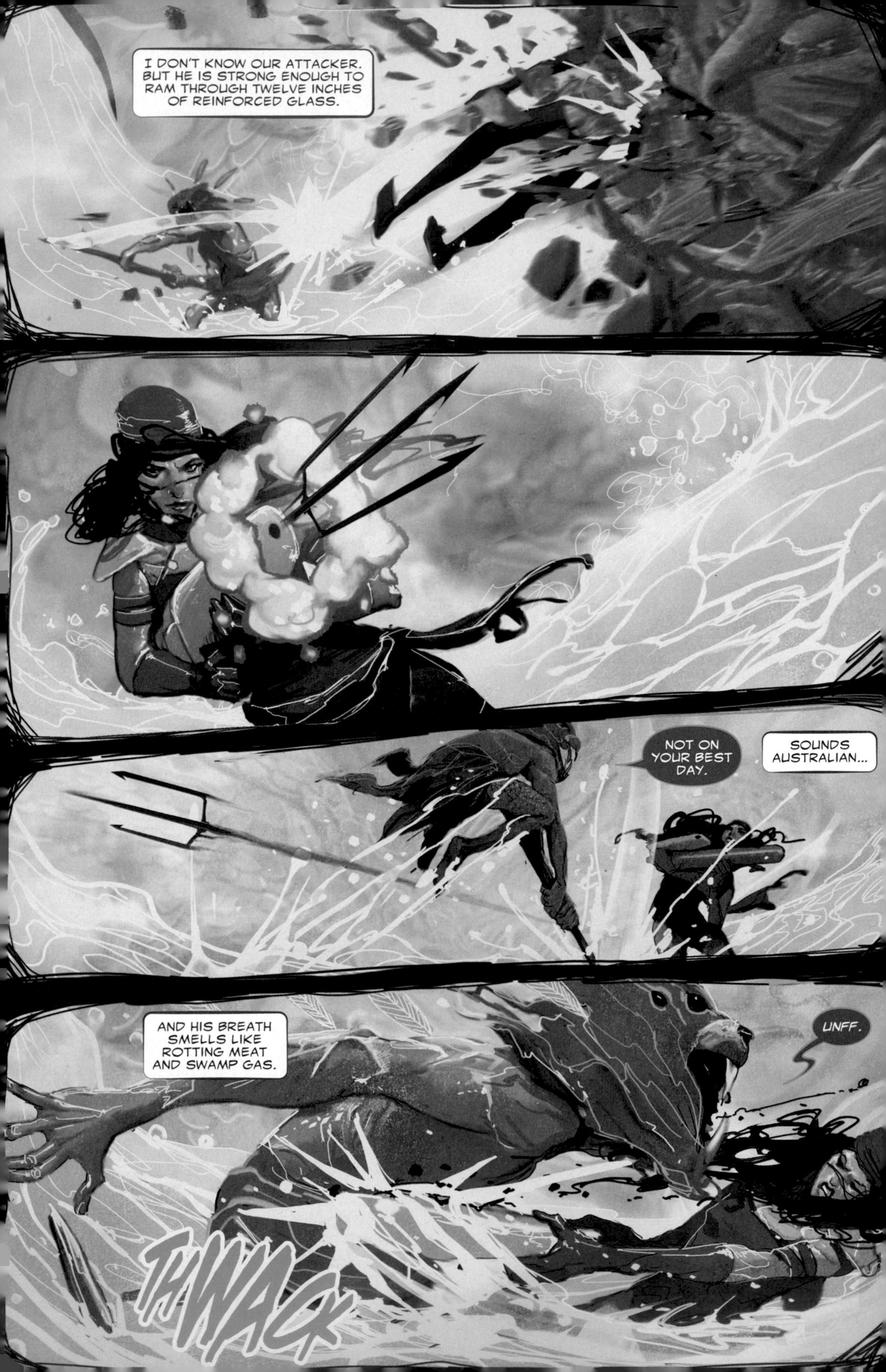

I DON'T KNOW OUR ATTACKER. BUT HE IS STRONG ENOUGH TO RAM THROUGH TWELVE INCHES OF REINFORCED GLASS.
NOT ON YOUR BEST DAY.
SOUNDS AUSTRALIAN...
AND HIS BREATH SMELLS LIKE ROTTING MEAT AND SWAMP GAS.
UNFF.
THWACK

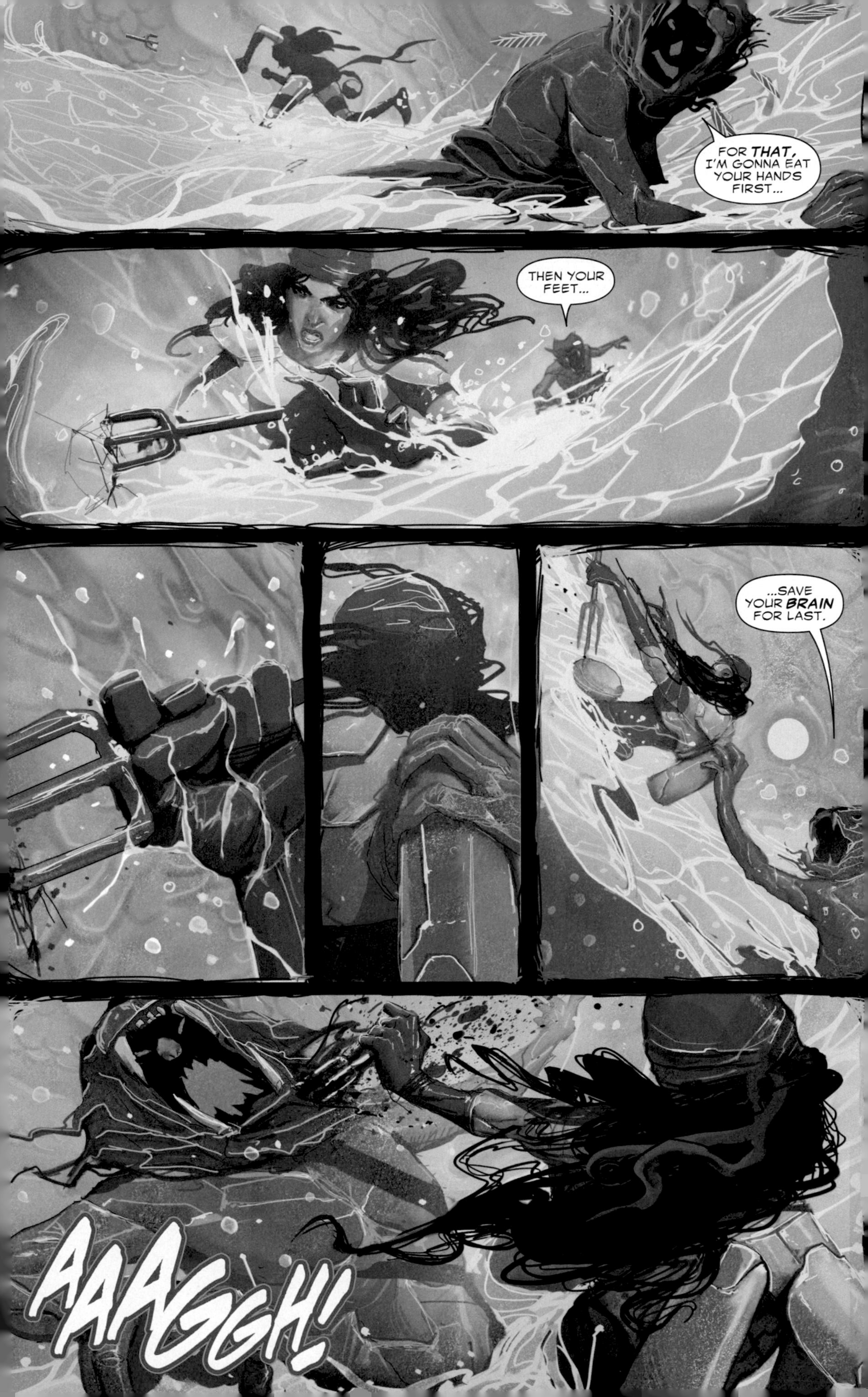
FOR THAT, I'M GONNA EAT YOUR HANDS FIRST...
THEN YOUR FEET...
...SAVE YOUR BRAIN FOR LAST.
AAAGGH!

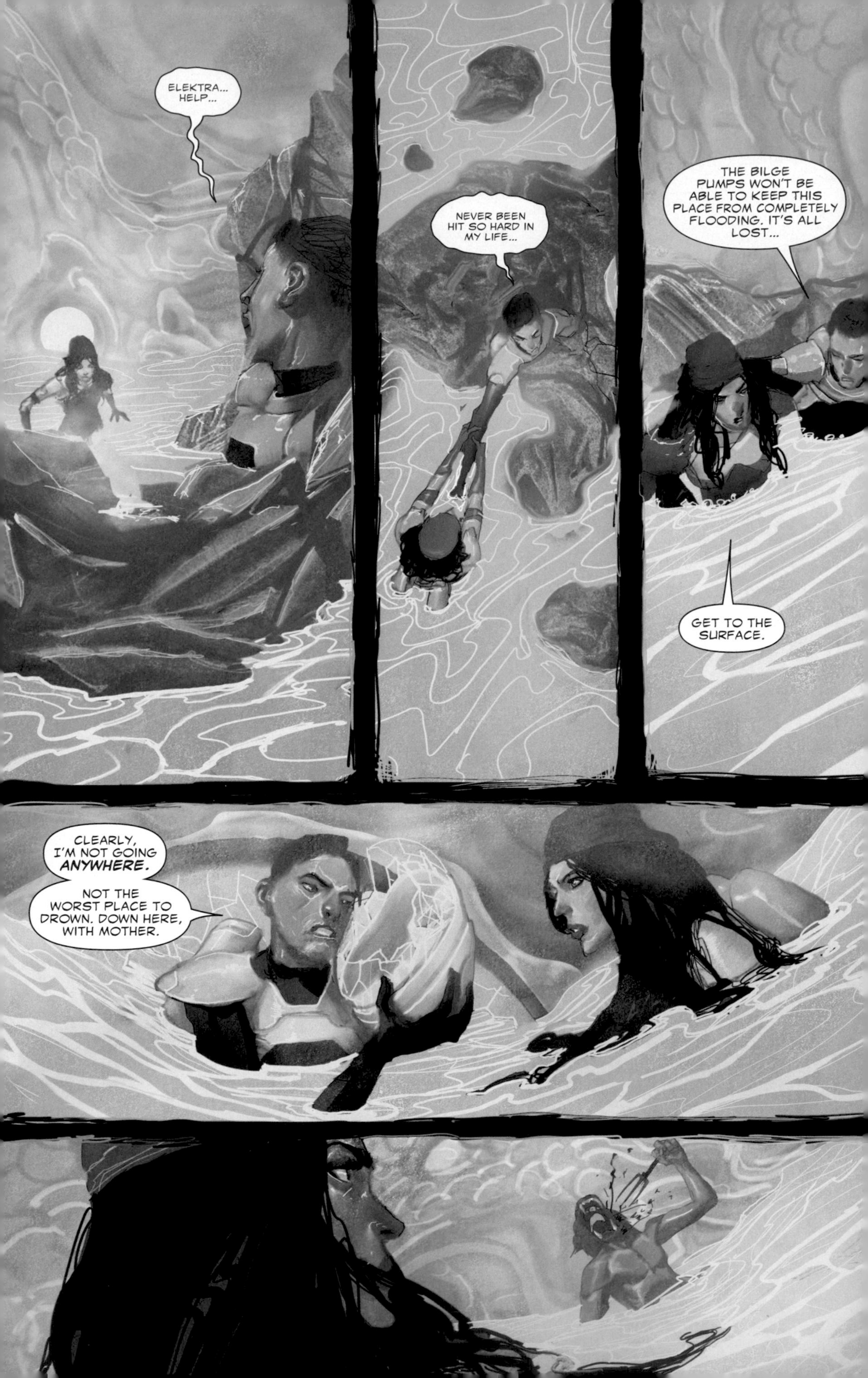
ELEKTRA... HELP...
NEVER BEEN HIT SO HARD IN MY LIFE...
THE BILGE PUMPS WON'T BE ABLE TO KEEP THIS PLACE FROM COMPLETELY FLOODING. IT'S ALL LOST...
GET TO THE SURFACE.
CLEARLY, I'M NOT GOING ANYWHERE.
NOT THE WORST PLACE TO DROWN. DOWN HERE, WITH MOTHER.

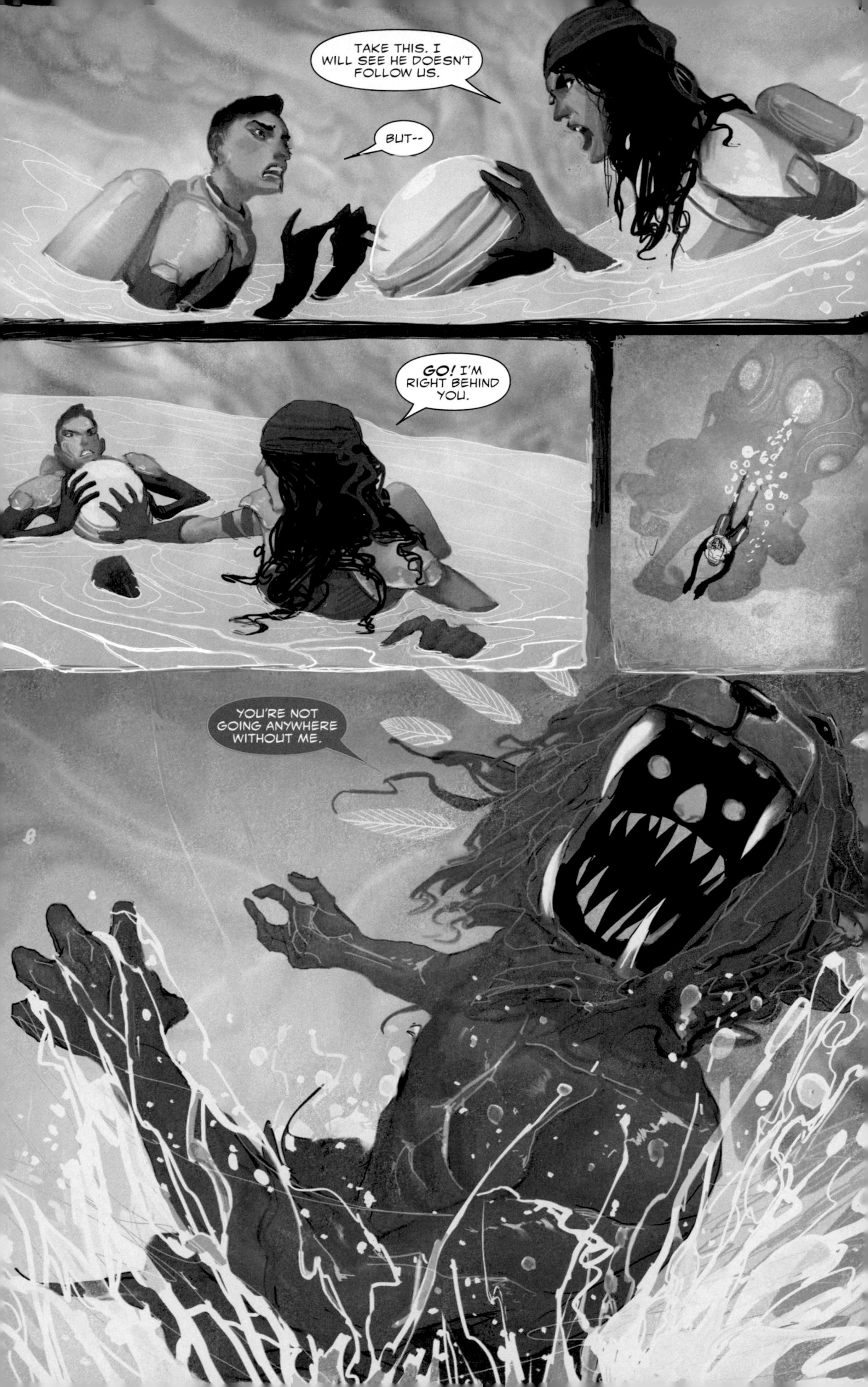
TAKE THIS. I WILL SEE HE DOESN'T FOLLOW US.
BUT--
GO! I'M RIGHT BEHIND YOU.
YOU'RE NOT GOING ANYWHERE WITHOUT ME.

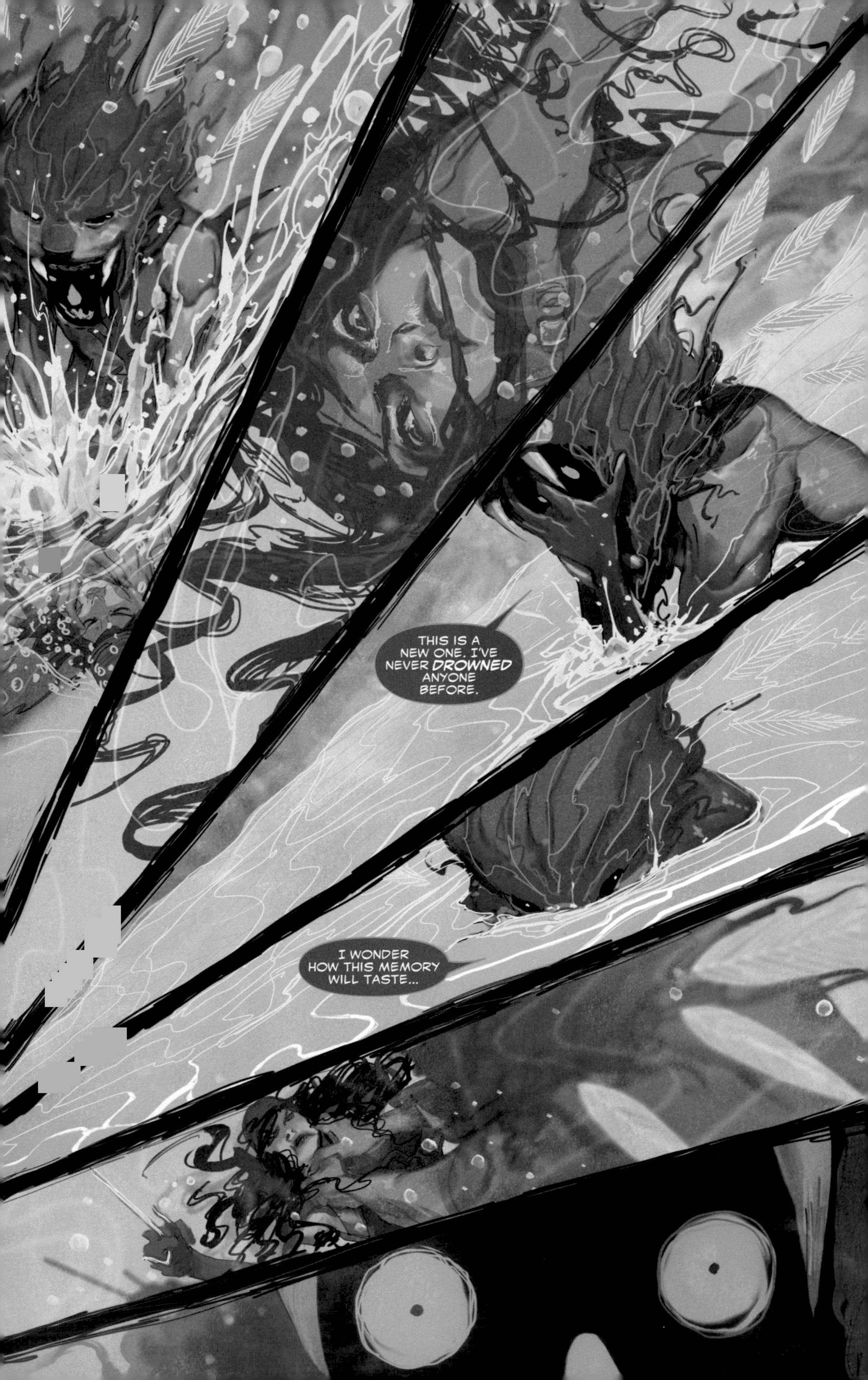
THIS IS A NEW ONE. I'VE NEVER DROWNED ANYONE BEFORE.
I WONDER HOW THIS MEMORY WILL TASTE...

I PIN HIS TONGUE TO HIS SKULL, JUST TO GET HIM TO STOP TALKING.
ALL I CAN SEE ARE FLASHES IN MY BRAIN...
AS HIS VOICE FADES, I CAN HEAR EVERYTHING ELSE...
RED YELLOW BLUE GREEN THEY BURN THE BACK OF MY EYES...
MY HEART HAMMERING IN MY HEAD...
SO BRIGHT CAN'T SEE CAN'T THINK CAN'T HEAL...
MY LUNGS SCREAMING...
ONE LAST FLASH THEN DARKNESS...
MY JAW POPS. THEN SILENCE...

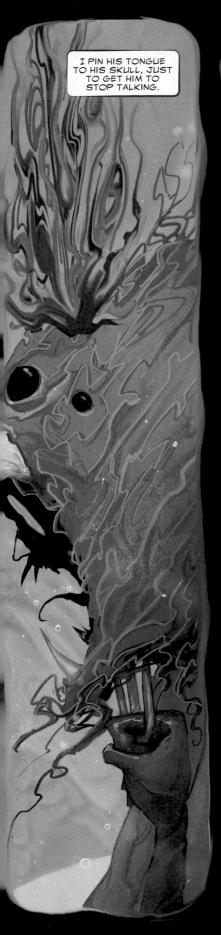

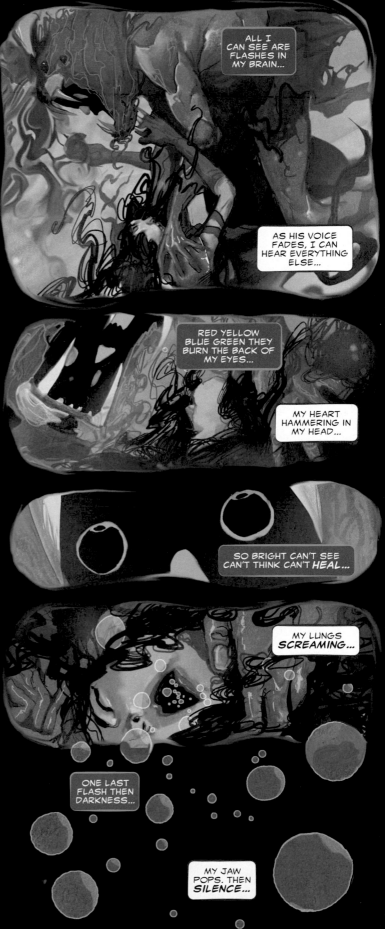

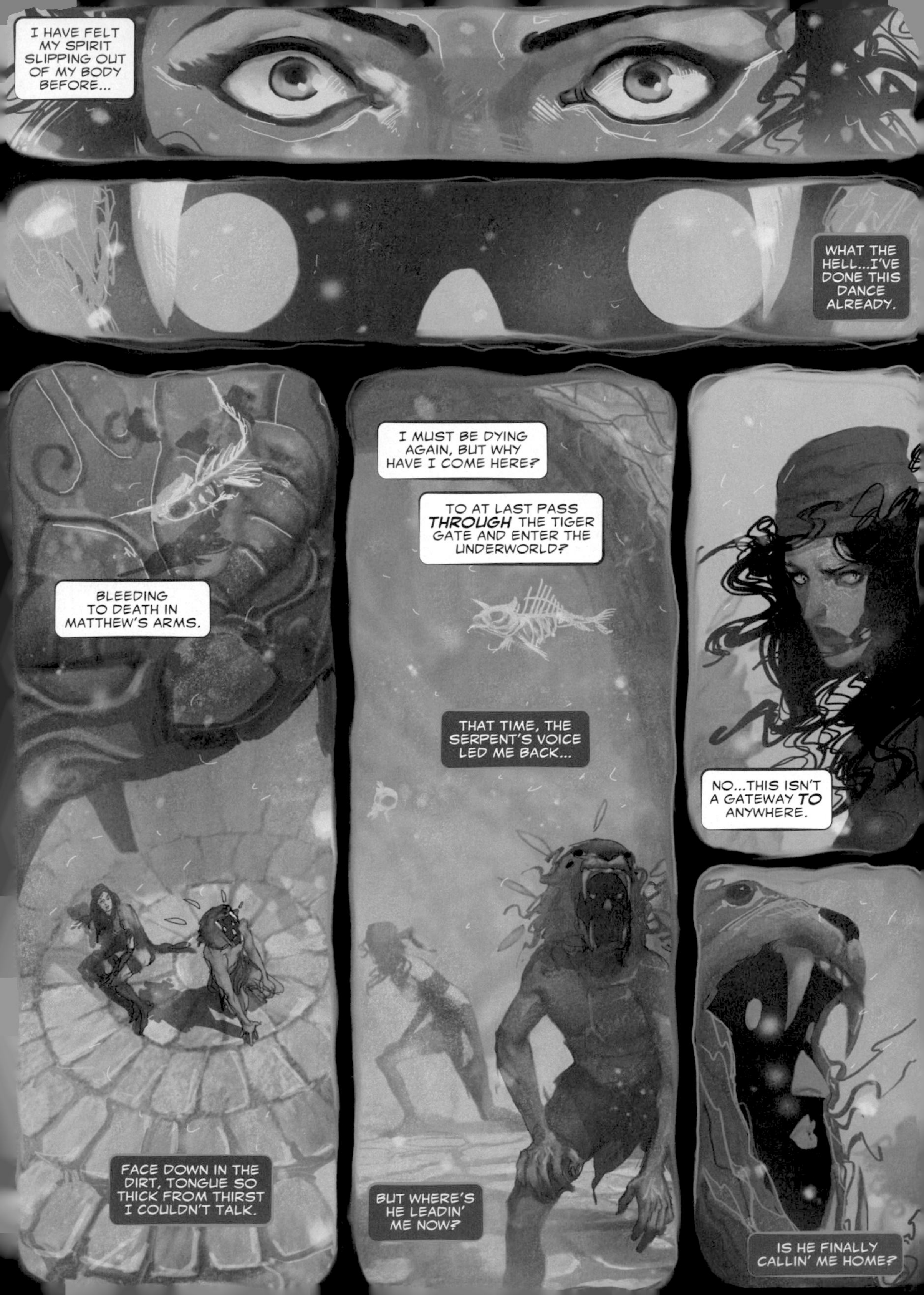
I HAVE FELT MY SPIRIT SLIPPING OUT OF MY BODY BEFORE...
WHAT THE HELL...I'VE DONE THIS DANCE ALREADY.
BLEEDING TO DEATH IN MATTHEW'S ARMS.
FACE DOWN IN THE DIRT, TONGUE SO THICK FROM THIRST I COULDN'T TALK.
I MUST BE DYING AGAIN, BUT WHY HAVE I COME HERE?
TO AT LAST PASS THROUGH THE TIGER GATE AND ENTER THE UNDERWORLD?
THAT TIME, THE SERPENT'S VOICE LED ME BACK...
BUT WHERE'S HE LEADIN' ME NOW?
NO...THIS ISN'T A GATEWAY TO ANYWHERE.
IS HE FINALLY CALLIN' ME HOME?

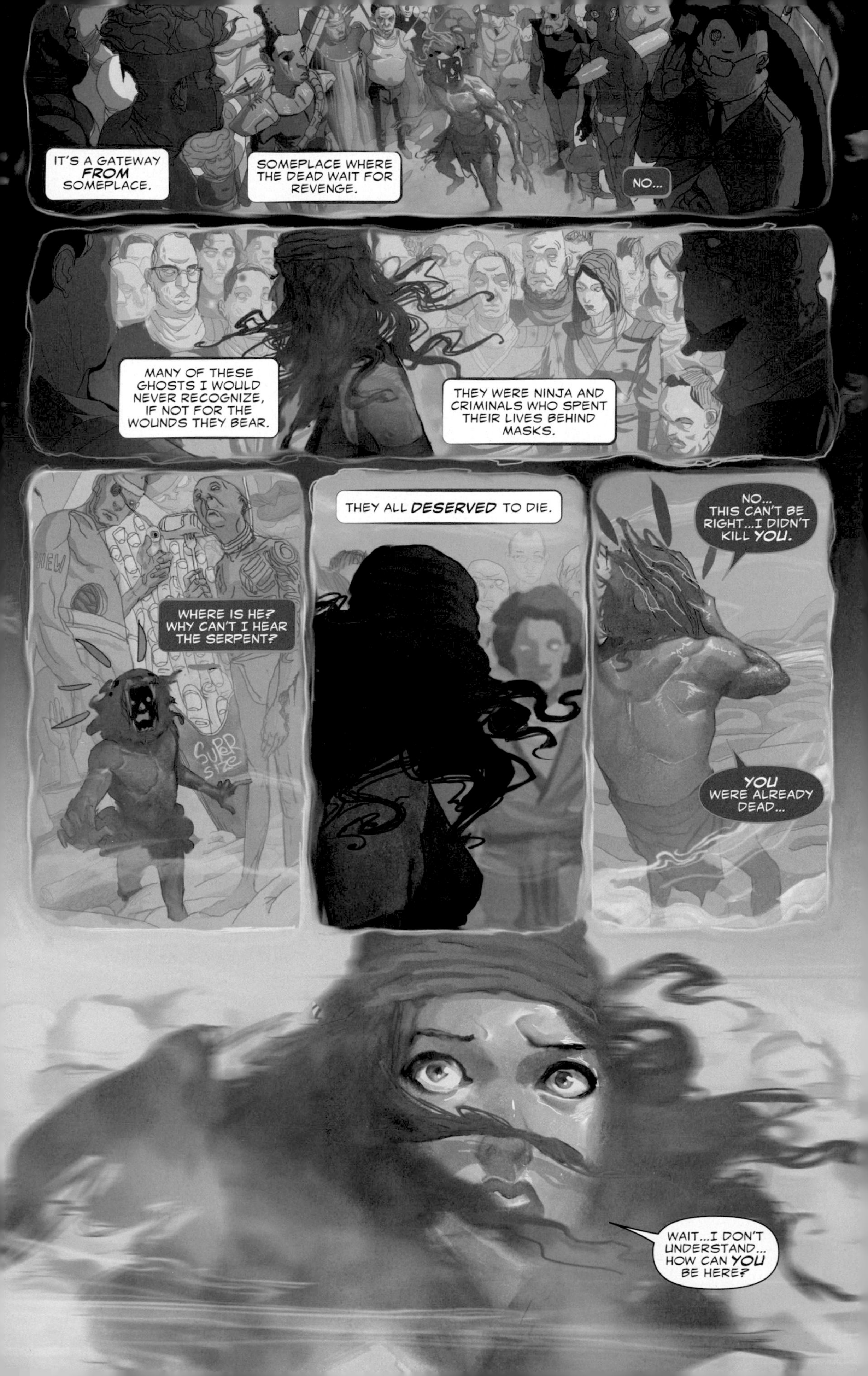
IT'S A GATEWAY *FROM* SOMEPLACE.
SOMEPLACE WHERE THE DEAD WAIT FOR REVENGE.
NO...
MANY OF THESE GHOSTS I WOULD NEVER RECOGNIZE, IF NOT FOR THE WOUNDS THEY BEAR.
THEY WERE NINJA AND CRIMINALS WHO SPENT THEIR LIVES BEHIND MASKS.
WHERE IS HE? WHY CAN'T I HEAR THE SERPENT?
SUPER SIZE
THEY ALL *DESERVED* TO DIE.
NO... THIS CAN'T BE RIGHT...I DIDN'T KILL *YOU.*
YOU WERE ALREADY DEAD...
WAIT...I DON'T UNDERSTAND... HOW CAN *YOU* BE HERE?

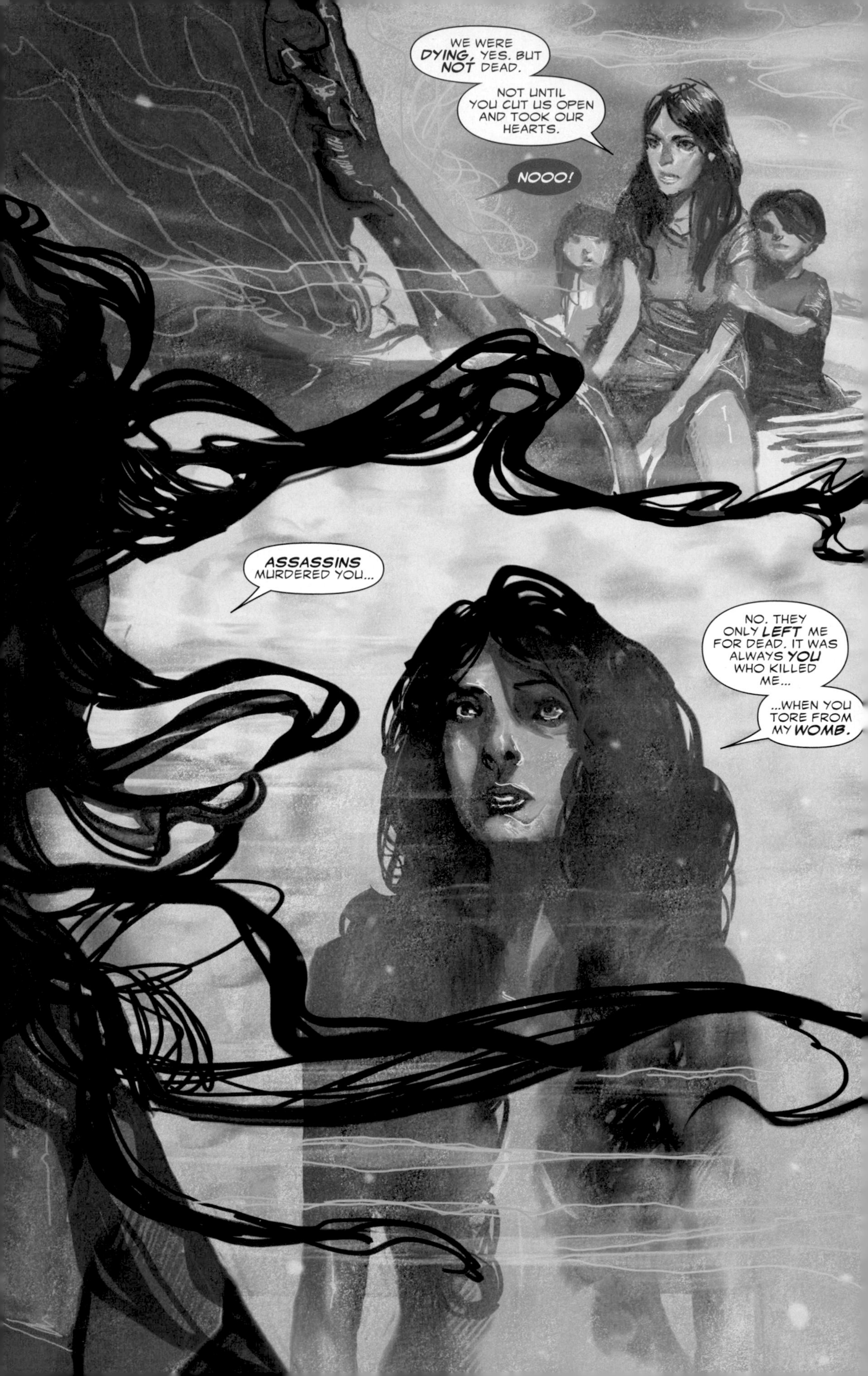
WE WERE DYING, YES. BUT NOT DEAD.
NOT UNTIL YOU CUT US OPEN AND TOOK OUR HEARTS.
NOOO!
ASSASSINS MURDERED YOU...
NO. THEY ONLY LEFT ME FOR DEAD. IT WAS ALWAYS YOU WHO KILLED ME...
...WHEN YOU TORE FROM MY WOMB.

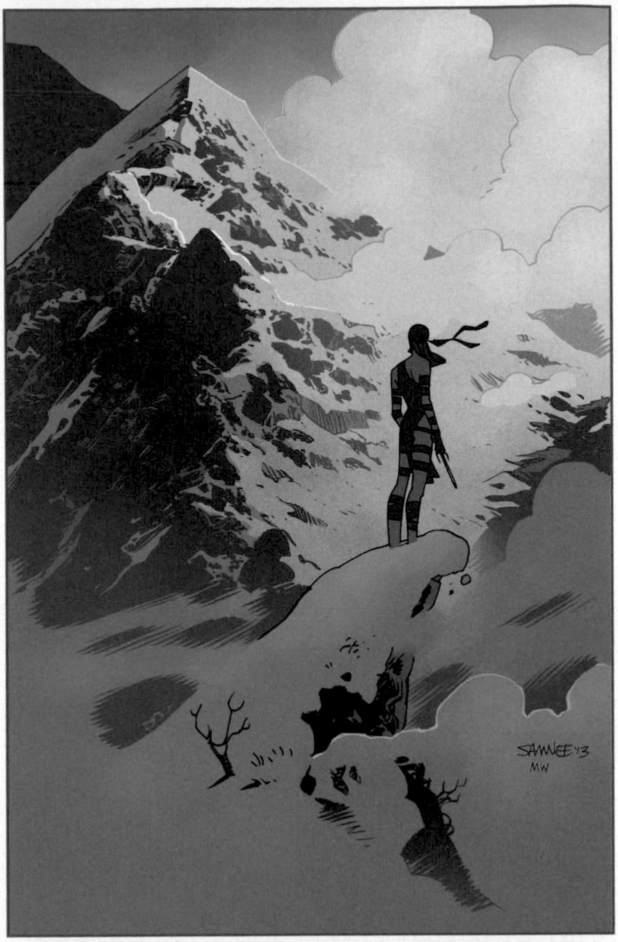
SAMNEE '13
MW

#2 VARIANT
BY CHRIS SAMNEE
& MATTHEW WILSON

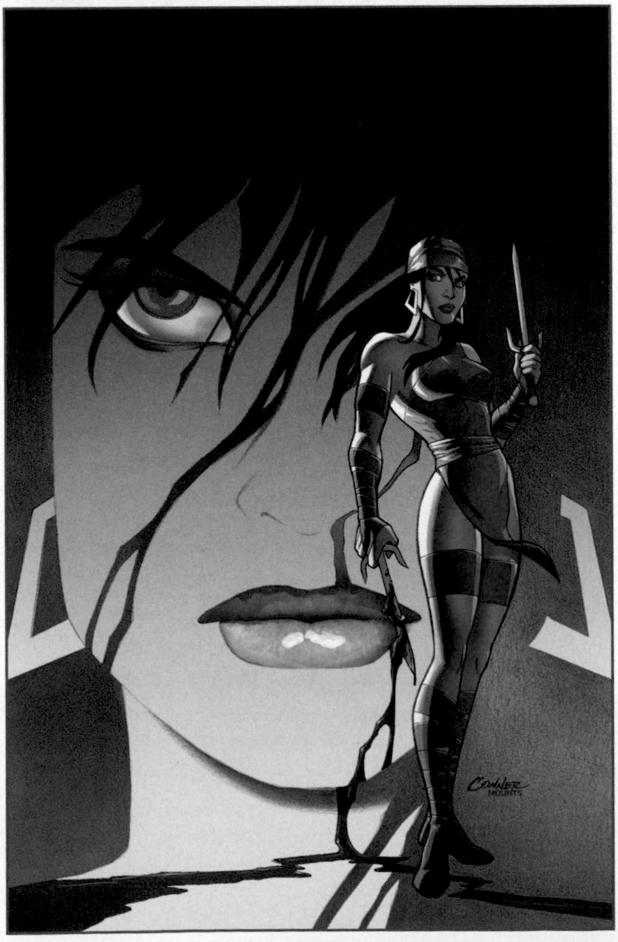

#3 VARIANT
BY AMANDA CONNER
& PAUL MOUNTS

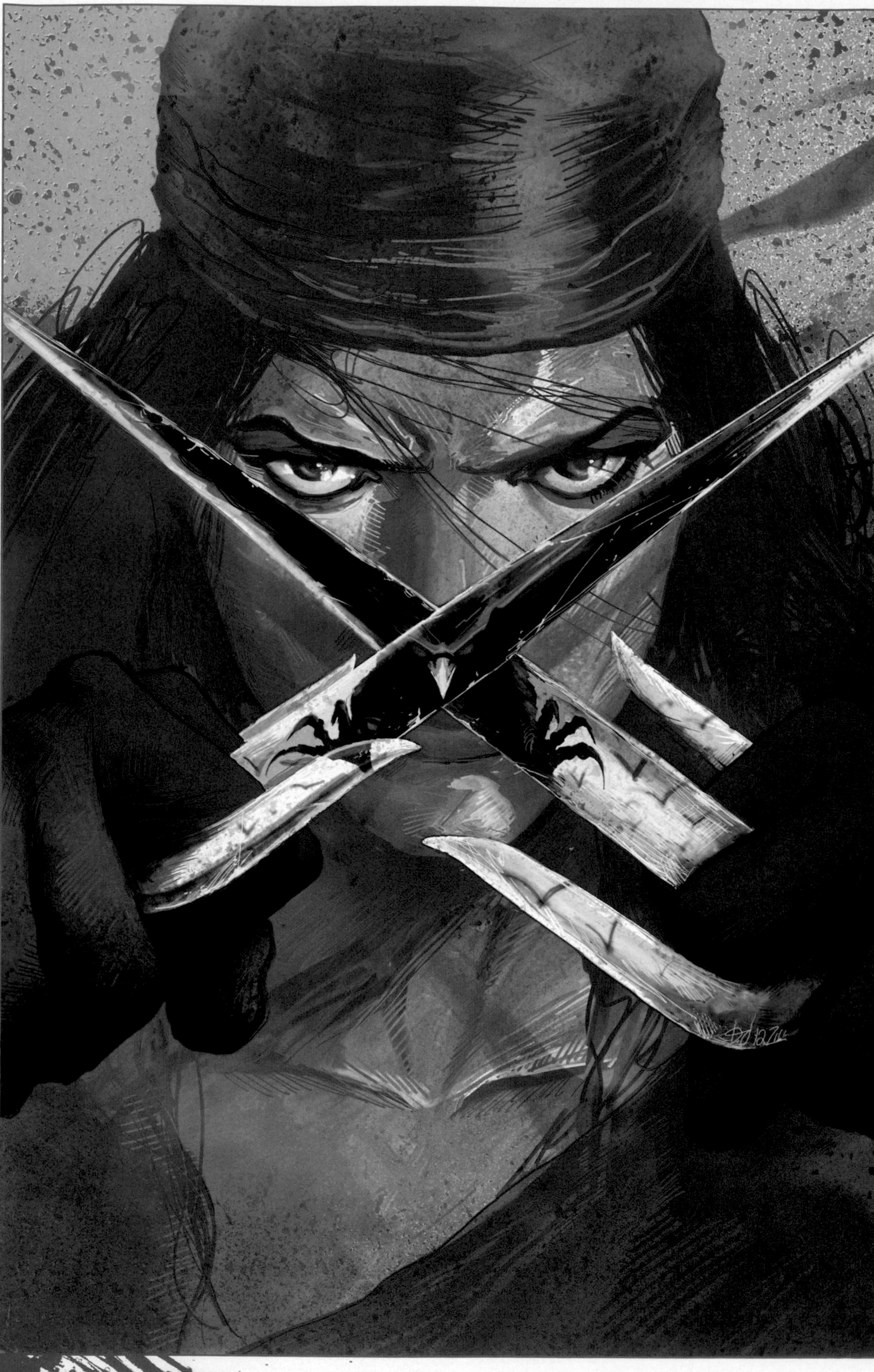

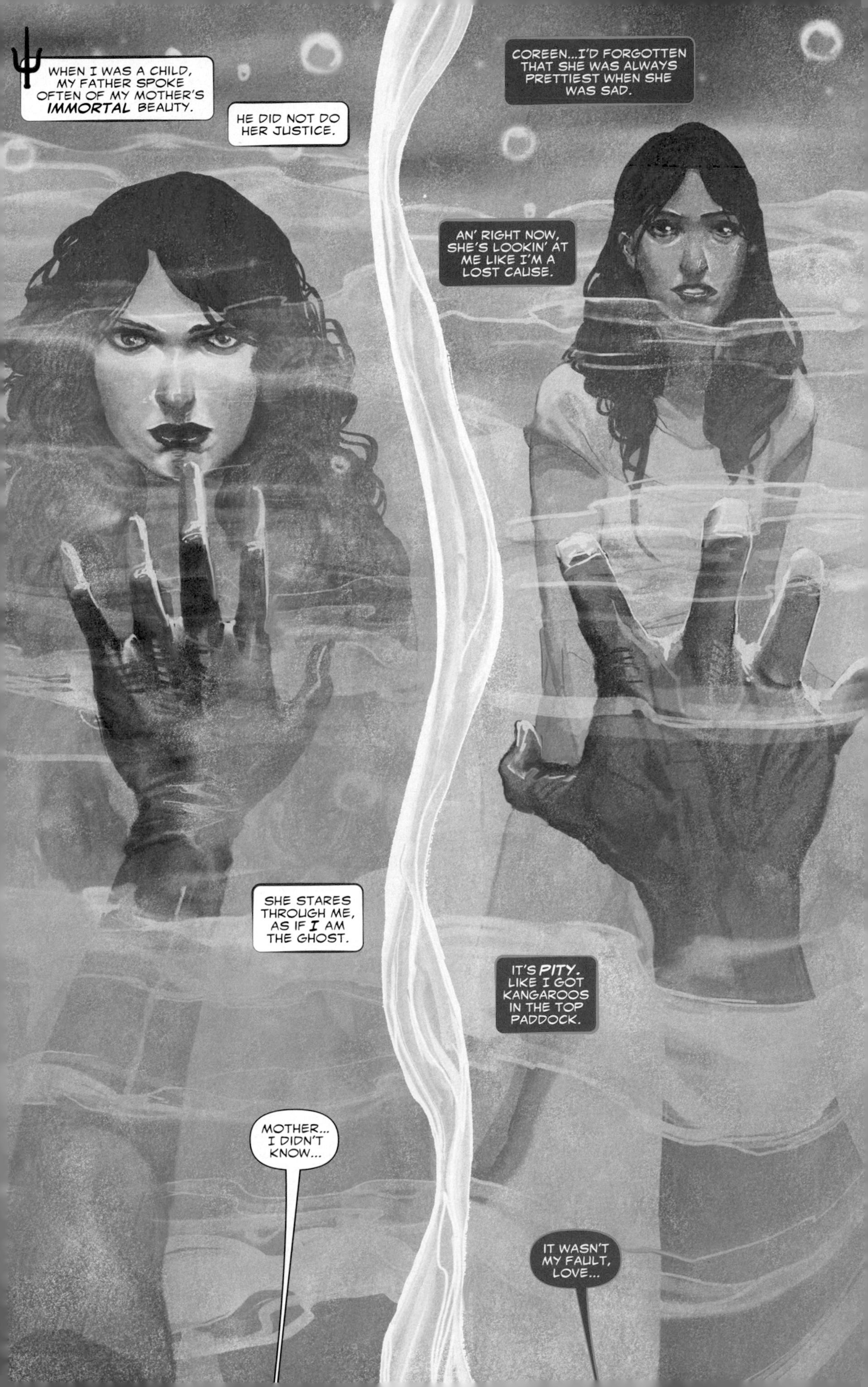
WHEN I WAS A CHILD, MY FATHER SPOKE OFTEN OF MY MOTHER'S *IMMORTAL* BEAUTY.
HE DID NOT DO HER JUSTICE.
SHE STARES THROUGH ME, AS IF *I* AM THE GHOST.
MOTHER... I DIDN'T KNOW...
COREEN...I'D FORGOTTEN THAT SHE WAS ALWAYS PRETTIEST WHEN SHE WAS SAD.
AN' RIGHT NOW, SHE'S LOOKIN' AT ME LIKE I'M A LOST CAUSE.
IT'S *PITY*. LIKE I GOT KANGAROOS IN THE TOP PADDOCK.
IT WASN'T MY FAULT, LOVE...

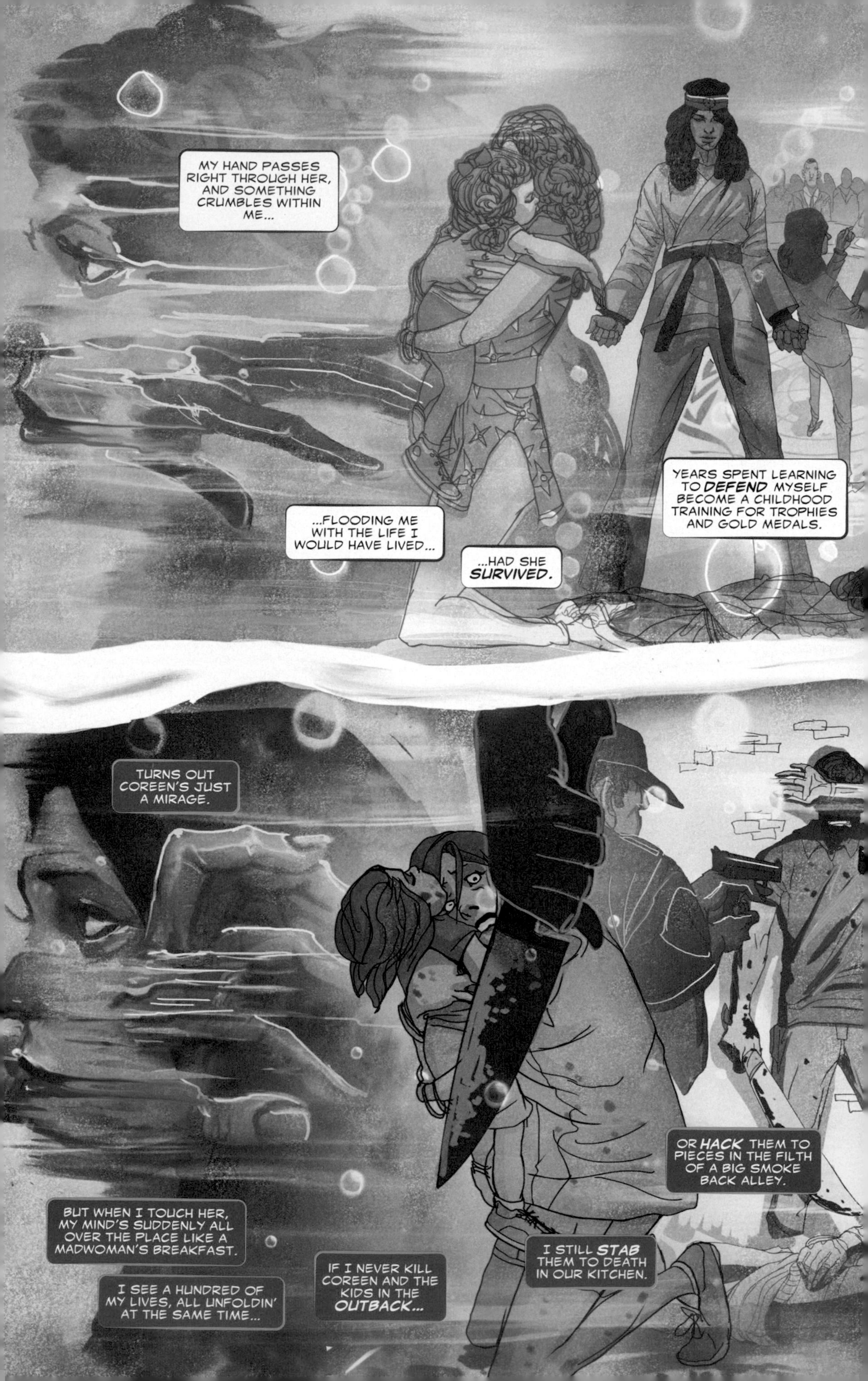
MY HAND PASSES RIGHT THROUGH HER, AND SOMETHING CRUMBLES WITHIN ME...
...FLOODING ME WITH THE LIFE I WOULD HAVE LIVED...
...HAD SHE SURVIVED.
YEARS SPENT LEARNING TO DEFEND MYSELF BECOME A CHILDHOOD TRAINING FOR TROPHIES AND GOLD MEDALS.
TURNS OUT COREEN'S JUST A MIRAGE.
BUT WHEN I TOUCH HER, MY MIND'S SUDDENLY ALL OVER THE PLACE LIKE A MADWOMAN'S BREAKFAST.
I SEE A HUNDRED OF MY LIVES, ALL UNFOLDIN' AT THE SAME TIME...
IF I NEVER KILL COREEN AND THE KIDS IN THE OUTBACK...
I STILL STAB THEM TO DEATH IN OUR KITCHEN.
OR HACK THEM TO PIECES IN THE FILTH OF A BIG SMOKE BACK ALLEY.

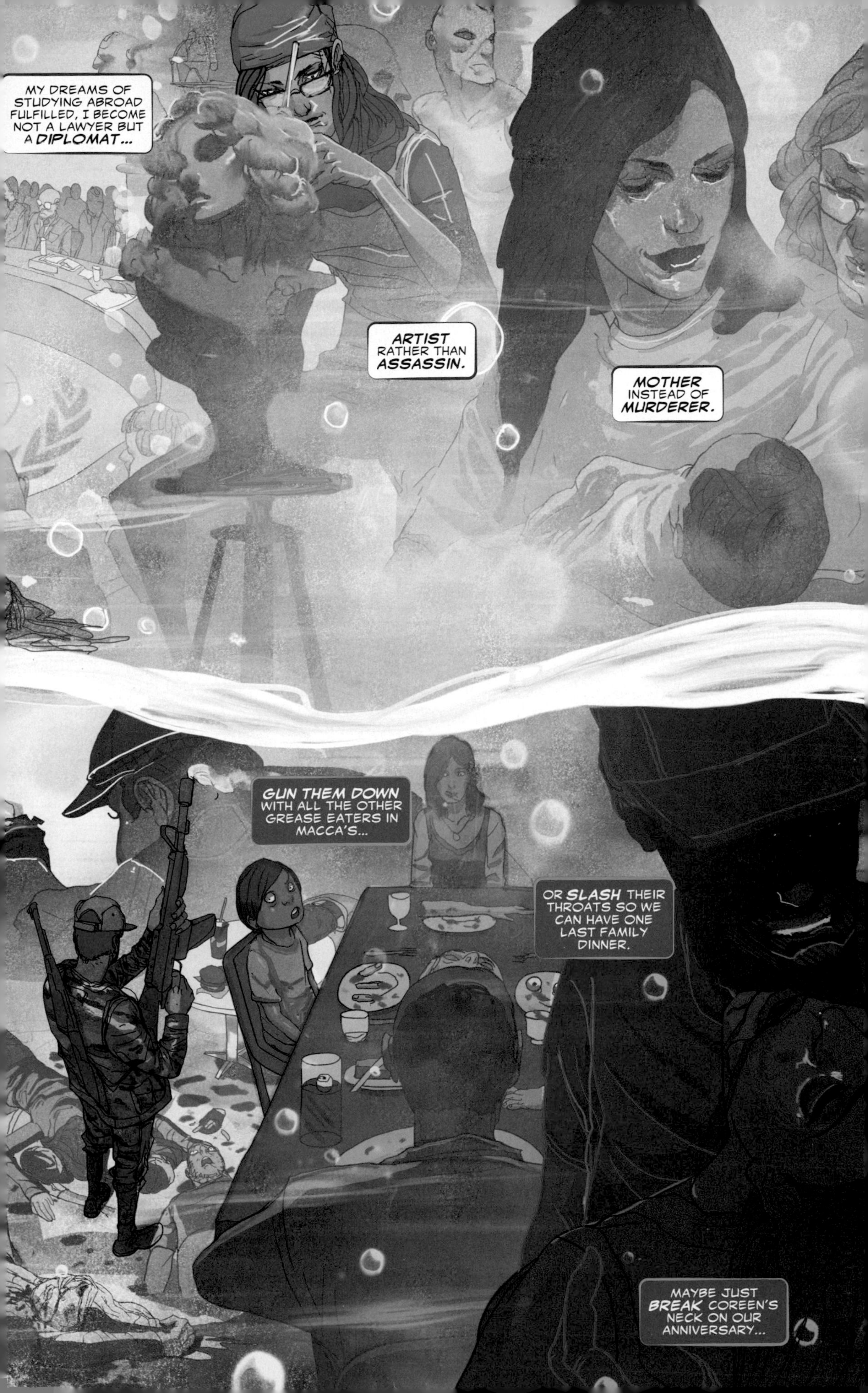
MY DREAMS OF STUDYING ABROAD FULFILLED, I BECOME NOT A LAWYER BUT A DIPLOMAT...
ARTIST RATHER THAN ASSASSIN.
MOTHER INSTEAD OF MURDERER.
GUN THEM DOWN WITH ALL THE OTHER GREASE EATERS IN MACCA'S...
OR SLASH THEIR THROATS SO WE CAN HAVE ONE LAST FAMILY DINNER.
MAYBE JUST BREAK COREEN'S NECK ON OUR ANNIVERSARY...

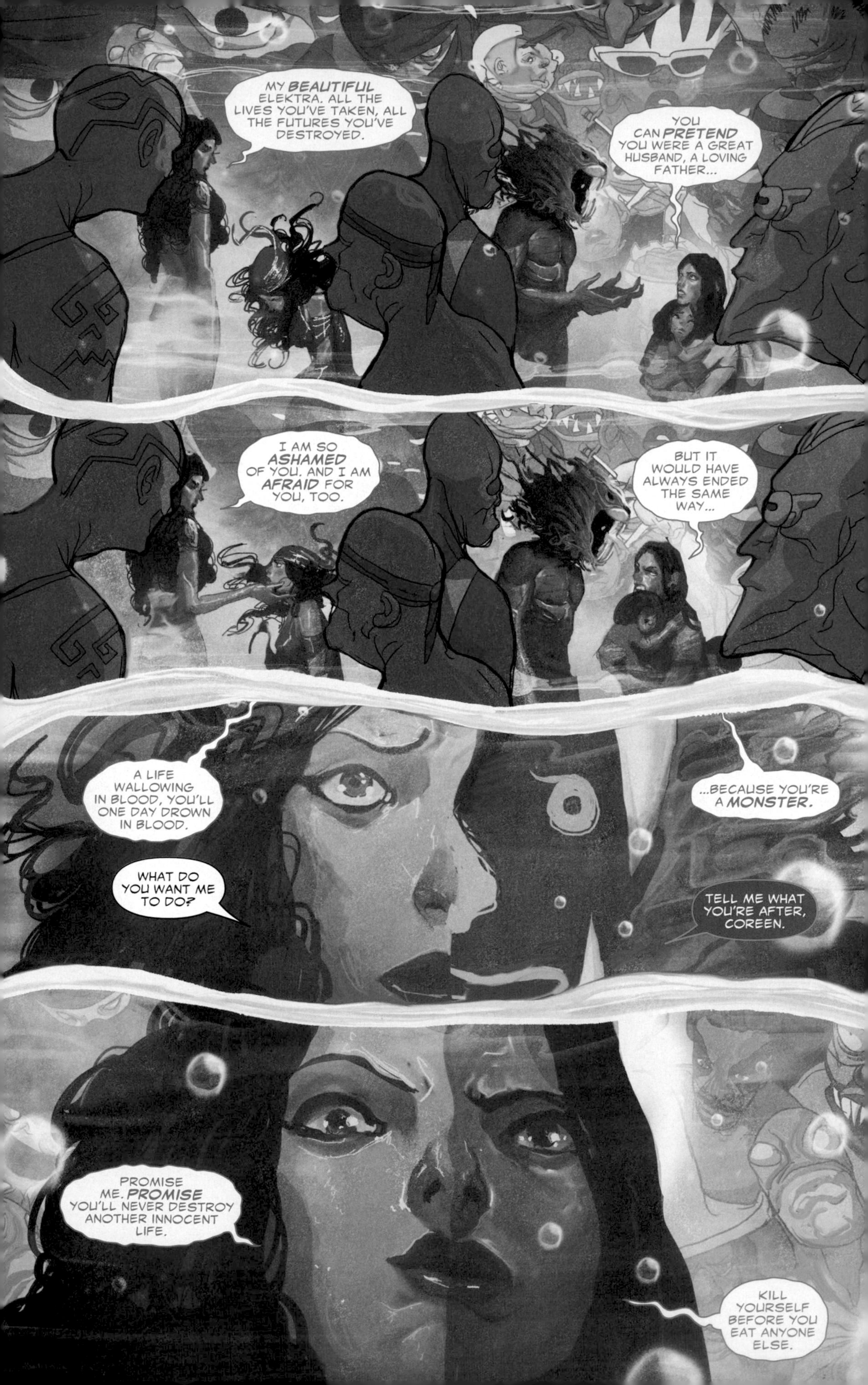
MY BEAUTIFUL ELEKTRA. ALL THE LIVES YOU'VE TAKEN, ALL THE FUTURES YOU'VE DESTROYED.
YOU CAN PRETEND YOU WERE A GREAT HUSBAND, A LOVING FATHER...
I AM SO ASHAMED OF YOU. AND I AM AFRAID FOR YOU, TOO.
BUT IT WOULD HAVE ALWAYS ENDED THE SAME WAY...
A LIFE WALLOWING IN BLOOD, YOU'LL ONE DAY DROWN IN BLOOD.
...BECAUSE YOU'RE A MONSTER.
WHAT DO YOU WANT ME TO DO?
TELL ME WHAT YOU'RE AFTER, COREEN.
PROMISE ME. PROMISE YOU'LL NEVER DESTROY ANOTHER INNOCENT LIFE.
KILL YOURSELF BEFORE YOU EAT ANYONE ELSE.

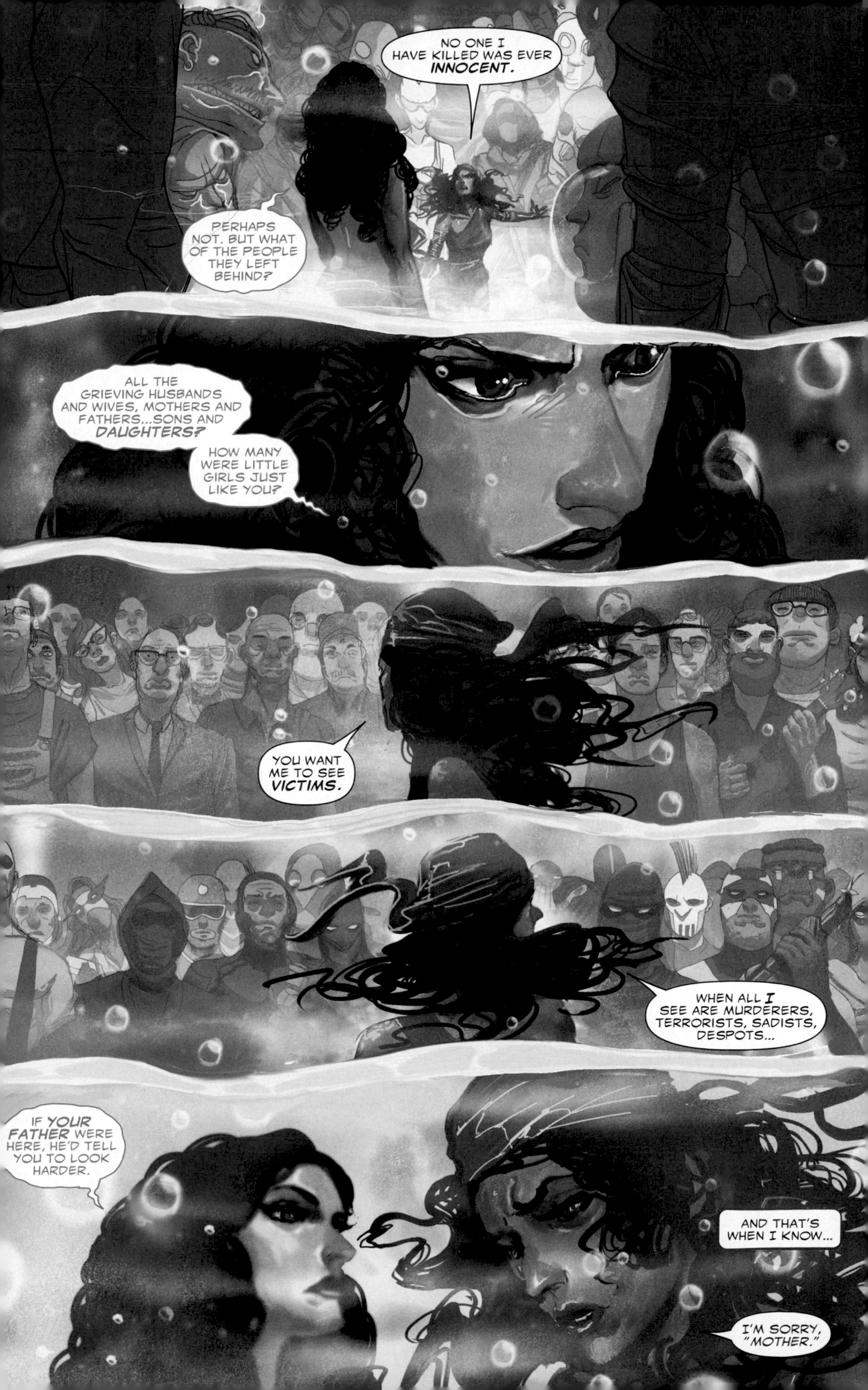
NO ONE I HAVE KILLED WAS EVER INNOCENT.
PERHAPS NOT. BUT WHAT OF THE PEOPLE THEY LEFT BEHIND?
ALL THE GRIEVING HUSBANDS AND WIVES, MOTHERS AND FATHERS...SONS AND DAUGHTERS?
HOW MANY WERE LITTLE GIRLS JUST LIKE YOU?
YOU WANT ME TO SEE VICTIMS.
WHEN ALL I SEE ARE MURDERERS, TERRORISTS, SADISTS, DESPOTS...
IF YOUR FATHER WERE HERE, HE'D TELL YOU TO LOOK HARDER.
AND THAT'S WHEN I KNOW...
I'M SORRY, "MOTHER."

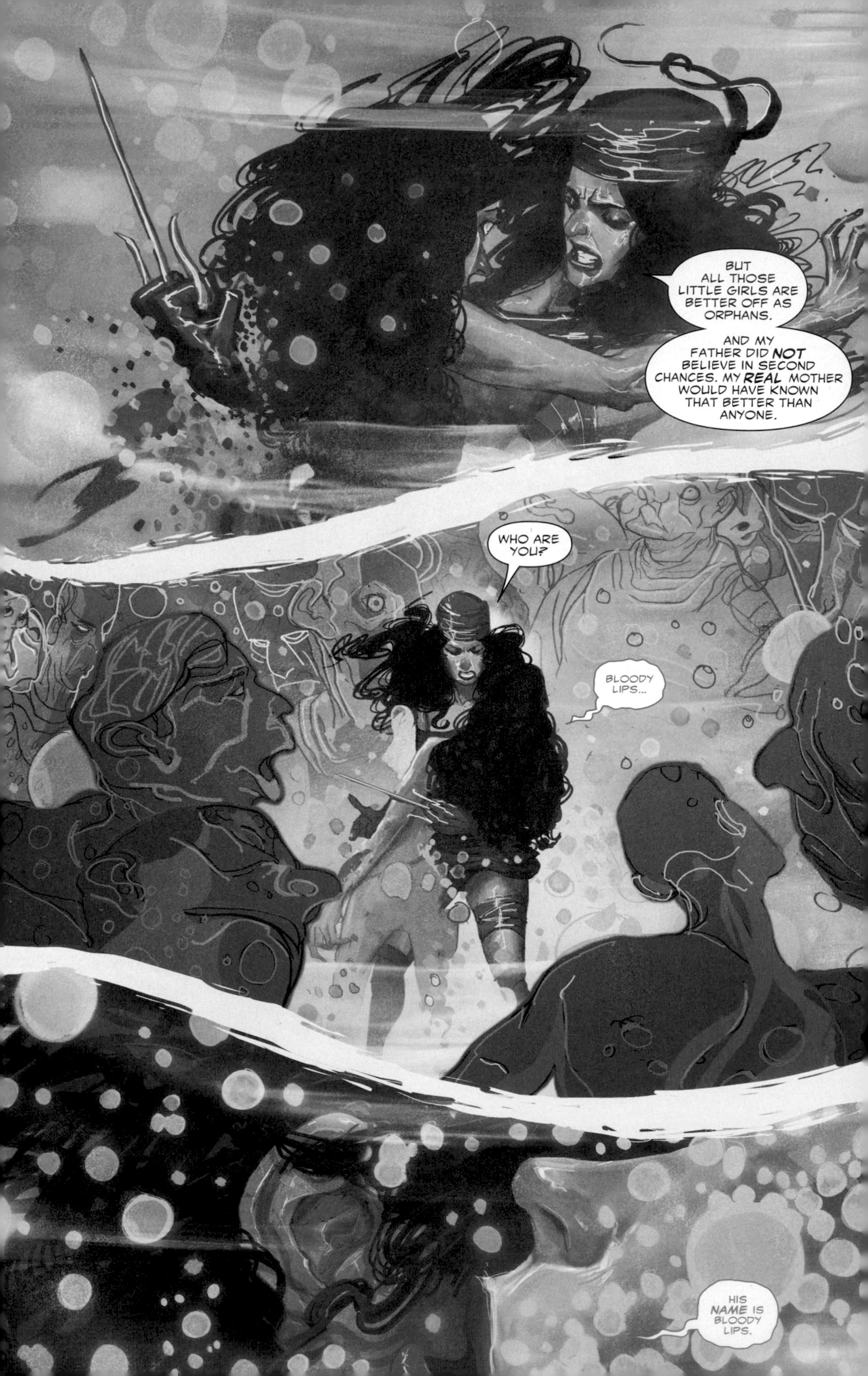
BUT ALL THOSE LITTLE GIRLS ARE BETTER OFF AS ORPHANS.
AND MY FATHER DID **NOT** BELIEVE IN SECOND CHANCES. MY ***REAL*** MOTHER WOULD HAVE KNOWN THAT BETTER THAN ANYONE.
WHO ARE YOU?
BLOODY LIPS...
HIS ***NAME*** IS BLOODY LIPS.

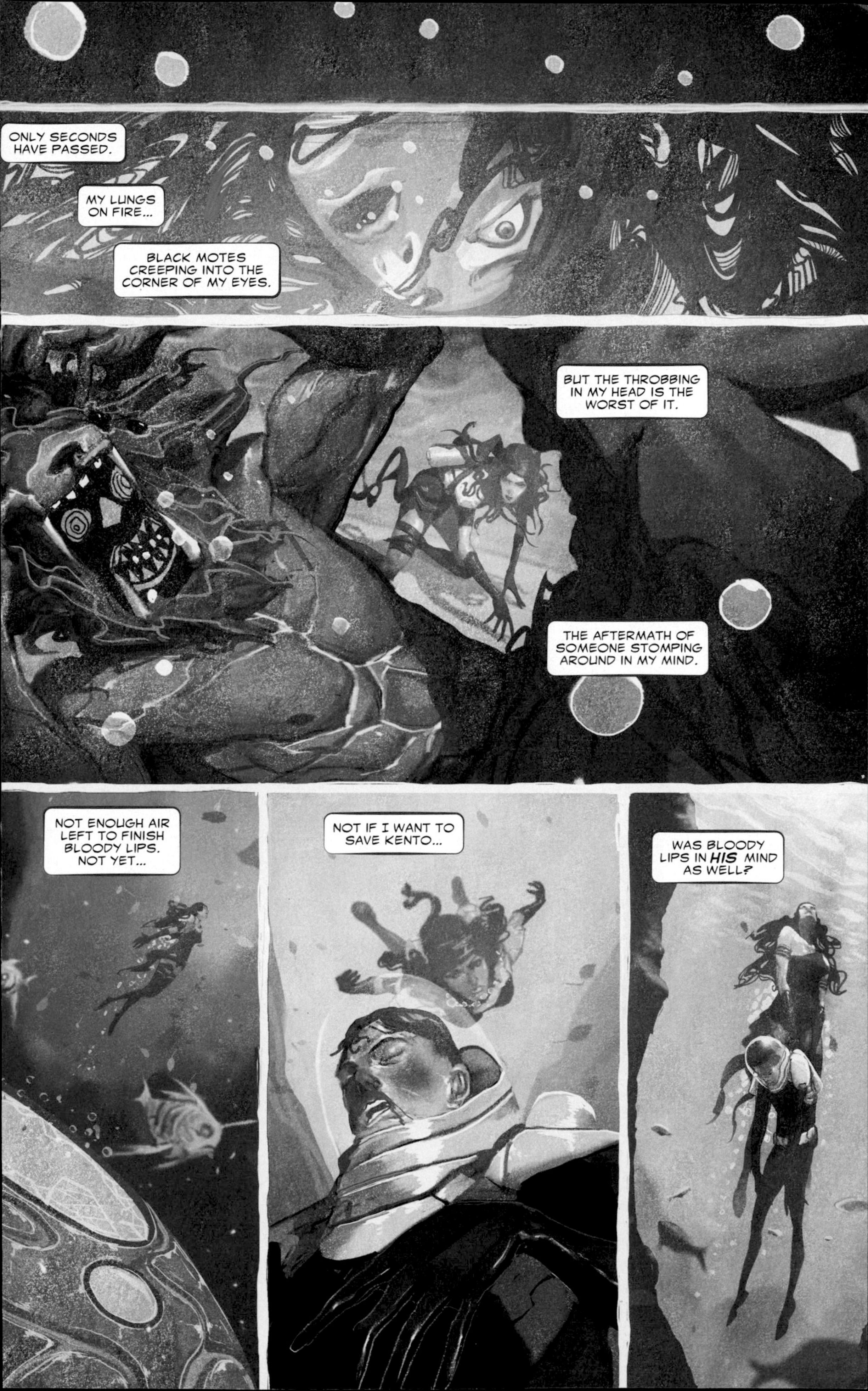
ONLY SECONDS HAVE PASSED.
MY LUNGS ON FIRE...
BLACK MOTES CREEPING INTO THE CORNER OF MY EYES.
BUT THE THROBBING IN MY HEAD IS THE WORST OF IT.
THE AFTERMATH OF SOMEONE STOMPING AROUND IN MY MIND.
NOT ENOUGH AIR LEFT TO FINISH BLOODY LIPS. NOT YET...
NOT IF I WANT TO SAVE KENTO...
WAS BLOODY LIPS IN ***HIS*** MIND AS WELL?

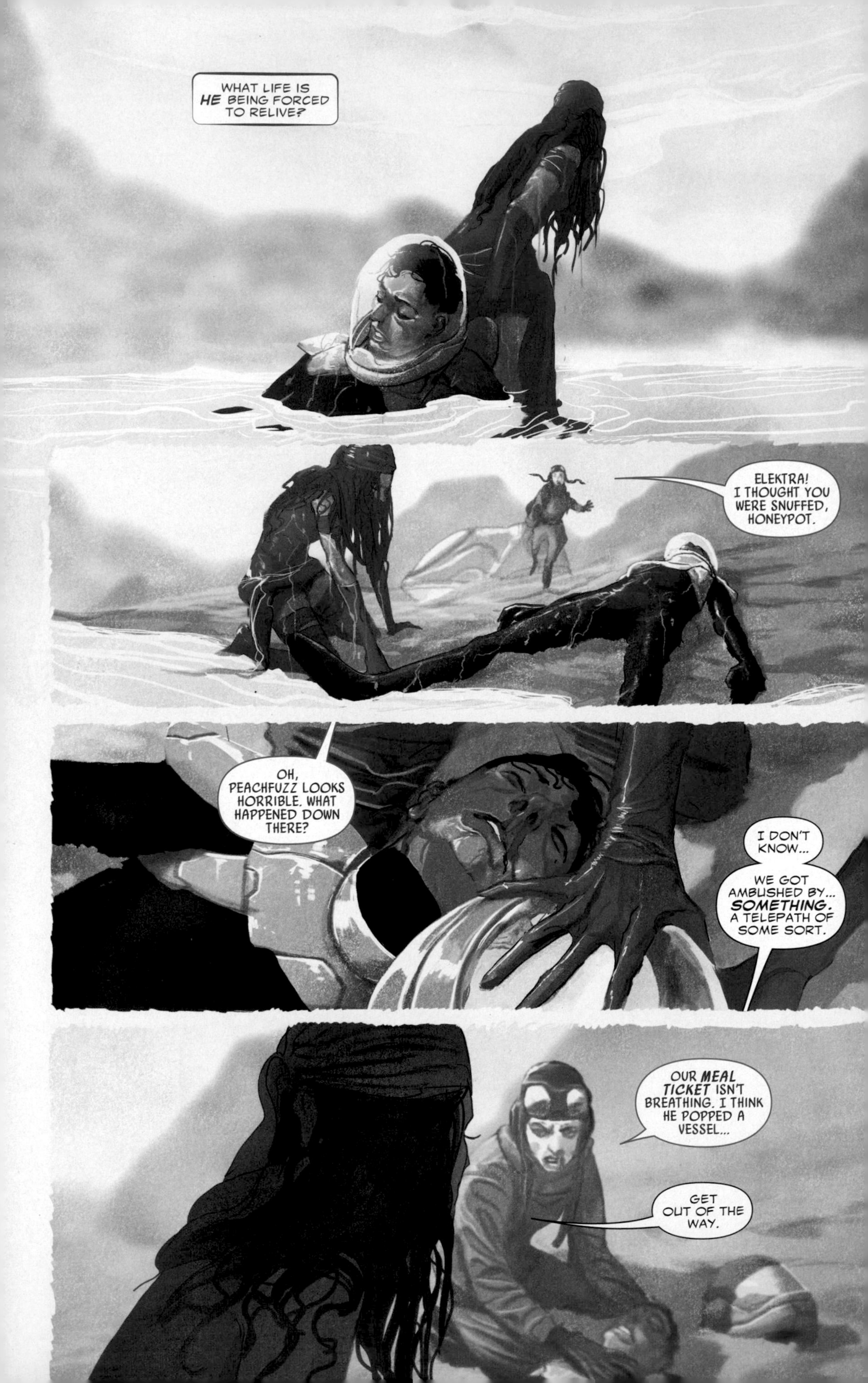
WHAT LIFE IS HE BEING FORCED TO RELIVE?
ELEKTRA! I THOUGHT YOU WERE SNUFFED, HONEYPOT.
OH, PEACHFUZZ LOOKS HORRIBLE. WHAT HAPPENED DOWN THERE?
I DON'T KNOW...
WE GOT AMBUSHED BY... SOMETHING. A TELEPATH OF SOME SORT.
OUR MEAL TICKET ISN'T BREATHING. I THINK HE POPPED A VESSEL...
GET OUT OF THE WAY.

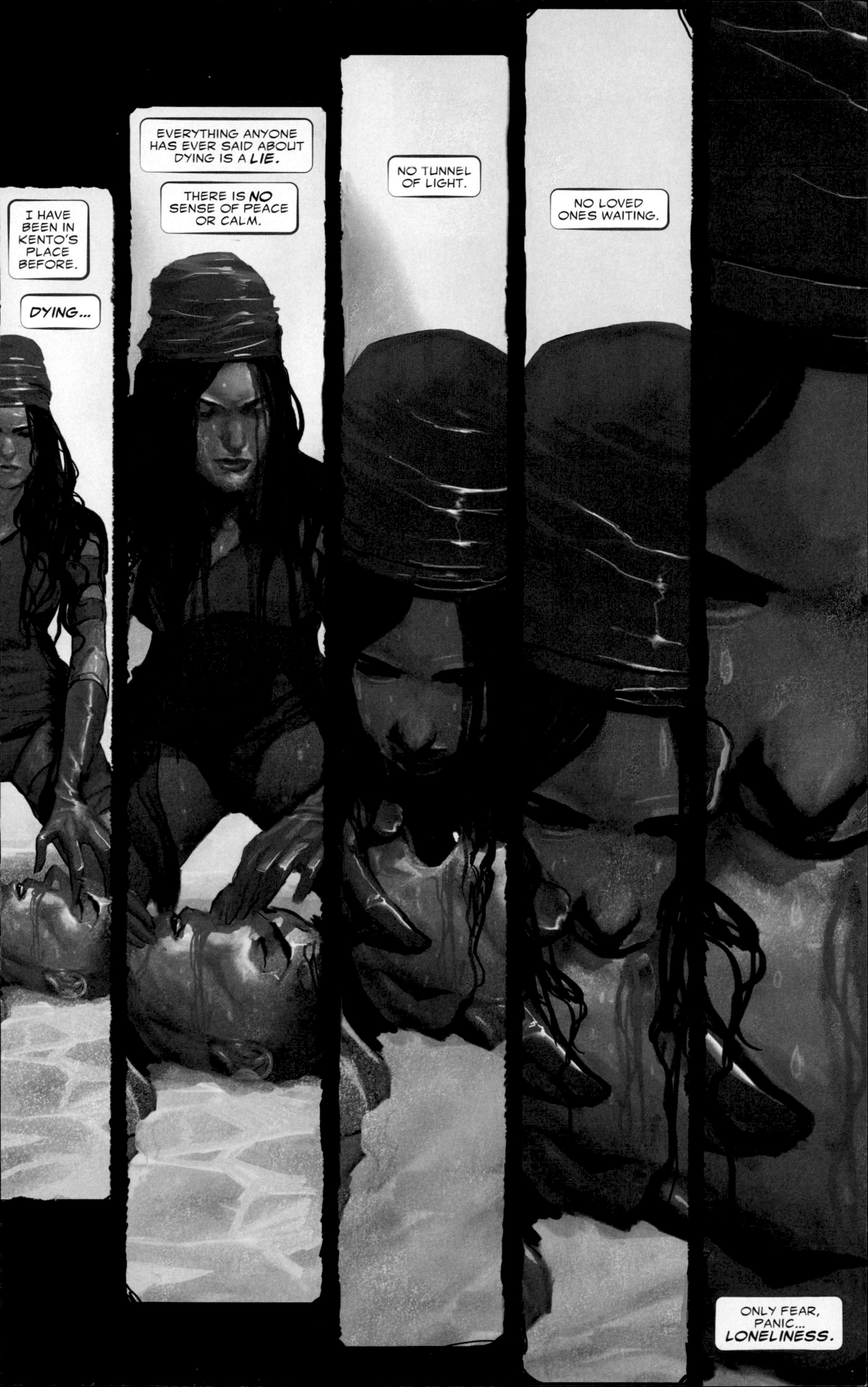
I HAVE BEEN IN KENTO'S PLACE BEFORE.
DYING...
EVERYTHING ANYONE HAS EVER SAID ABOUT DYING IS A LIE.
THERE IS NO SENSE OF PEACE OR CALM.
NO TUNNEL OF LIGHT.
NO LOVED ONES WAITING.
ONLY FEAR, PANIC... LONELINESS.

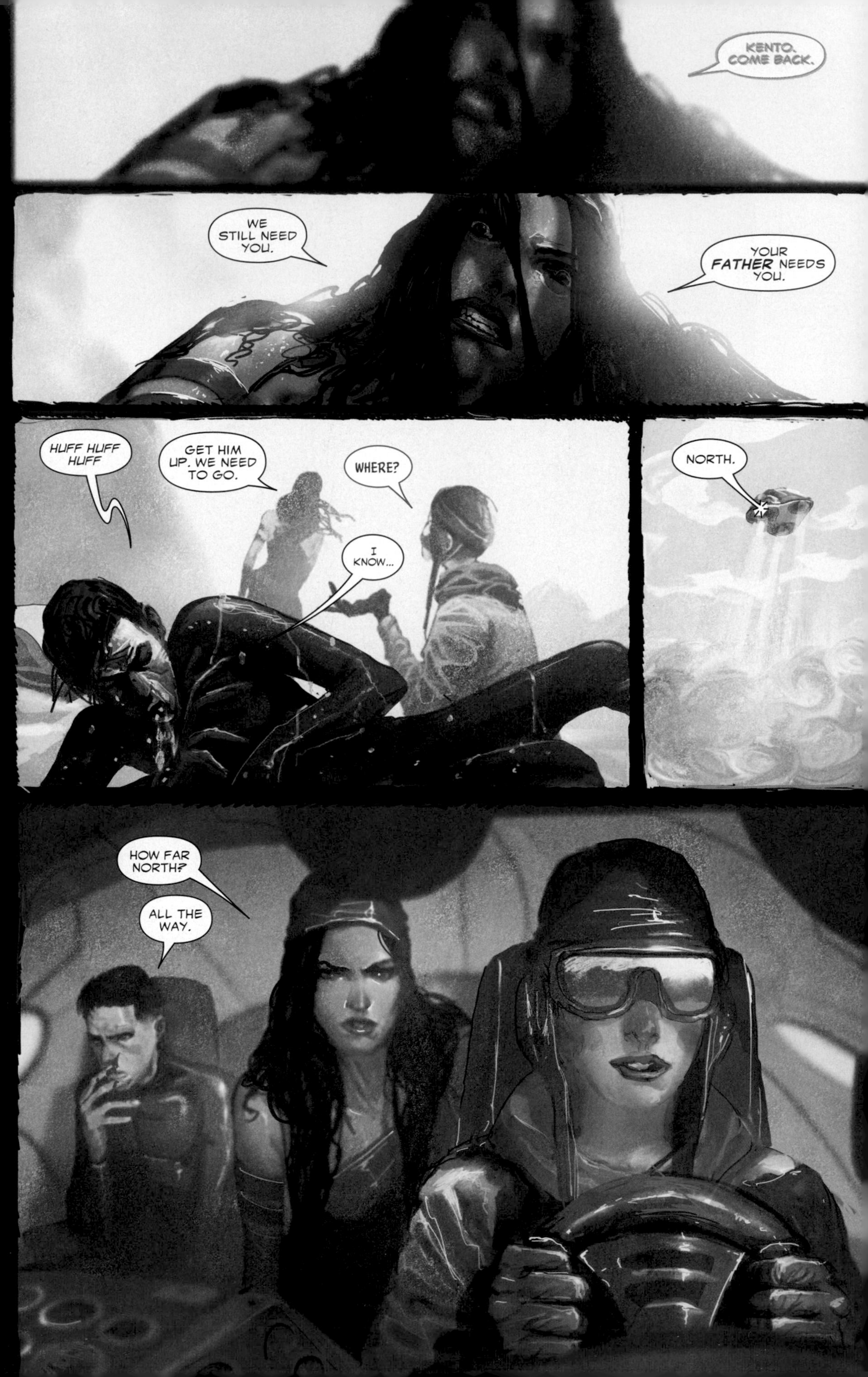
KENTO. COME BACK.
WE STILL NEED YOU.
YOUR FATHER NEEDS YOU.
HUFF HUFF HUFF
GET HIM UP. WE NEED TO GO.
WHERE?
I KNOW...
NORTH.
HOW FAR NORTH?
ALL THE WAY.

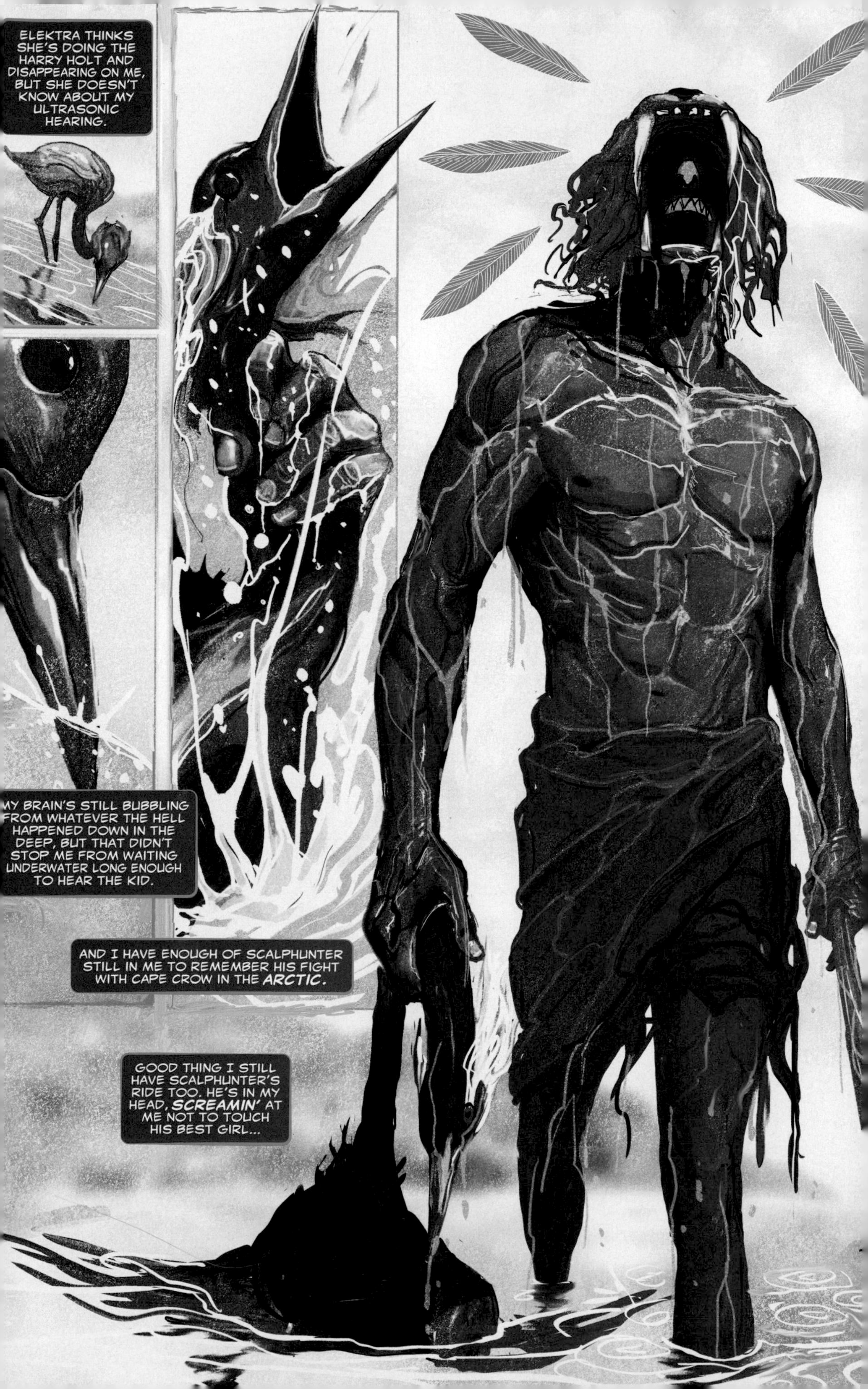
ELEKTRA THINKS SHE'S DOING THE HARRY HOLT AND DISAPPEARING ON ME, BUT SHE DOESN'T KNOW ABOUT MY ULTRASONIC HEARING.
MY BRAIN'S STILL BUBBLING FROM WHATEVER THE HELL HAPPENED DOWN IN THE DEEP, BUT THAT DIDN'T STOP ME FROM WAITING UNDERWATER LONG ENOUGH TO HEAR THE KID.
AND I HAVE ENOUGH OF SCALPHUNTER STILL IN ME TO REMEMBER HIS FIGHT WITH CAPE CROW IN THE ARCTIC.
GOOD THING I STILL HAVE SCALPHUNTER'S RIDE TOO. HE'S IN MY HEAD, SCREAMIN' AT ME NOT TO TOUCH HIS BEST GIRL...

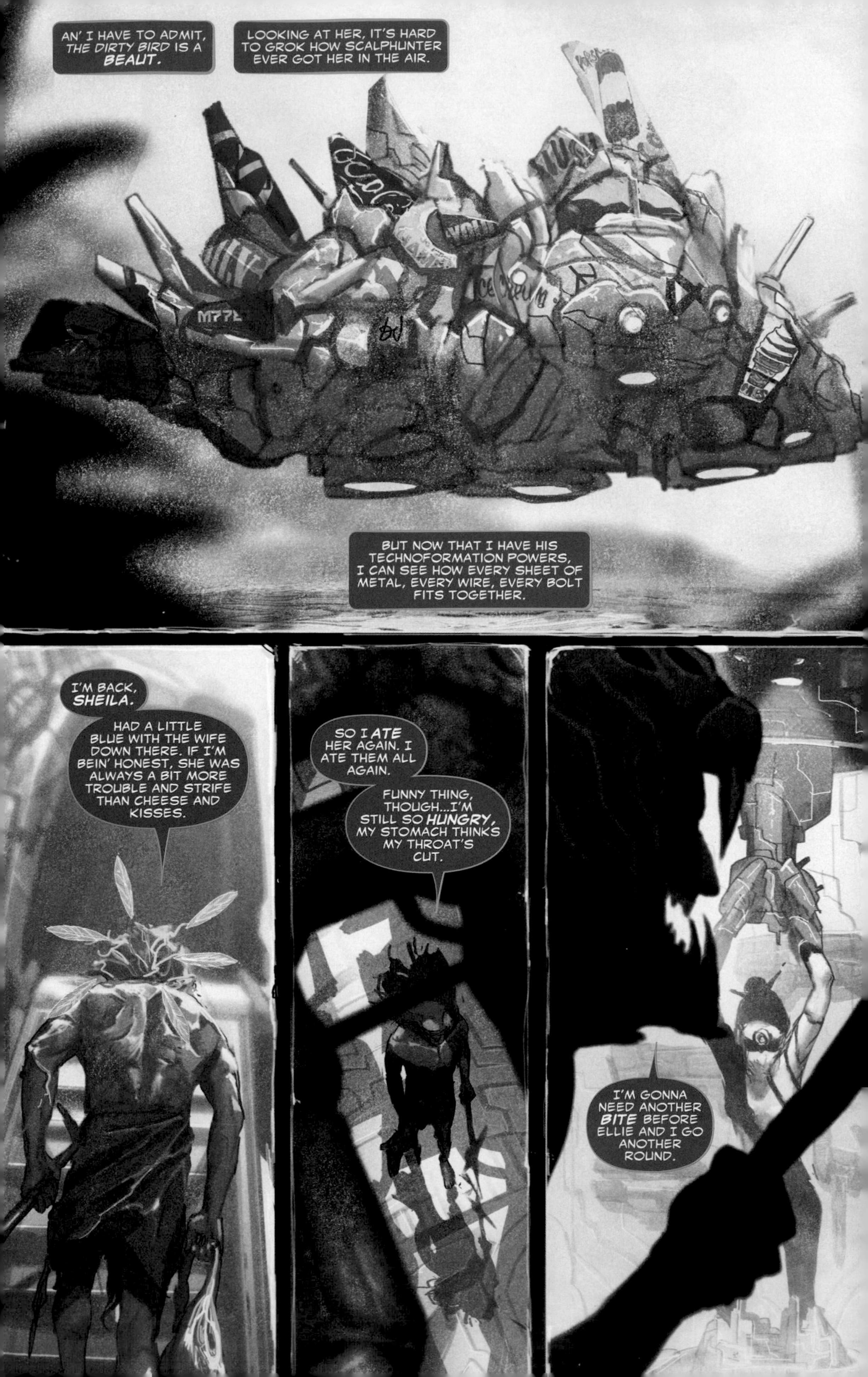
AN' I HAVE TO ADMIT, THE DIRTY BIRD IS A BEAUT.
LOOKING AT HER, IT'S HARD TO GROK HOW SCALPHUNTER EVER GOT HER IN THE AIR.
BUT NOW THAT I HAVE HIS TECHNOFORMATION POWERS, I CAN SEE HOW EVERY SHEET OF METAL, EVERY WIRE, EVERY BOLT FITS TOGETHER.
I'M BACK, SHEILA.
HAD A LITTLE BLUE WITH THE WIFE DOWN THERE. IF I'M BEIN' HONEST, SHE WAS ALWAYS A BIT MORE TROUBLE AND STRIFE THAN CHEESE AND KISSES.
SO I ATE HER AGAIN. I ATE THEM ALL AGAIN.
FUNNY THING, THOUGH...I'M STILL SO HUNGRY, MY STOMACH THINKS MY THROAT'S CUT.
I'M GONNA NEED ANOTHER BITE BEFORE ELLIE AND I GO ANOTHER ROUND.

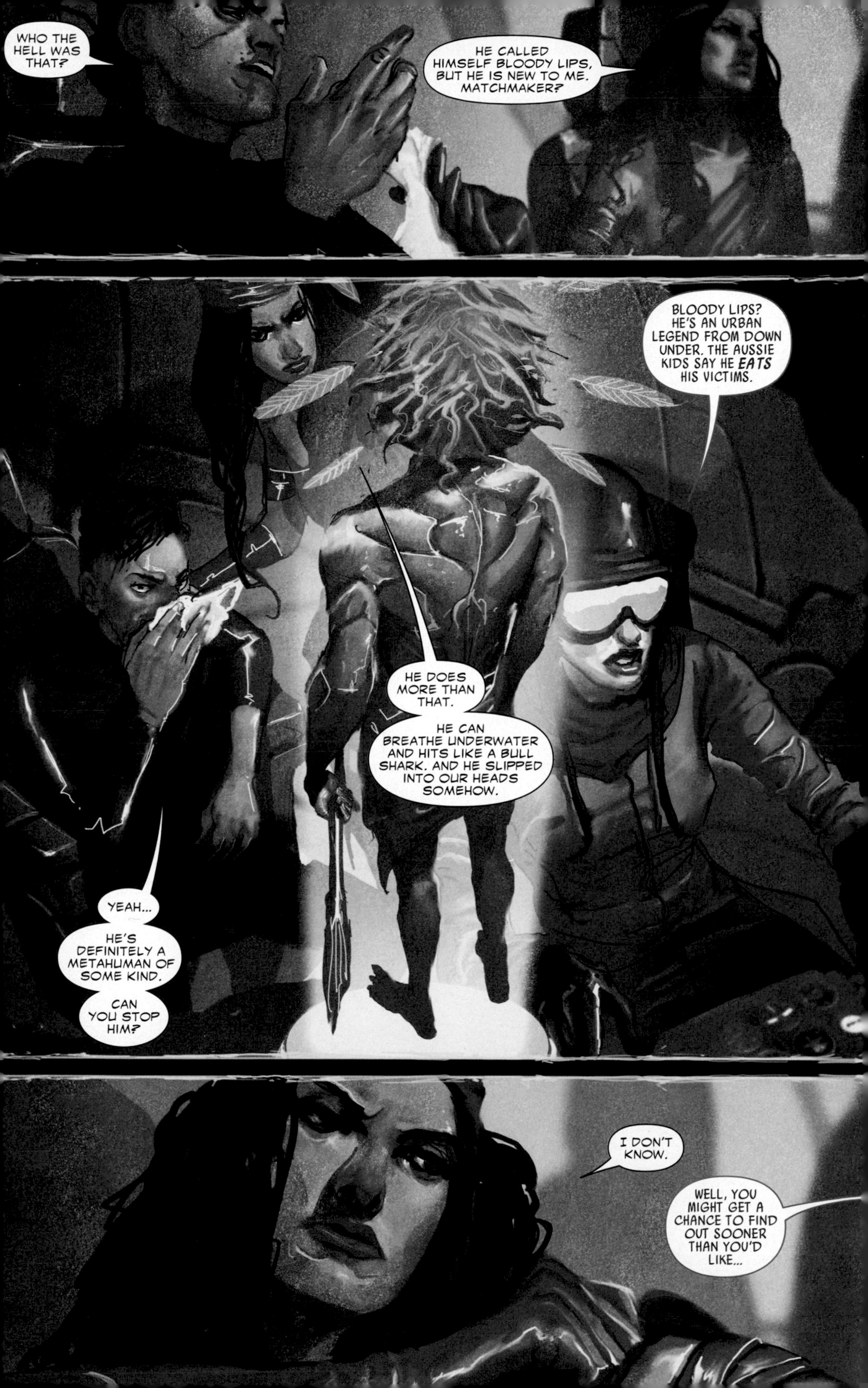
WHO THE HELL WAS THAT?
HE CALLED HIMSELF BLOODY LIPS, BUT HE IS NEW TO ME. MATCHMAKER?
BLOODY LIPS? HE'S AN URBAN LEGEND FROM DOWN UNDER. THE AUSSIE KIDS SAY HE EATS HIS VICTIMS.
HE DOES MORE THAN THAT.
HE CAN BREATHE UNDERWATER AND HITS LIKE A BULL SHARK. AND HE SLIPPED INTO OUR HEADS SOMEHOW.
YEAH...
HE'S DEFINITELY A METAHUMAN OF SOME KIND.
CAN YOU STOP HIM?
I DON'T KNOW.
WELL, YOU MIGHT GET A CHANCE TO FIND OUT SOONER THAN YOU'D LIKE...

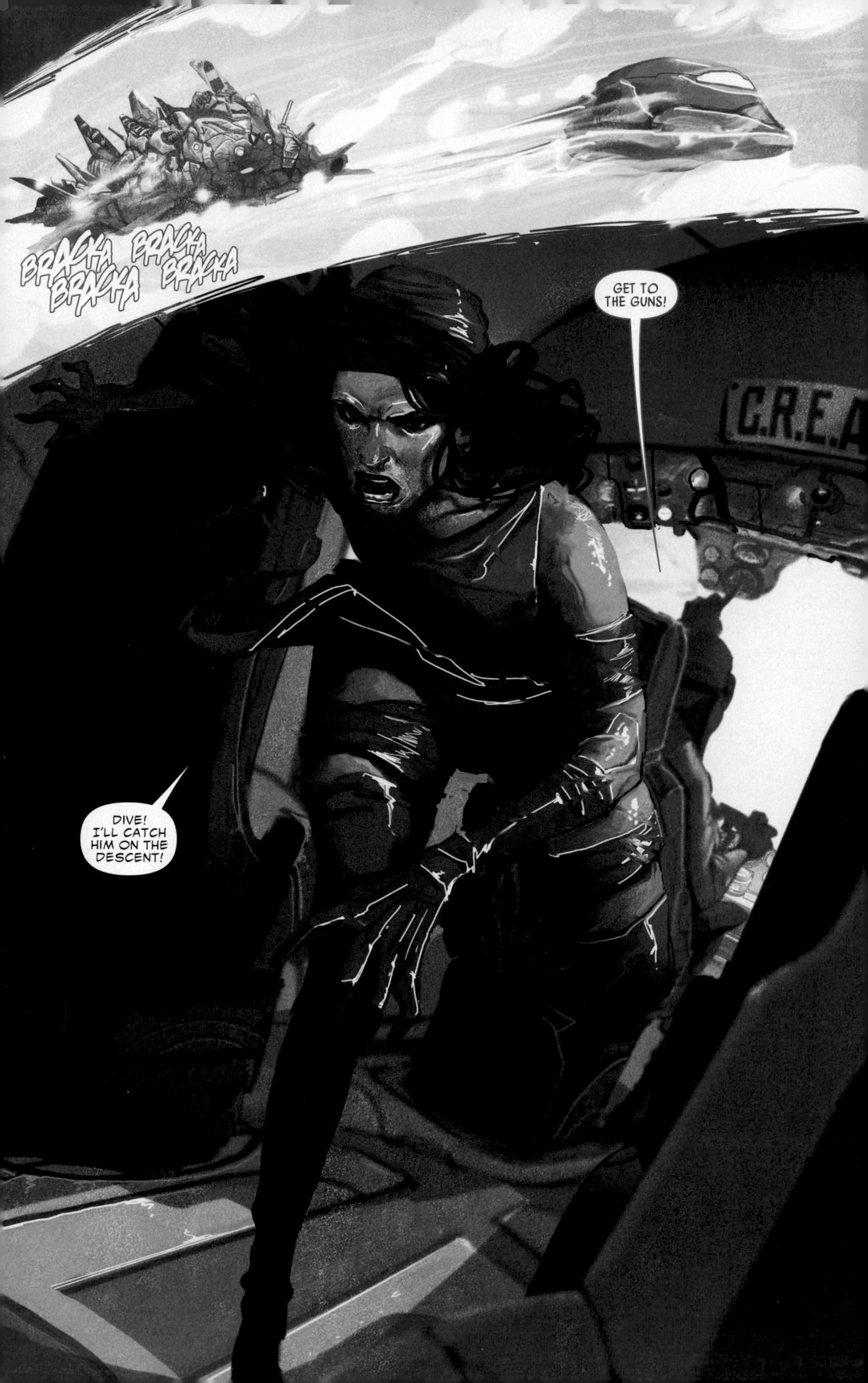
BRACKA BRACKA BRACKA BRACKA
GET TO THE GUNS!
C.R.E.A
DIVE! I'LL CATCH HIM ON THE DESCENT!

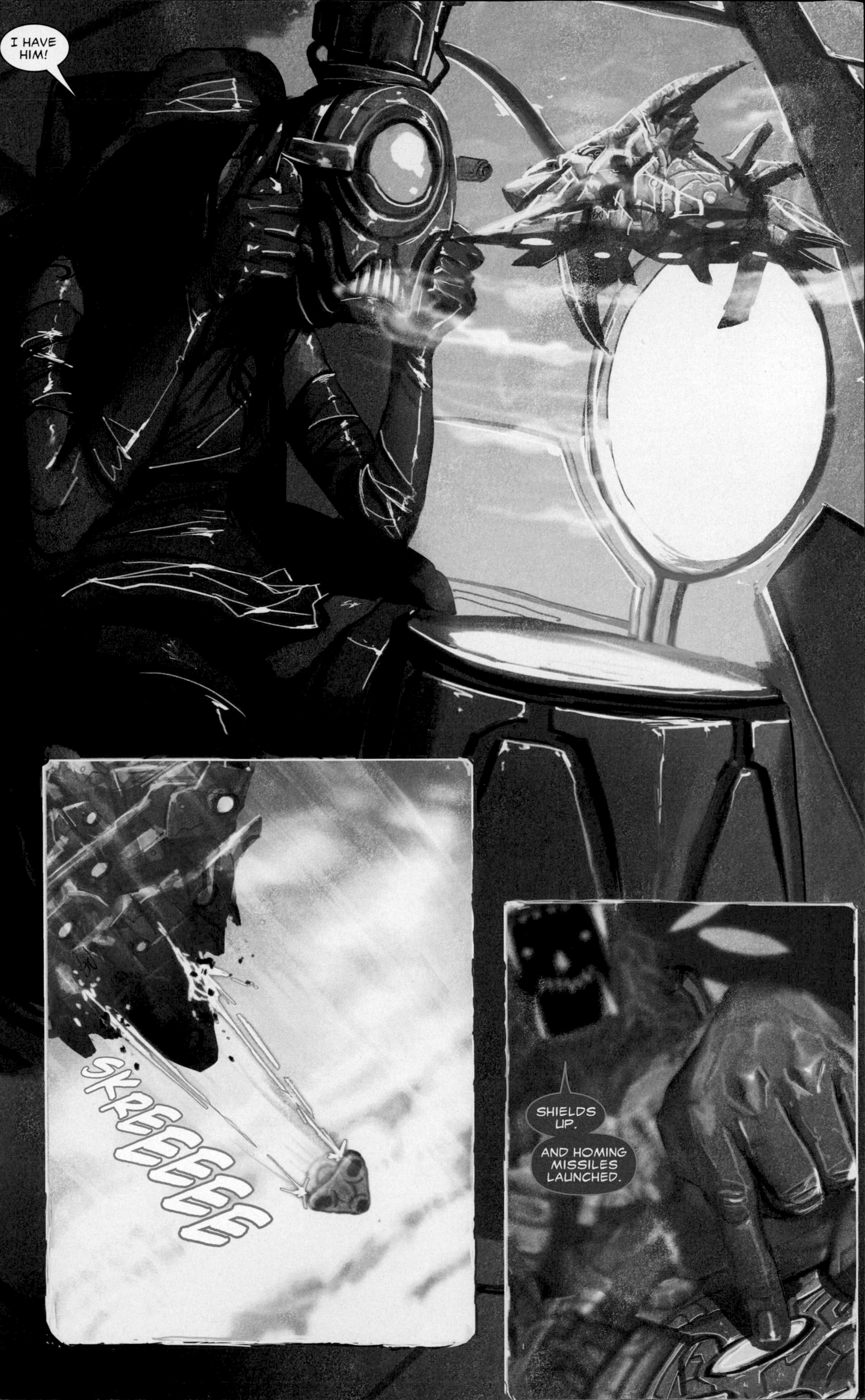
I HAVE HIM!
SKREEEEE
SHIELDS UP.
AND HOMING MISSILES LAUNCHED.

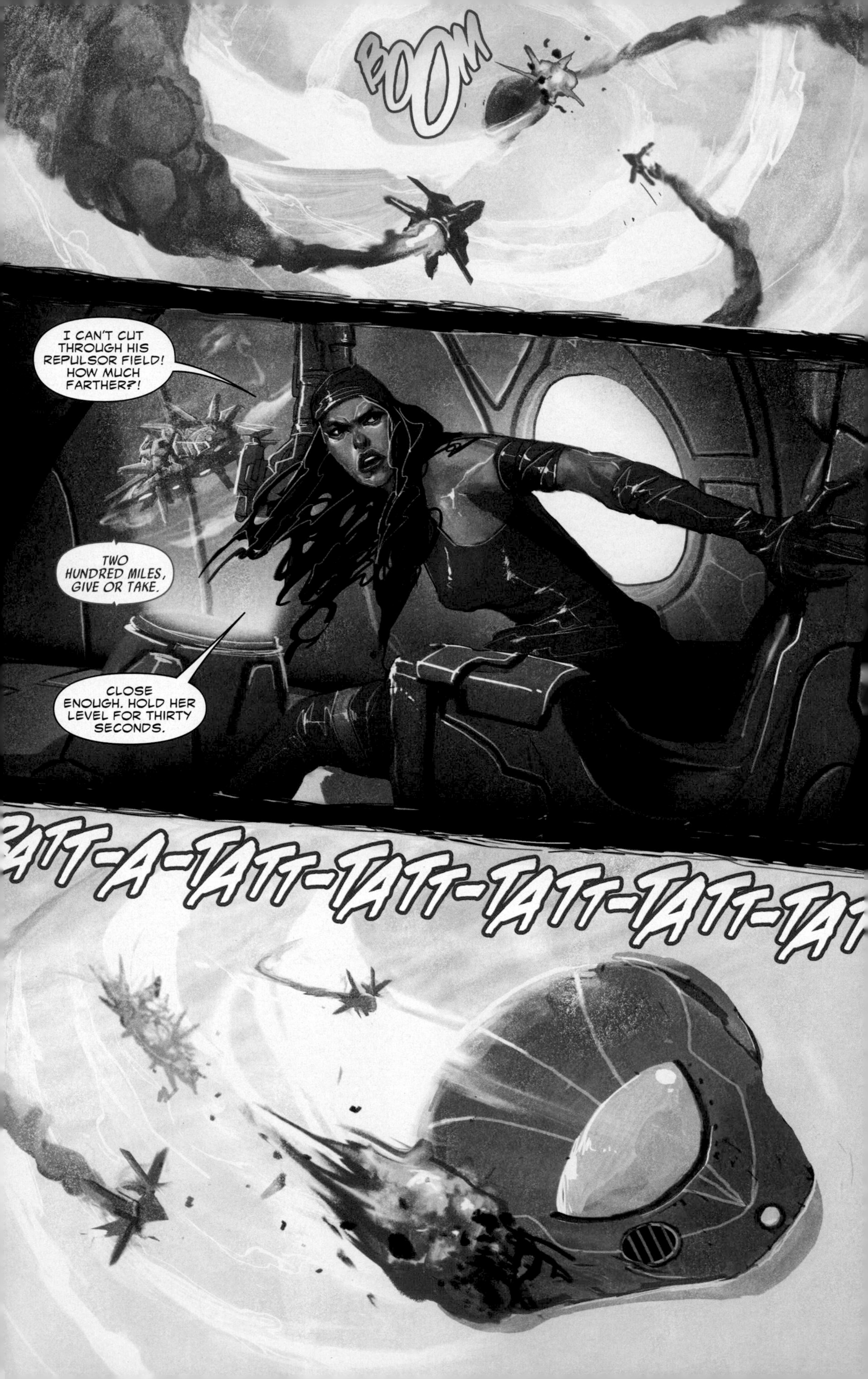
BOOM
I CAN'T CUT THROUGH HIS REPULSOR FIELD! HOW MUCH FARTHER?!
TWO HUNDRED MILES, GIVE OR TAKE.
CLOSE ENOUGH. HOLD HER LEVEL FOR THIRTY SECONDS.
ATT-A-TATT-TATT-TATT-TATT-TATT-TAT

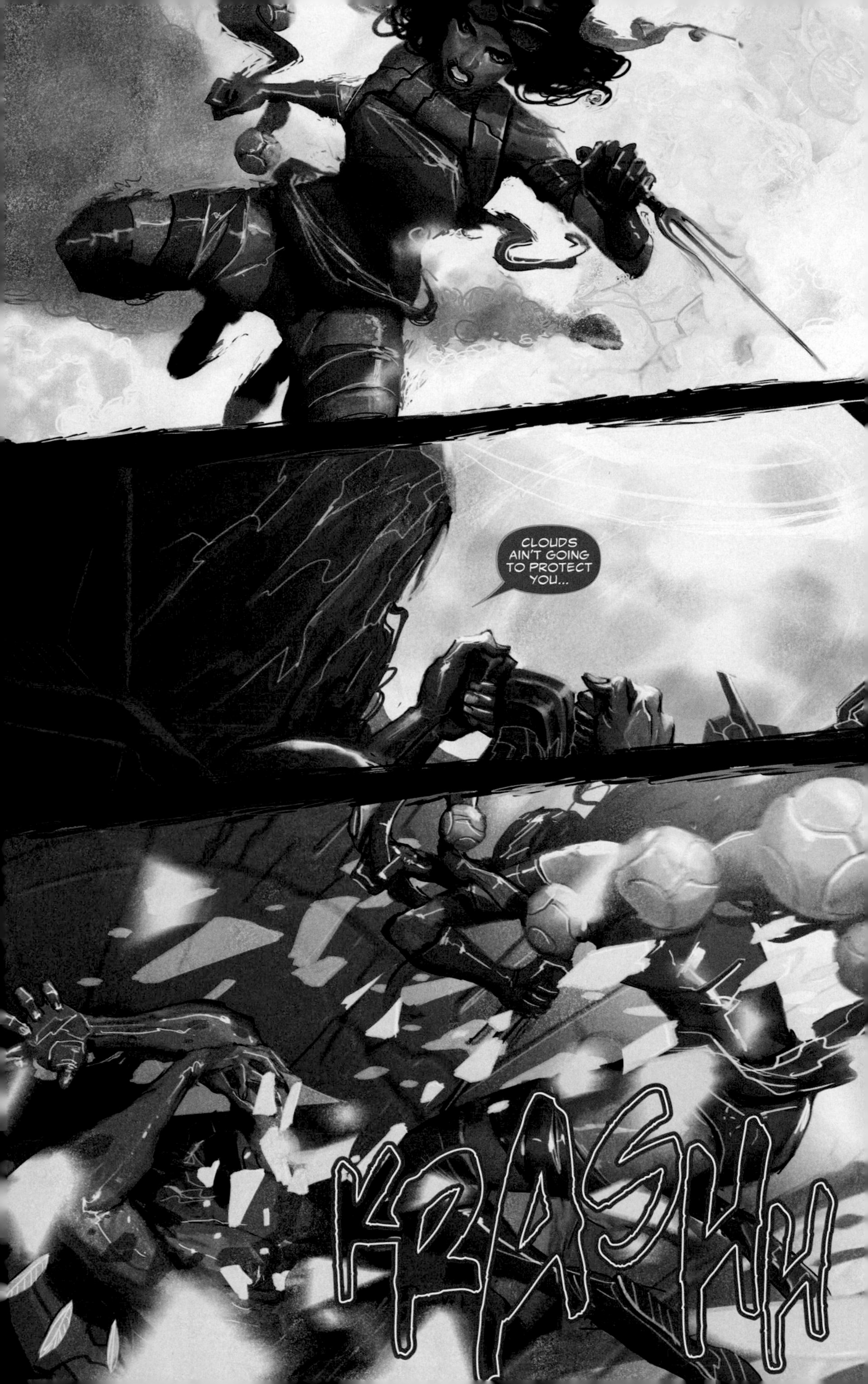
CLOUDS AIN'T GOING TO PROTECT YOU...
KRASHH

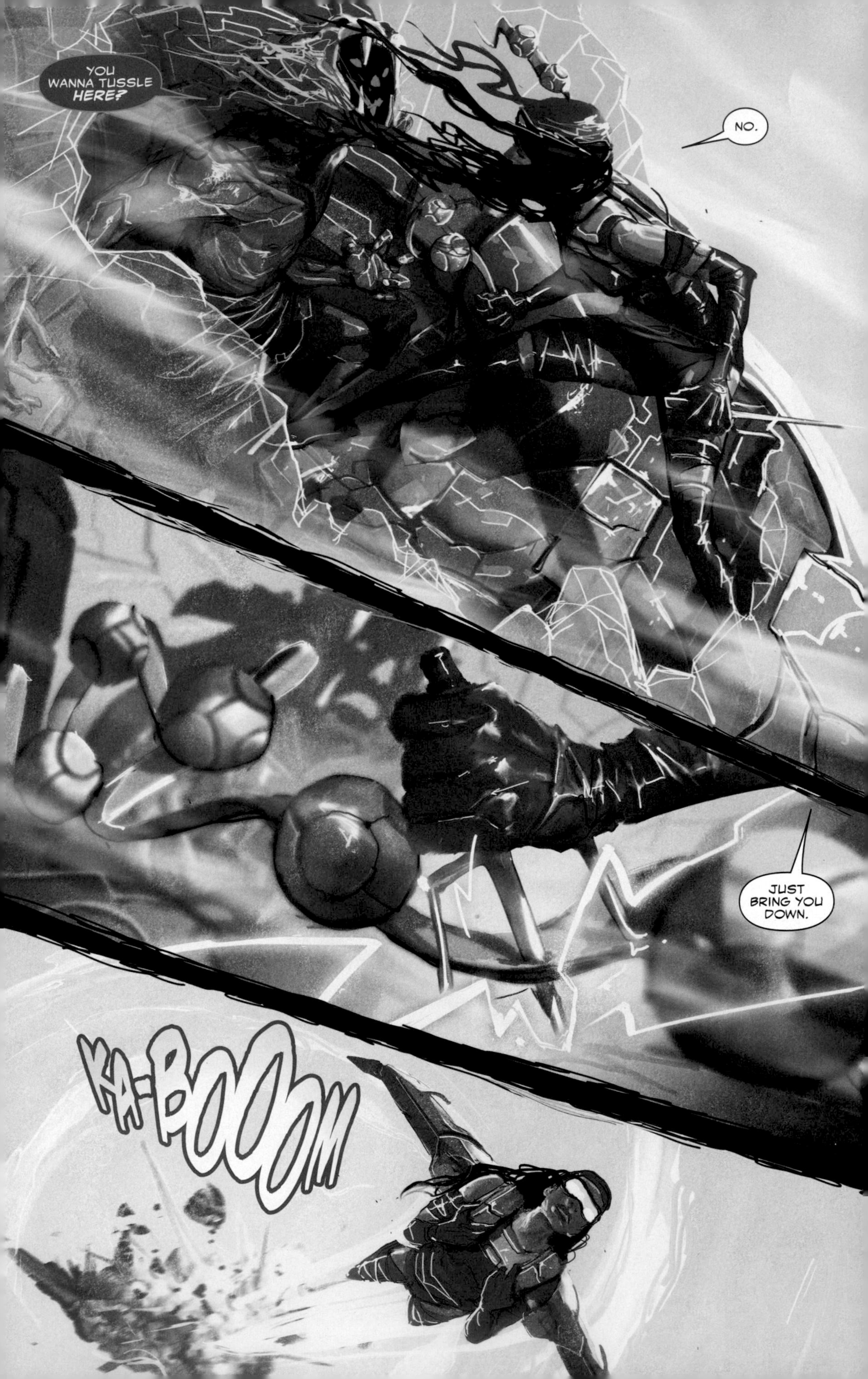
YOU WANNA TUSSLE HERE?
NO.
JUST BRING YOU DOWN.
KA-BOOOM

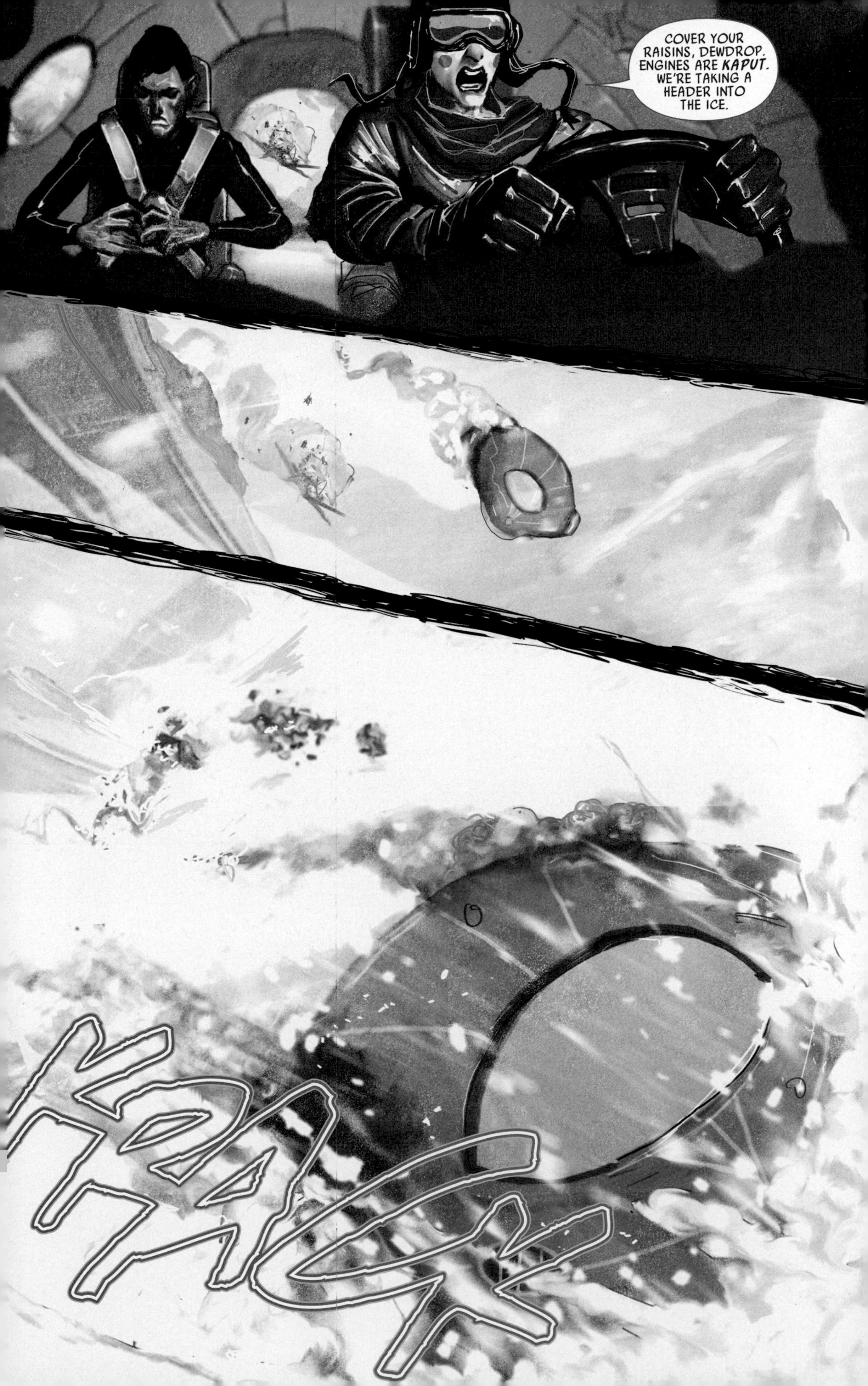
COVER YOUR RAISINS, DEWDROP. ENGINES ARE KAPUT. WE'RE TAKING A HEADER INTO THE ICE.
KRAKK

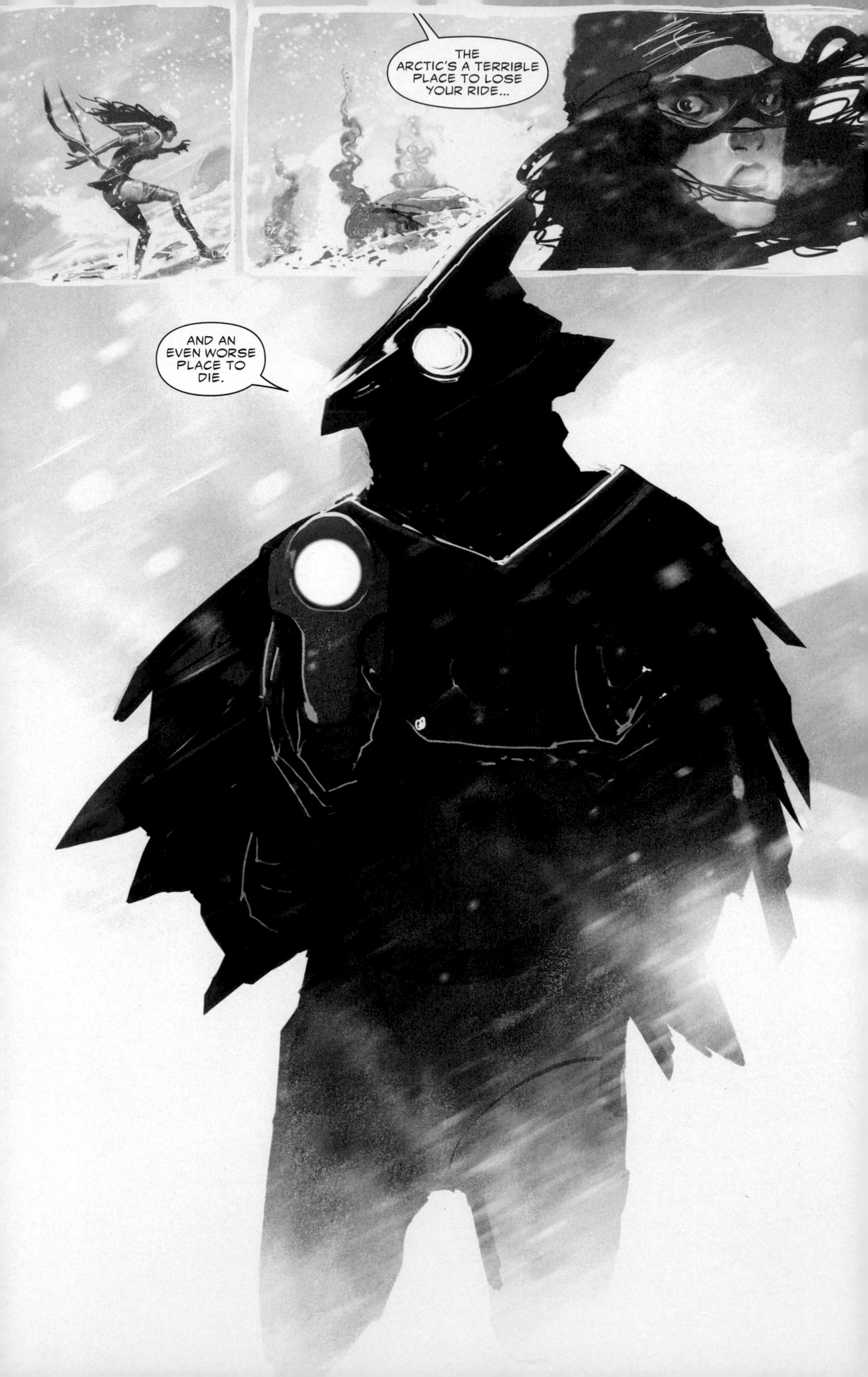
THE ARCTIC'S A TERRIBLE PLACE TO LOSE YOUR RIDE...
AND AN EVEN WORSE PLACE TO DIE.

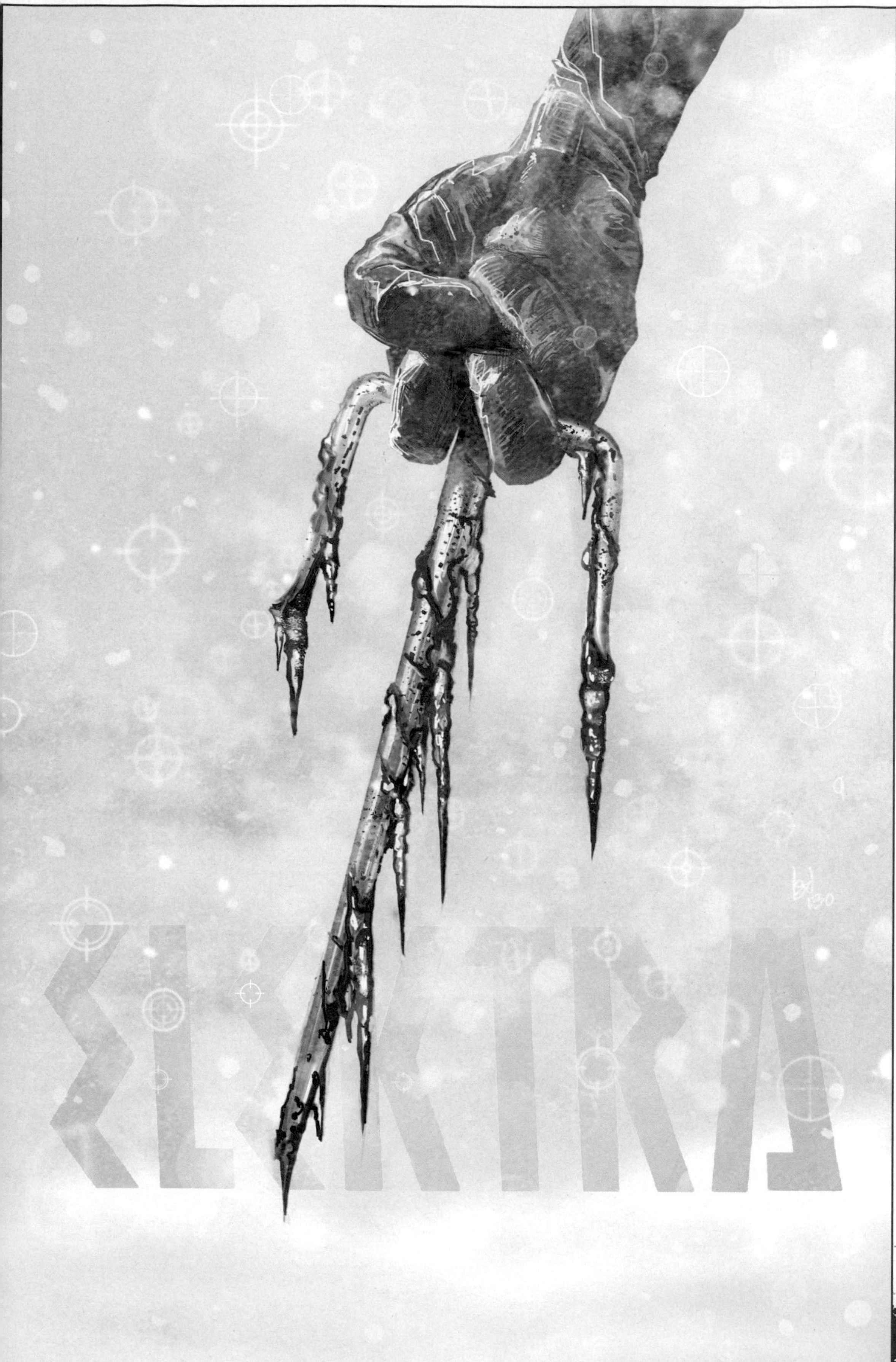
ELEKTRA

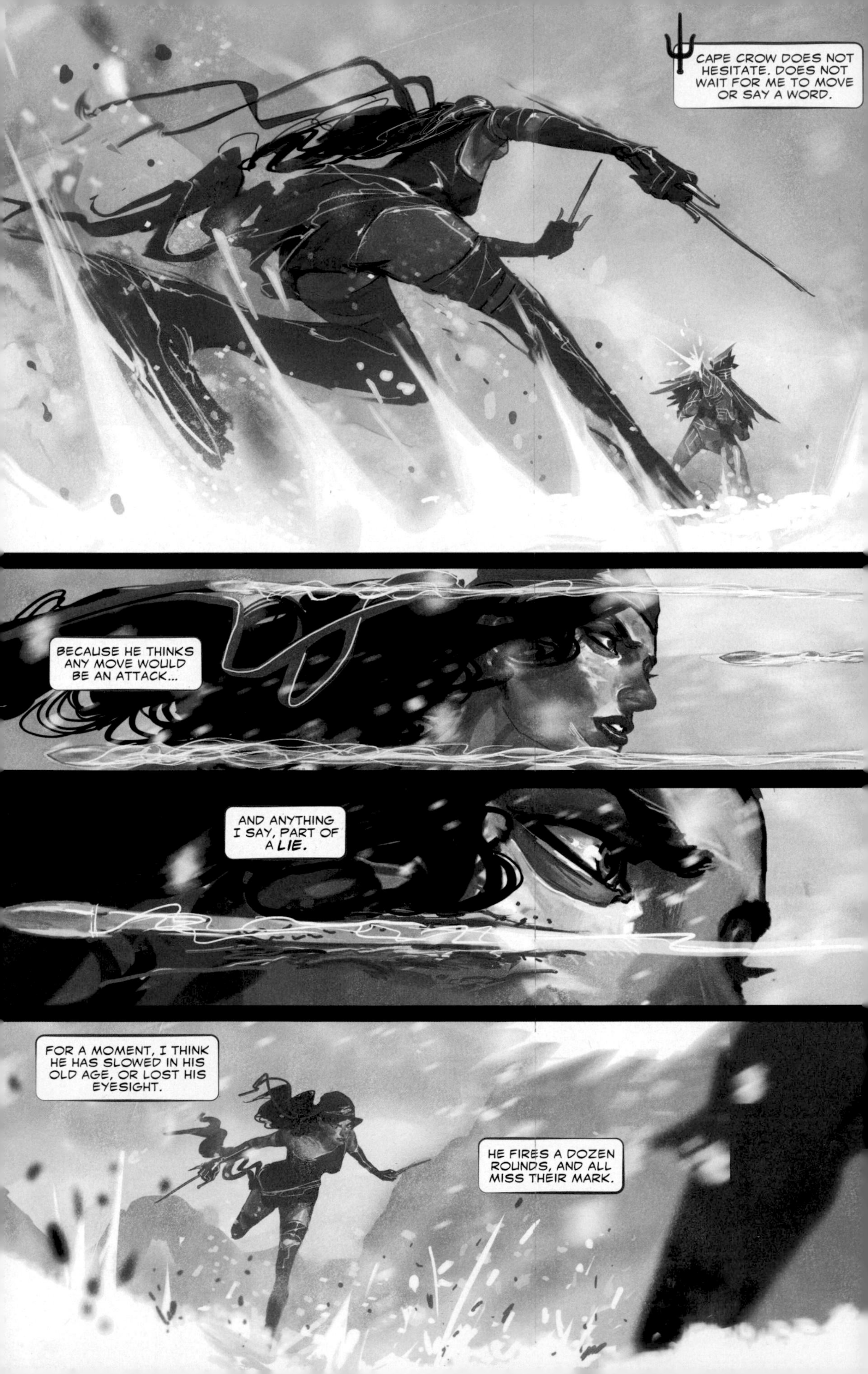
CAPE CROW DOES NOT HESITATE. DOES NOT WAIT FOR ME TO MOVE OR SAY A WORD.
BECAUSE HE THINKS ANY MOVE WOULD BE AN ATTACK...
AND ANYTHING I SAY, PART OF A LIE.
FOR A MOMENT, I THINK HE HAS SLOWED IN HIS OLD AGE, OR LOST HIS EYESIGHT.
HE FIRES A DOZEN ROUNDS, AND ALL MISS THEIR MARK.

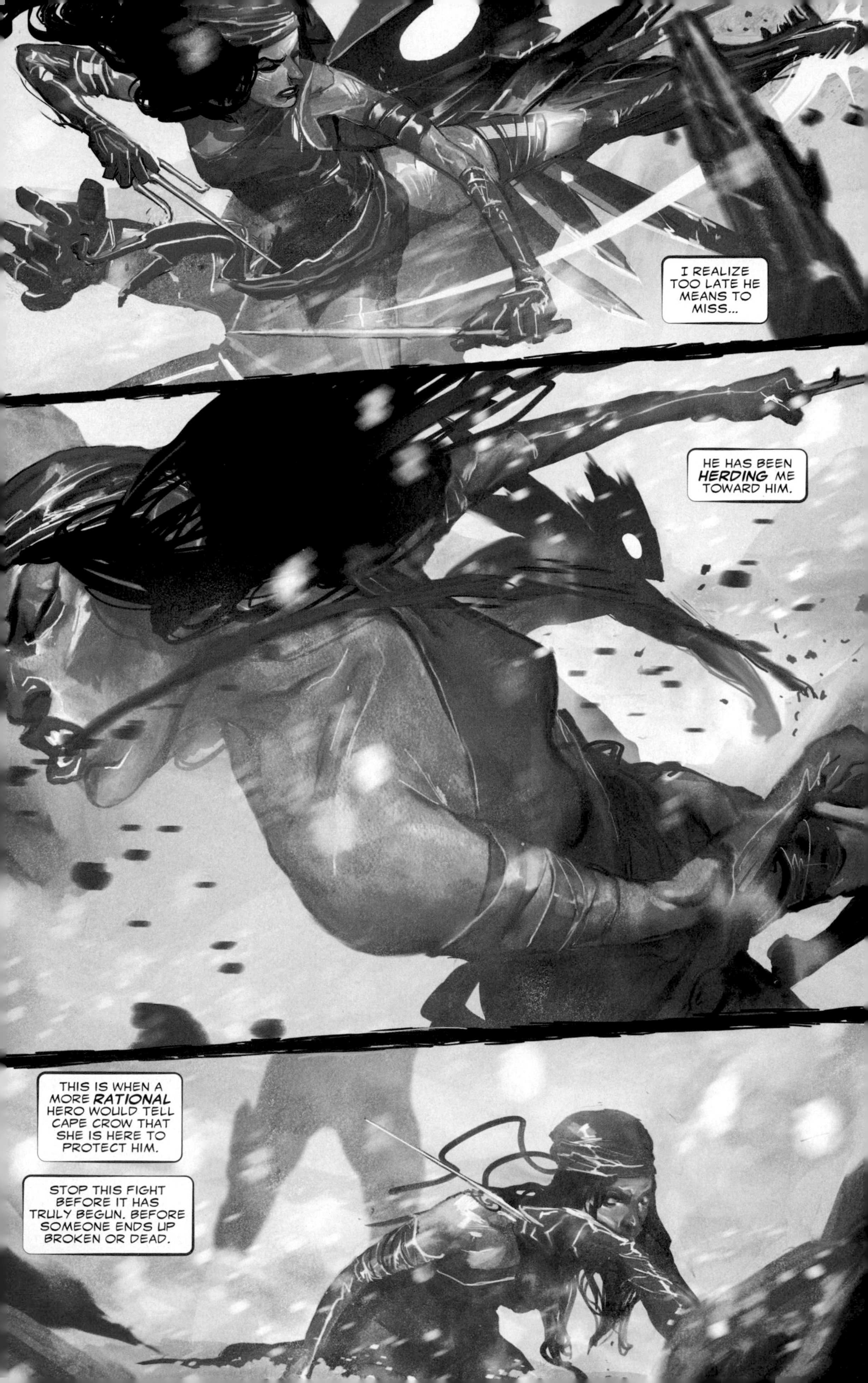
I REALIZE TOO LATE HE MEANS TO MISS...
HE HAS BEEN HERDING ME TOWARD HIM.
THIS IS WHEN A MORE RATIONAL HERO WOULD TELL CAPE CROW THAT SHE IS HERE TO PROTECT HIM.
STOP THIS FIGHT BEFORE IT HAS TRULY BEGUN. BEFORE SOMEONE ENDS UP BROKEN OR DEAD.

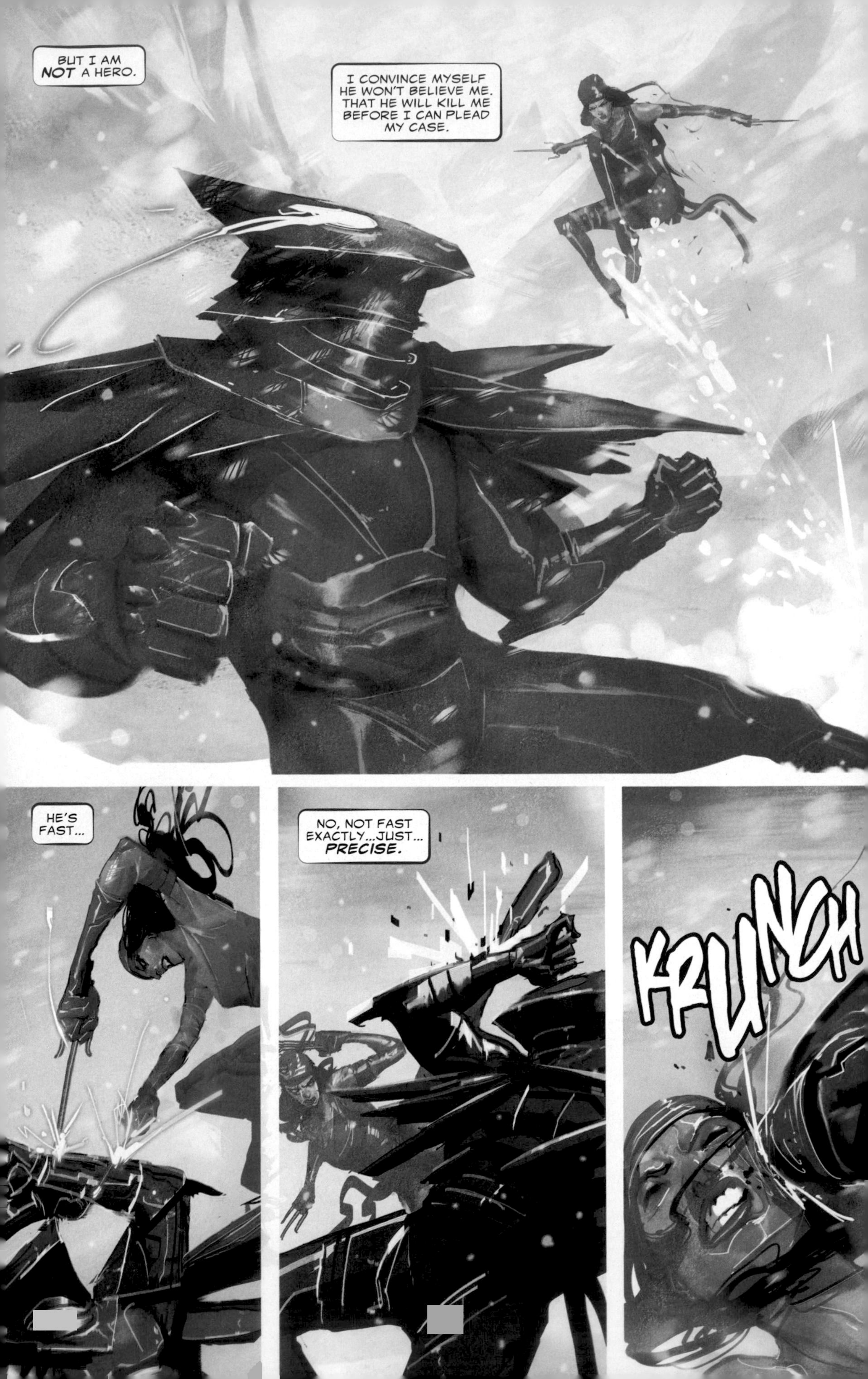
BUT I AM NOT A HERO.
I CONVINCE MYSELF HE WON'T BELIEVE ME. THAT HE WILL KILL ME BEFORE I CAN PLEAD MY CASE.
HE'S FAST...
NO, NOT FAST EXACTLY...JUST... PRECISE.
KRUNCH

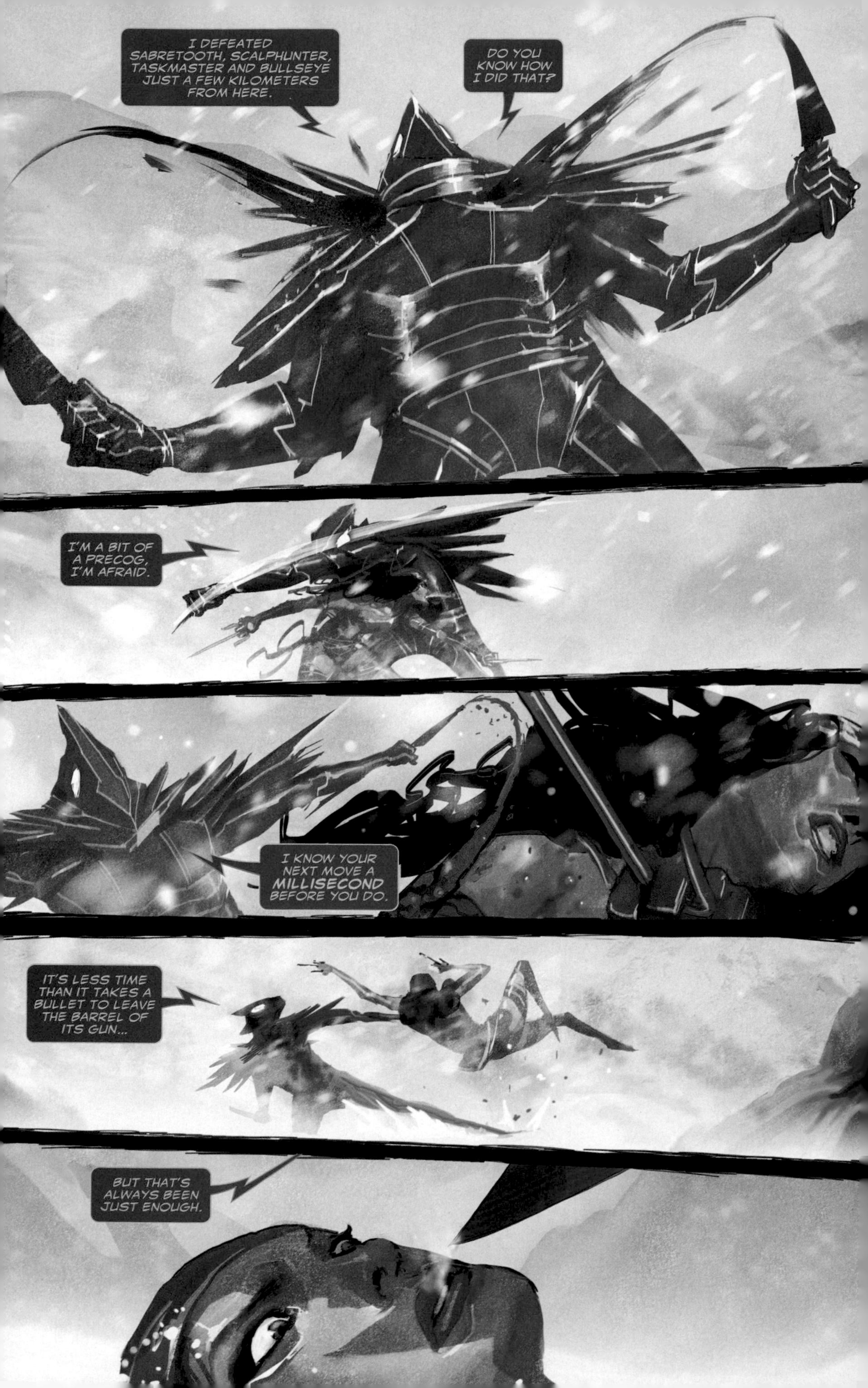
I DEFEATED SABRETOOTH, SCALPHUNTER, TASKMASTER AND BULLSEYE JUST A FEW KILOMETERS FROM HERE.
DO YOU KNOW HOW I DID THAT?
I'M A BIT OF A PRECOG, I'M AFRAID.
I KNOW YOUR NEXT MOVE A **MILLISECOND** BEFORE YOU DO.
IT'S LESS TIME THAN IT TAKES A BULLET TO LEAVE THE BARREL OF ITS GUN...
BUT THAT'S ALWAYS BEEN JUST ENOUGH.

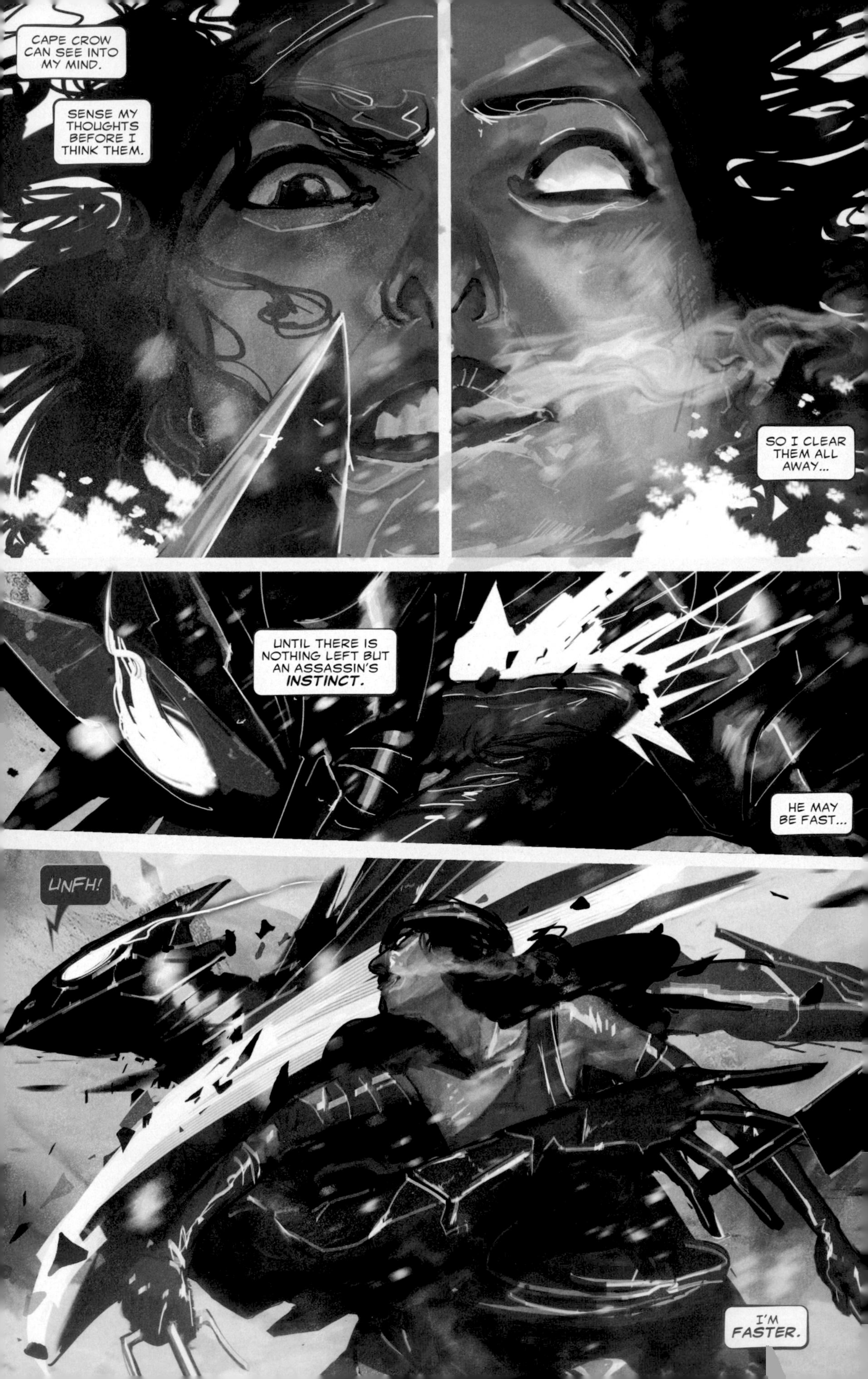
CAPE CROW CAN SEE INTO MY MIND.
SENSE MY THOUGHTS BEFORE I THINK THEM.
SO I CLEAR THEM ALL AWAY...
UNTIL THERE IS NOTHING LEFT BUT AN ASSASSIN'S *INSTINCT.*
HE MAY BE FAST...
UNFH!
I'M *FASTER.*

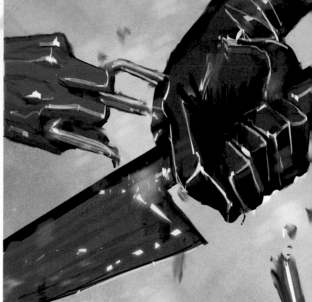

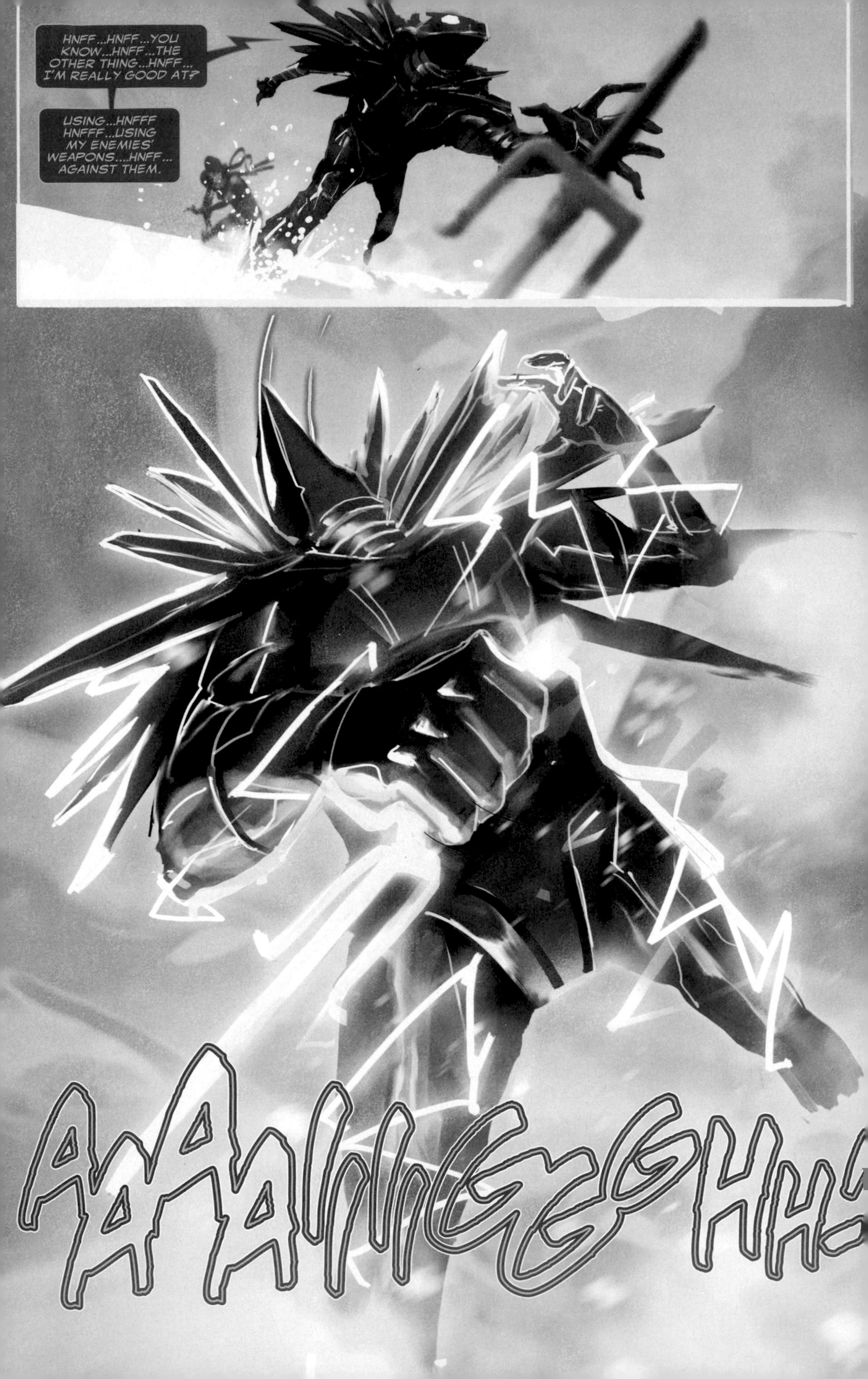
HNFF...HNFF...YOU KNOW...HNFF...THE OTHER THING...HNFF... I'M REALLY GOOD AT?
USING...HNFFF HNFFF...USING MY ENEMIES' WEAPONS....HNFF... AGAINST THEM.
AAAAHHGGGHH

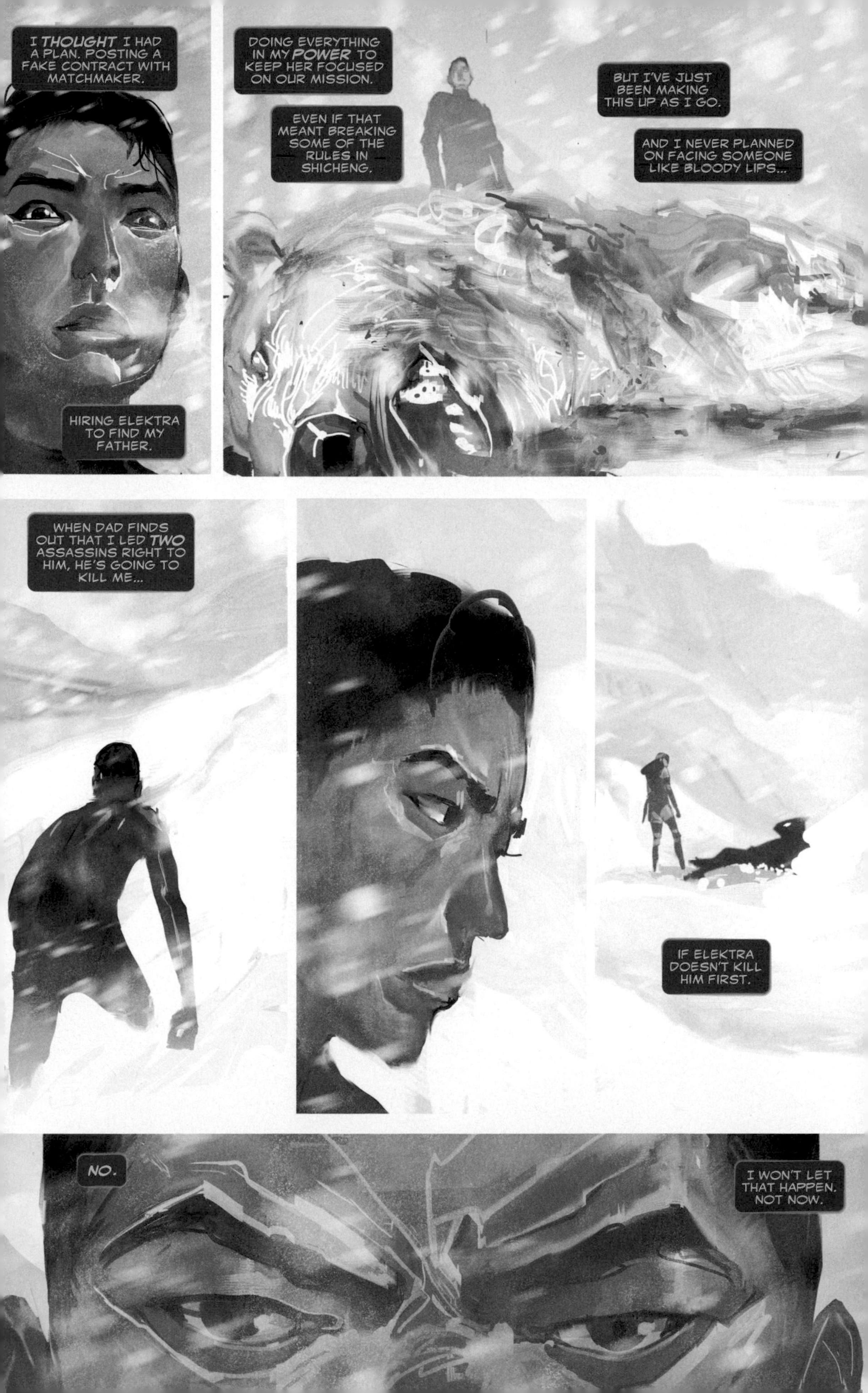
I THOUGHT I HAD A PLAN. POSTING A FAKE CONTRACT WITH MATCHMAKER.
HIRING ELEKTRA TO FIND MY FATHER.
DOING EVERYTHING IN MY POWER TO KEEP HER FOCUSED ON OUR MISSION.
EVEN IF THAT MEANT BREAKING SOME OF THE RULES IN SHICHENG.
BUT I'VE JUST BEEN MAKING THIS UP AS I GO.
AND I NEVER PLANNED ON FACING SOMEONE LIKE BLOODY LIPS...
WHEN DAD FINDS OUT THAT I LED TWO ASSASSINS RIGHT TO HIM, HE'S GOING TO KILL ME...
IF ELEKTRA DOESN'T KILL HIM FIRST.
NO.
I WON'T LET THAT HAPPEN. NOT NOW.

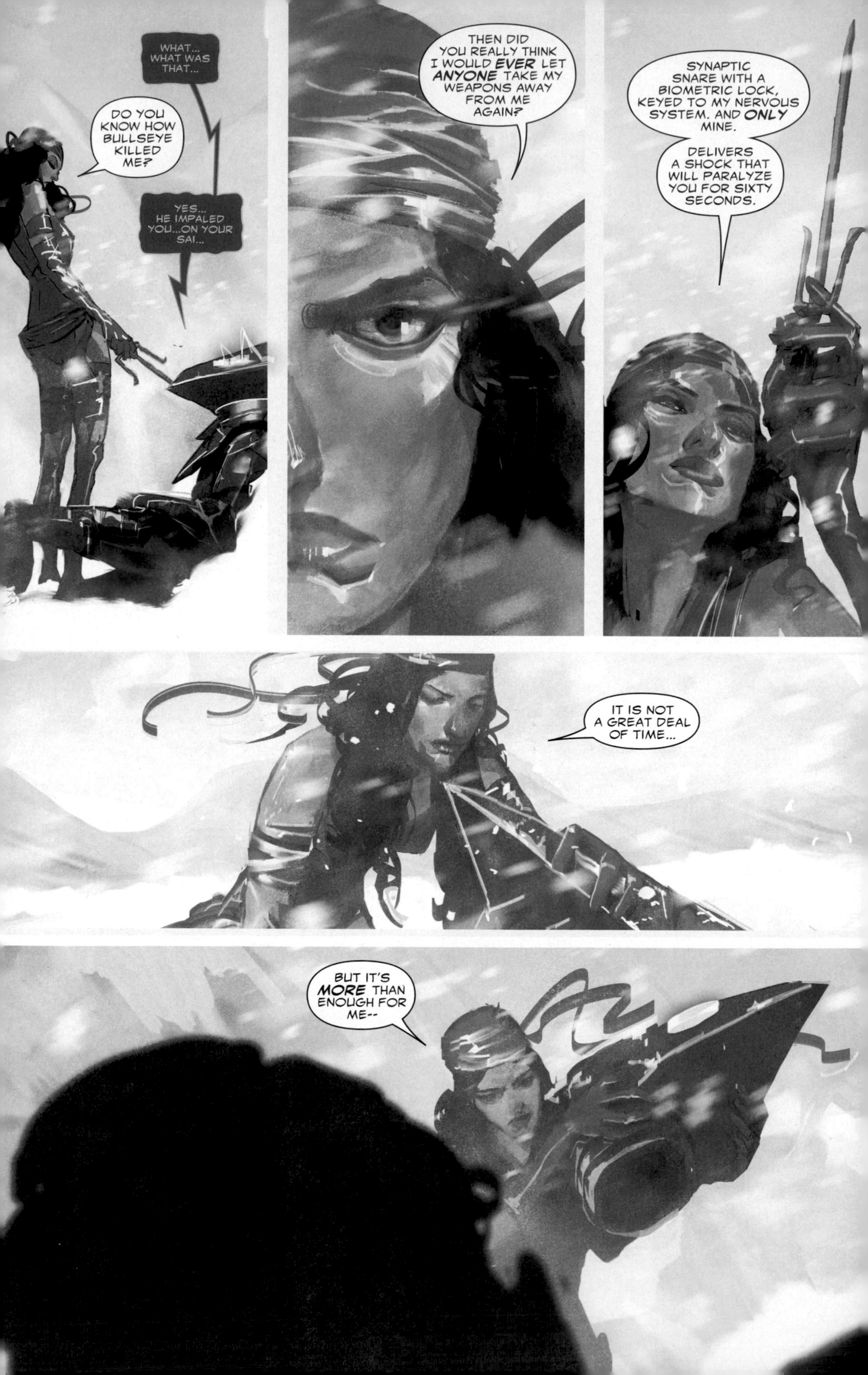
WHAT... WHAT WAS THAT...
DO YOU KNOW HOW BULLSEYE KILLED ME?
YES... HE IMPALED YOU...ON YOUR SAI...
THEN DID YOU REALLY THINK I WOULD EVER LET ANYONE TAKE MY WEAPONS AWAY FROM ME AGAIN?
SYNAPTIC SNARE WITH A BIOMETRIC LOCK, KEYED TO MY NERVOUS SYSTEM. AND ONLY MINE.
DELIVERS A SHOCK THAT WILL PARALYZE YOU FOR SIXTY SECONDS.
IT IS NOT A GREAT DEAL OF TIME...
BUT IT'S MORE THAN ENOUGH FOR ME--

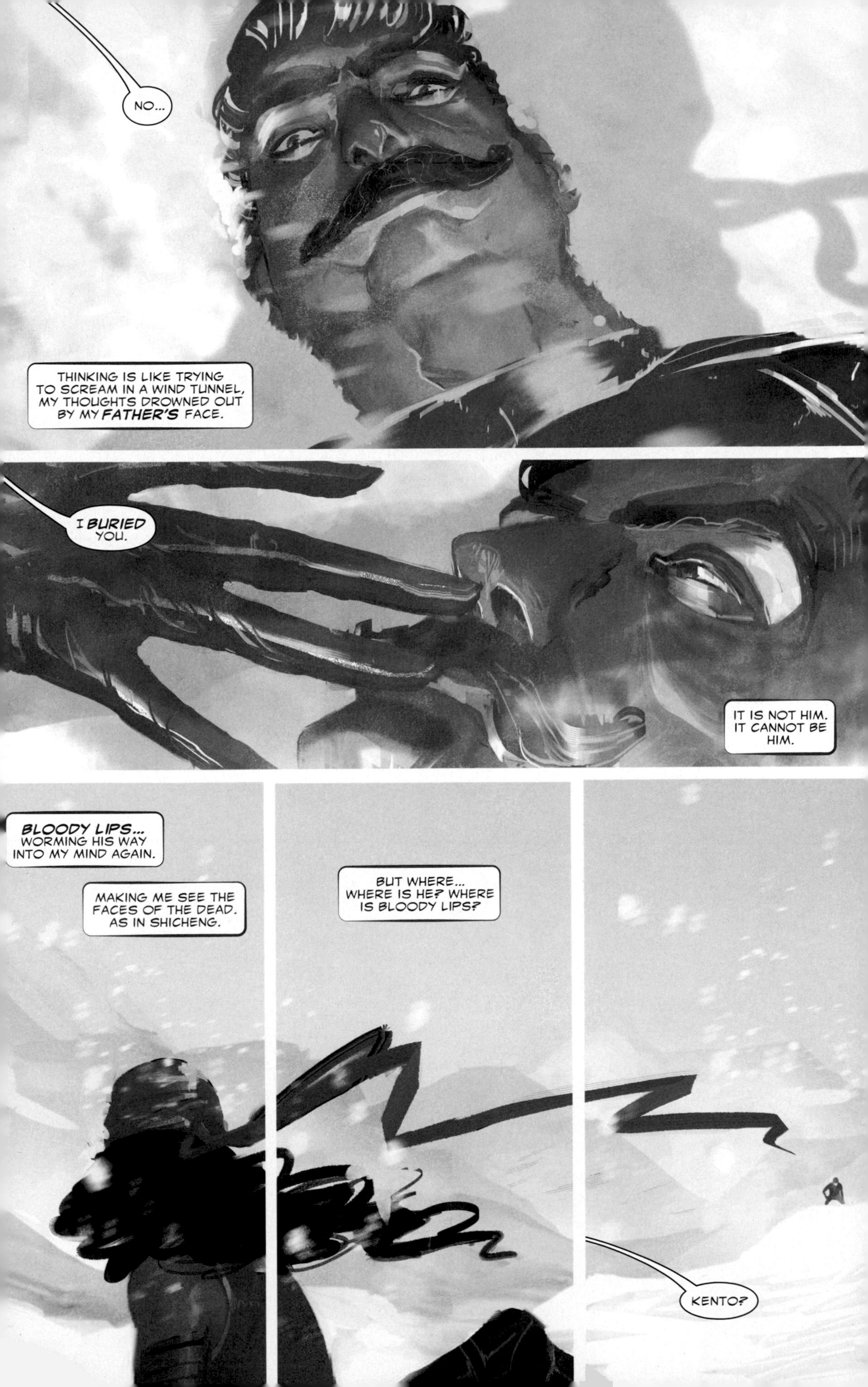
NO...
THINKING IS LIKE TRYING TO SCREAM IN A WIND TUNNEL, MY THOUGHTS DROWNED OUT BY MY FATHER'S FACE.
I BURIED YOU.
IT IS NOT HIM. IT CANNOT BE HIM.
BLOODY LIPS... WORMING HIS WAY INTO MY MIND AGAIN.
MAKING ME SEE THE FACES OF THE DEAD. AS IN SHICHENG.
BUT WHERE... WHERE IS HE? WHERE IS BLOODY LIPS?
KENTO?

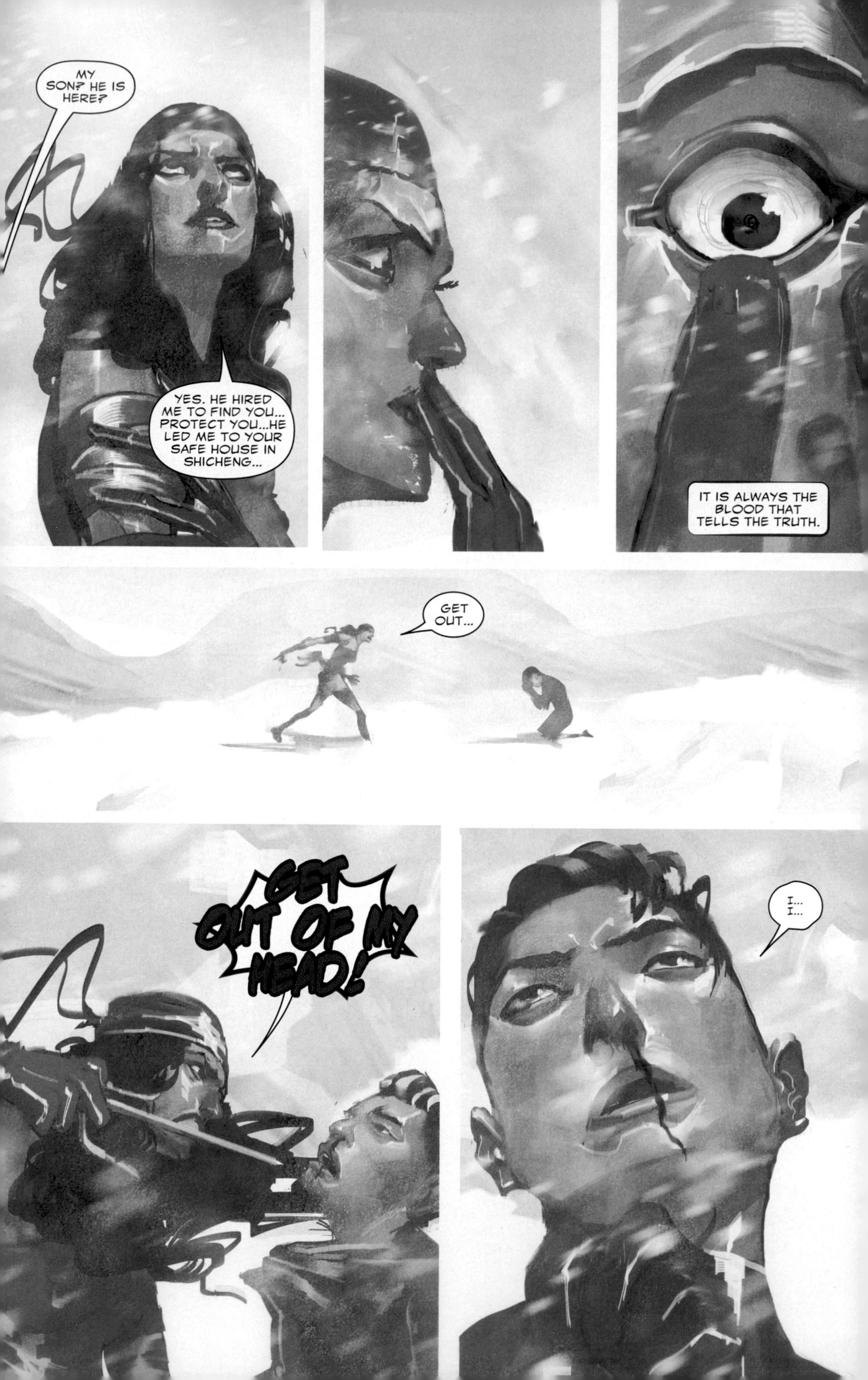
MY SON? HE IS HERE?
YES. HE HIRED ME TO FIND YOU... PROTECT YOU...HE LED ME TO YOUR SAFE HOUSE IN SHICHENG...
IT IS ALWAYS THE BLOOD THAT TELLS THE TRUTH.
GET OUT...
GET OUT OF MY HEAD!
I... I...

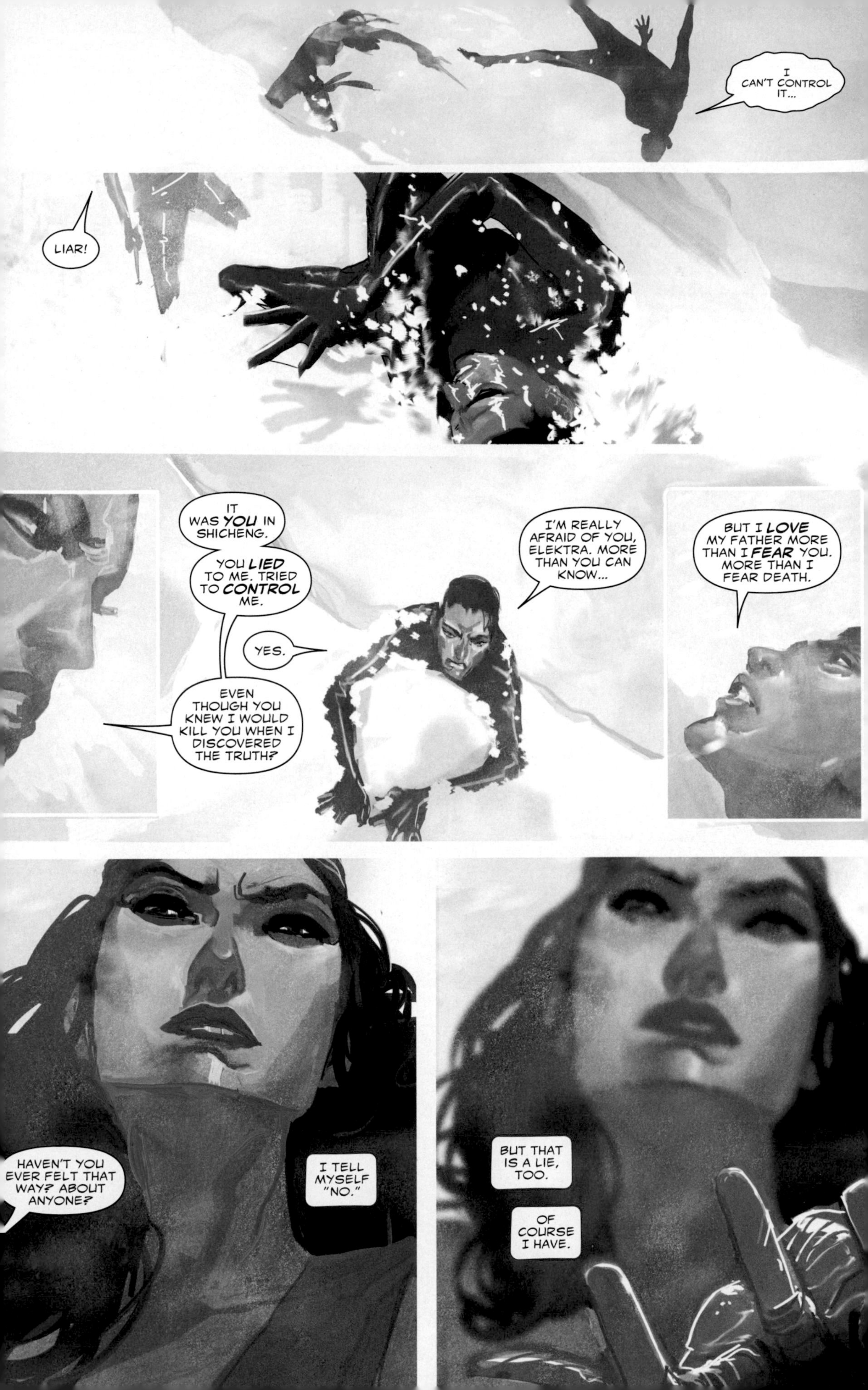
I CAN'T CONTROL IT...
LIAR!
IT WAS YOU IN SHICHENG.
YOU LIED TO ME. TRIED TO CONTROL ME.
EVEN THOUGH YOU KNEW I WOULD KILL YOU WHEN I DISCOVERED THE TRUTH?
YES.
I'M REALLY AFRAID OF YOU, ELEKTRA. MORE THAN YOU CAN KNOW...
BUT I LOVE MY FATHER MORE THAN I FEAR YOU. MORE THAN I FEAR DEATH.
HAVEN'T YOU EVER FELT THAT WAY? ABOUT ANYONE?
I TELL MYSELF "NO."
BUT THAT IS A LIE, TOO.
OF COURSE I HAVE.

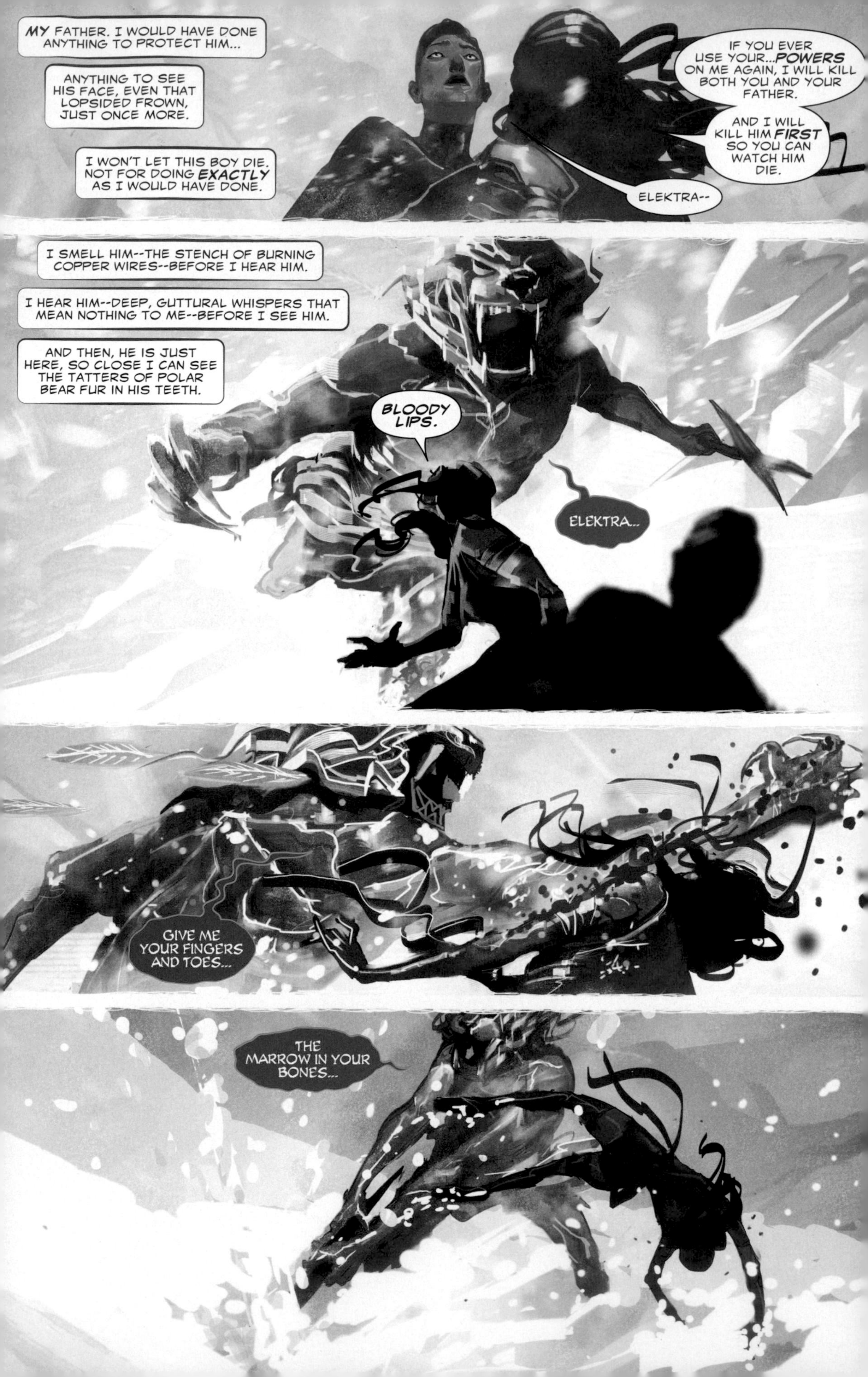
MY FATHER. I WOULD HAVE DONE ANYTHING TO PROTECT HIM...
ANYTHING TO SEE HIS FACE, EVEN THAT LOPSIDED FROWN, JUST ONCE MORE.
I WON'T LET THIS BOY DIE. NOT FOR DOING EXACTLY AS I WOULD HAVE DONE.
IF YOU EVER USE YOUR...POWERS ON ME AGAIN, I WILL KILL BOTH YOU AND YOUR FATHER.
AND I WILL KILL HIM FIRST SO YOU CAN WATCH HIM DIE.
ELEKTRA--
I SMELL HIM--THE STENCH OF BURNING COPPER WIRES--BEFORE I HEAR HIM.
I HEAR HIM--DEEP, GUTTURAL WHISPERS THAT MEAN NOTHING TO ME--BEFORE I SEE HIM.
AND THEN, HE IS JUST HERE, SO CLOSE I CAN SEE THE TATTERS OF POLAR BEAR FUR IN HIS TEETH.
BLOODY LIPS.
ELEKTRA...
GIVE ME YOUR FINGERS AND TOES...
THE MARROW IN YOUR BONES...

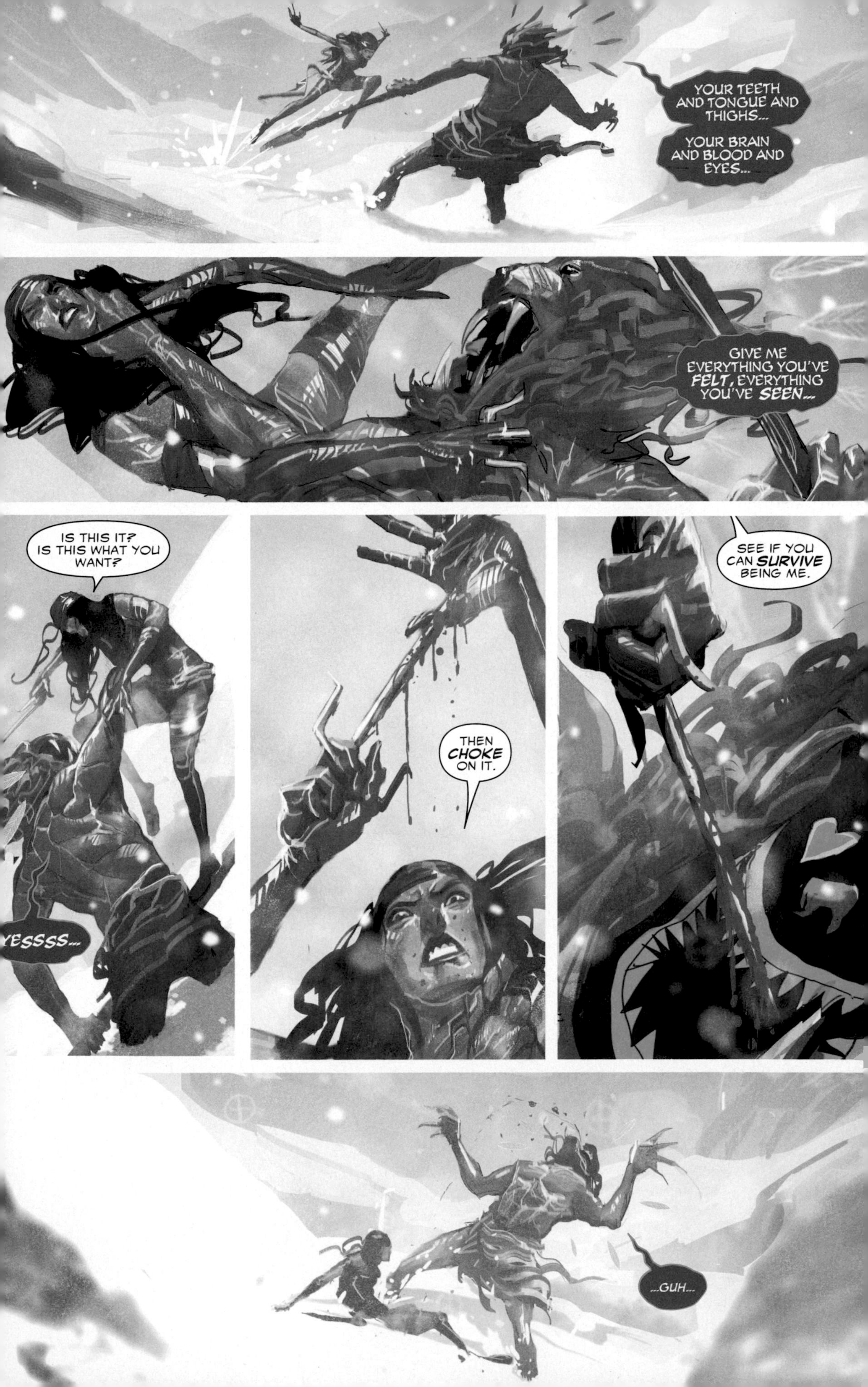
YOUR TEETH AND TONGUE AND THIGHS...
YOUR BRAIN AND BLOOD AND EYES...
GIVE ME EVERYTHING YOU'VE FELT, EVERYTHING YOU'VE SEEN...
IS THIS IT? IS THIS WHAT YOU WANT?
YESSSS...
THEN CHOKE ON IT.
SEE IF YOU CAN SURVIVE BEING ME.
...GUH...

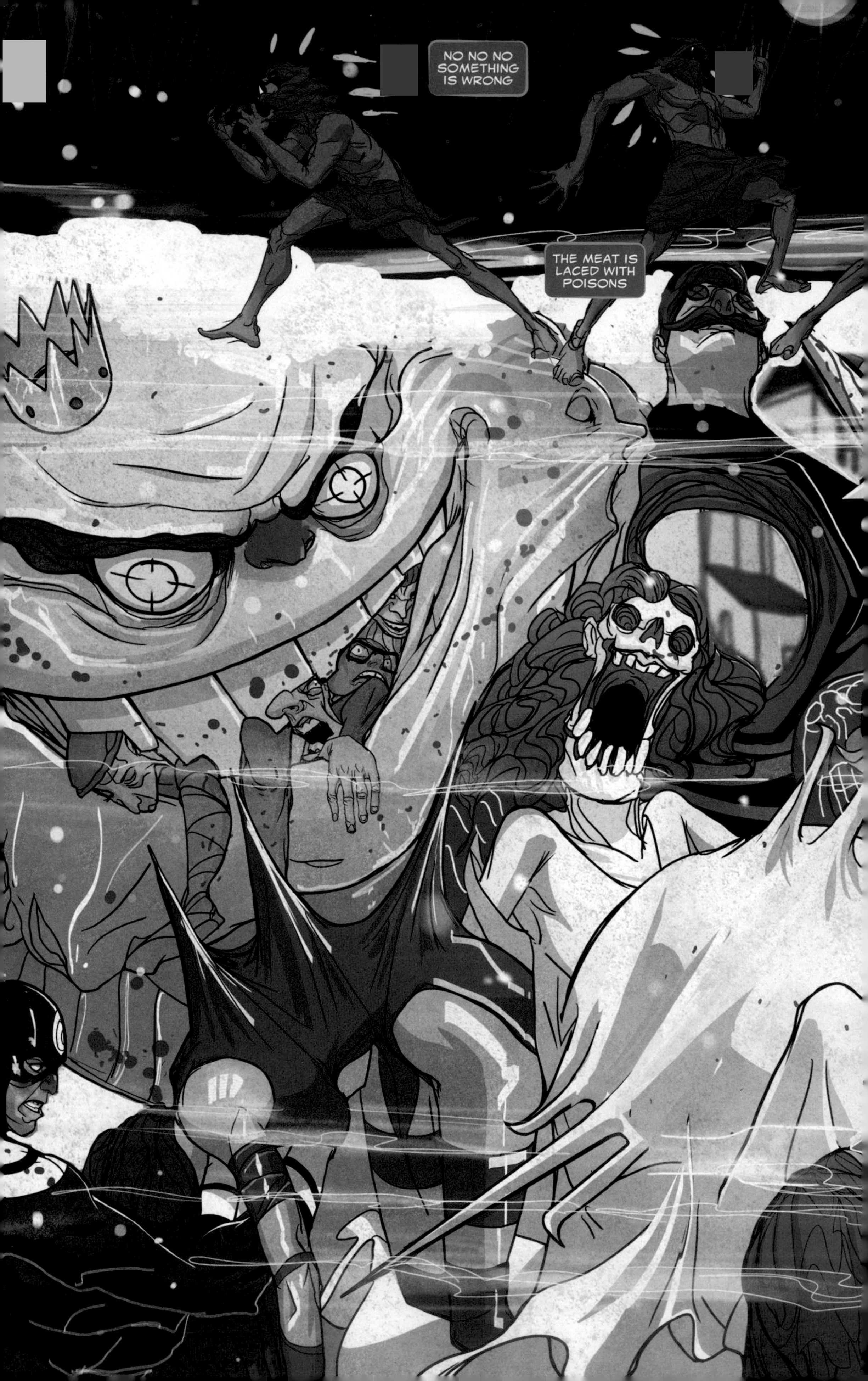
NO NO NO SOMETHING IS WRONG
THE MEAT IS LACED WITH POISONS

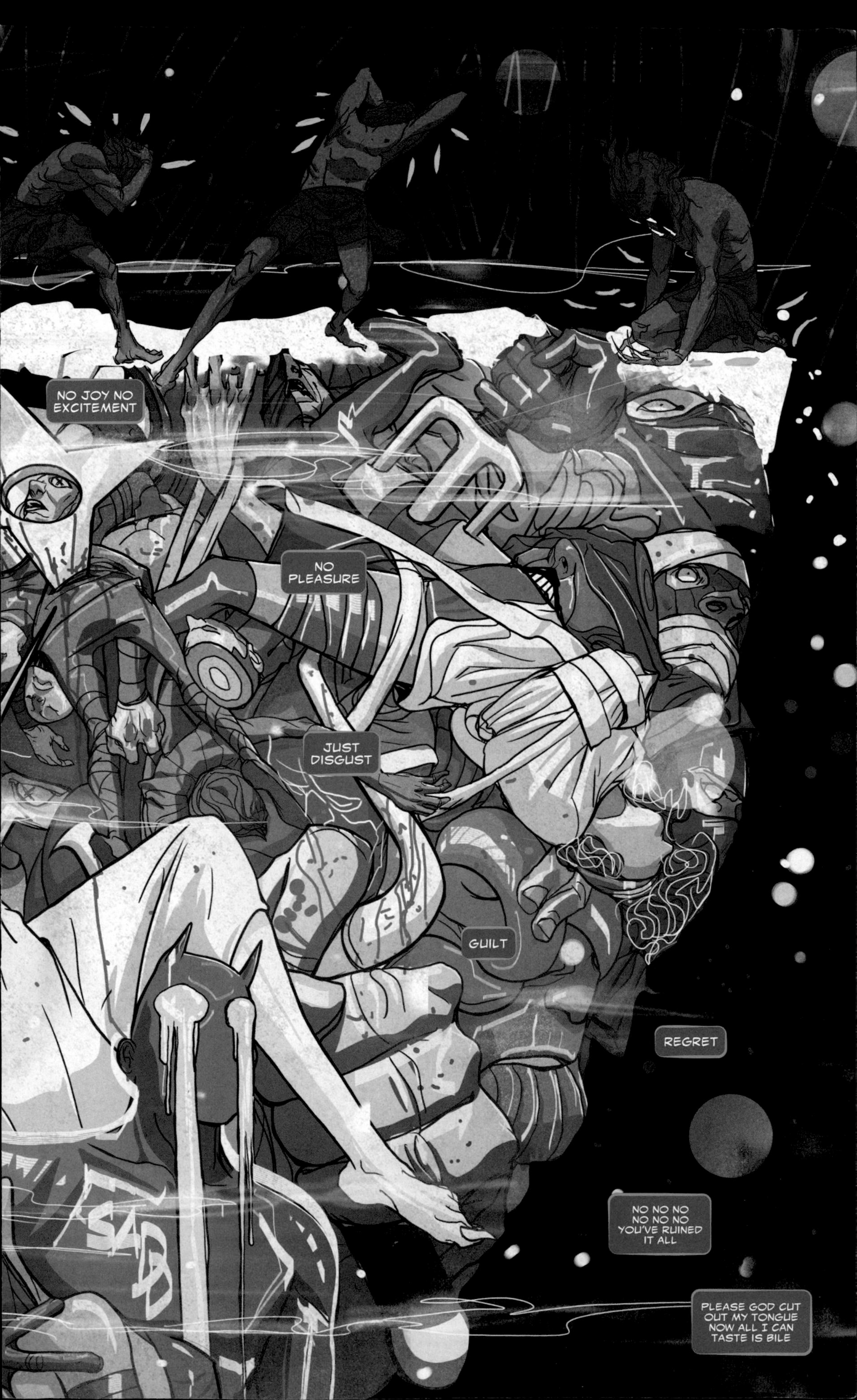
NO JOY NO EXCITEMENT
NO PLEASURE
JUST DISGUST
GUILT
REGRET
NO NO NO NO NO NO YOU'VE RUINED IT ALL
PLEASE GOD CUT OUT MY TONGUE NOW ALL I CAN TASTE IS BILE
SAD

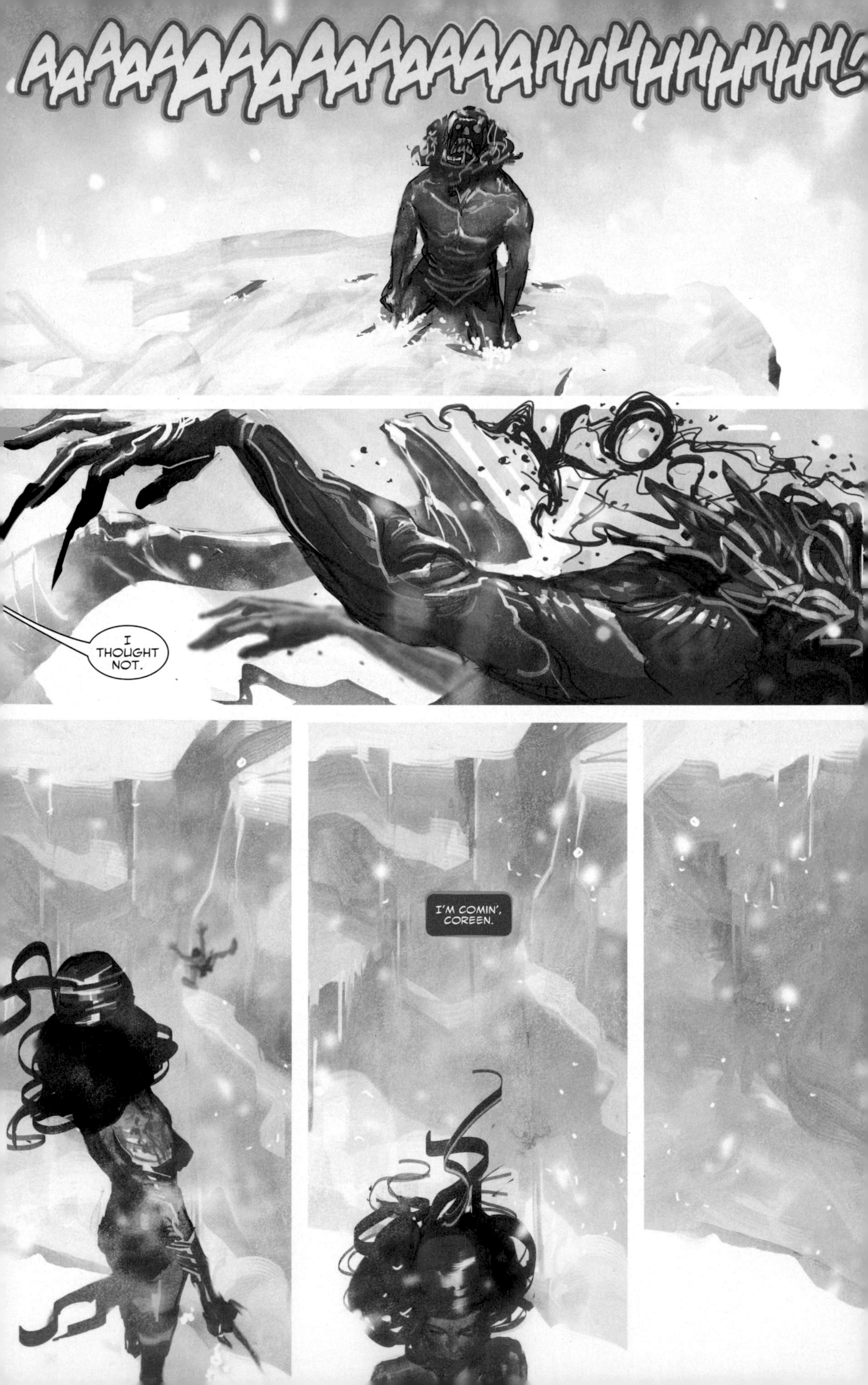
AAAAAAAAAAAAAAAAHHHHHHHH!
I THOUGHT NOT.
I'M COMIN', COREEN.

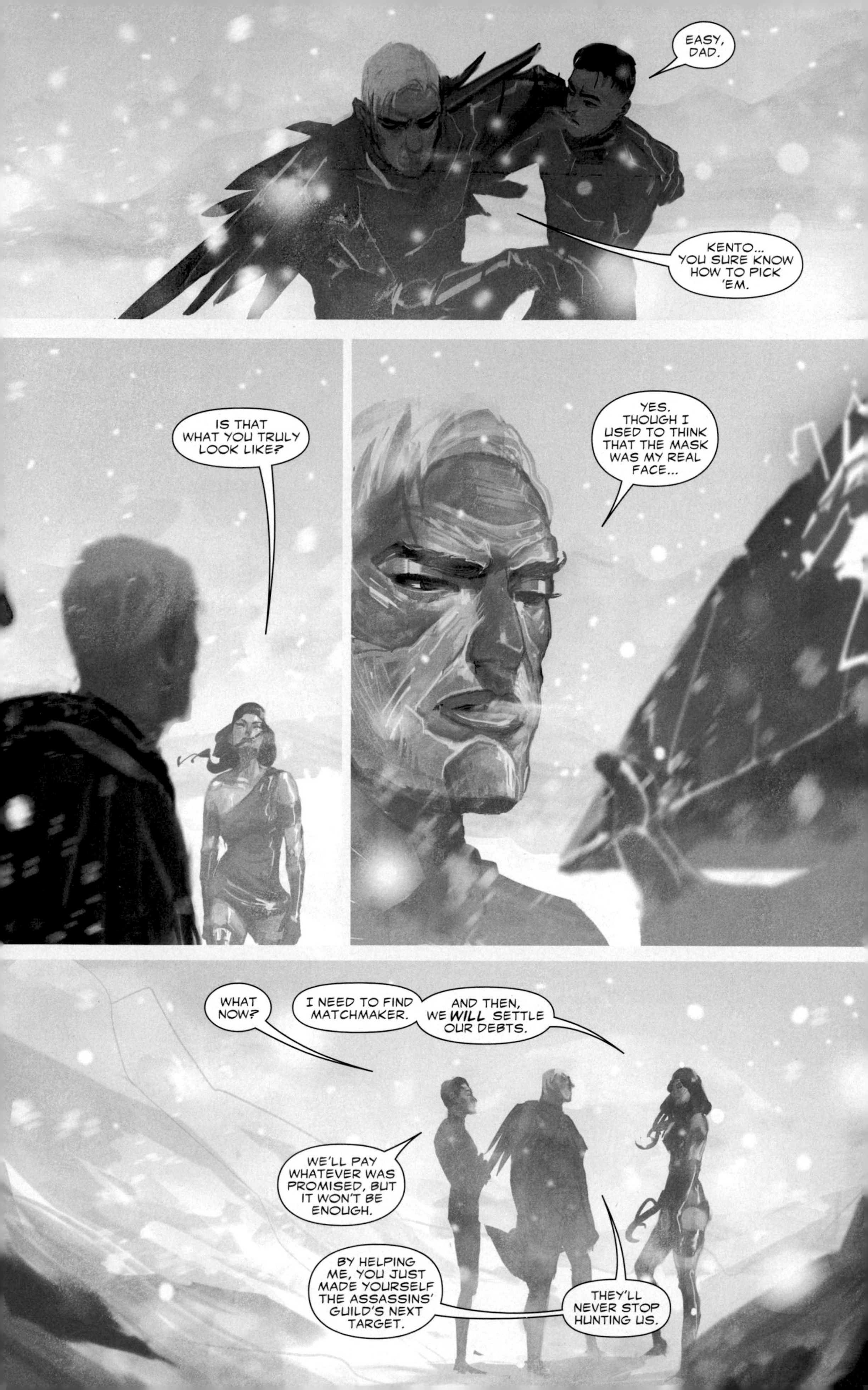
EASY, DAD.
KENTO... YOU SURE KNOW HOW TO PICK 'EM.
IS THAT WHAT YOU TRULY LOOK LIKE?
YES. THOUGH I USED TO THINK THAT THE MASK WAS MY REAL FACE...
WHAT NOW?
I NEED TO FIND MATCHMAKER.
AND THEN, WE WILL SETTLE OUR DEBTS.
WE'LL PAY WHATEVER WAS PROMISED, BUT IT WON'T BE ENOUGH.
BY HELPING ME, YOU JUST MADE YOURSELF THE ASSASSINS' GUILD'S NEXT TARGET.
THEY'LL NEVER STOP HUNTING US.

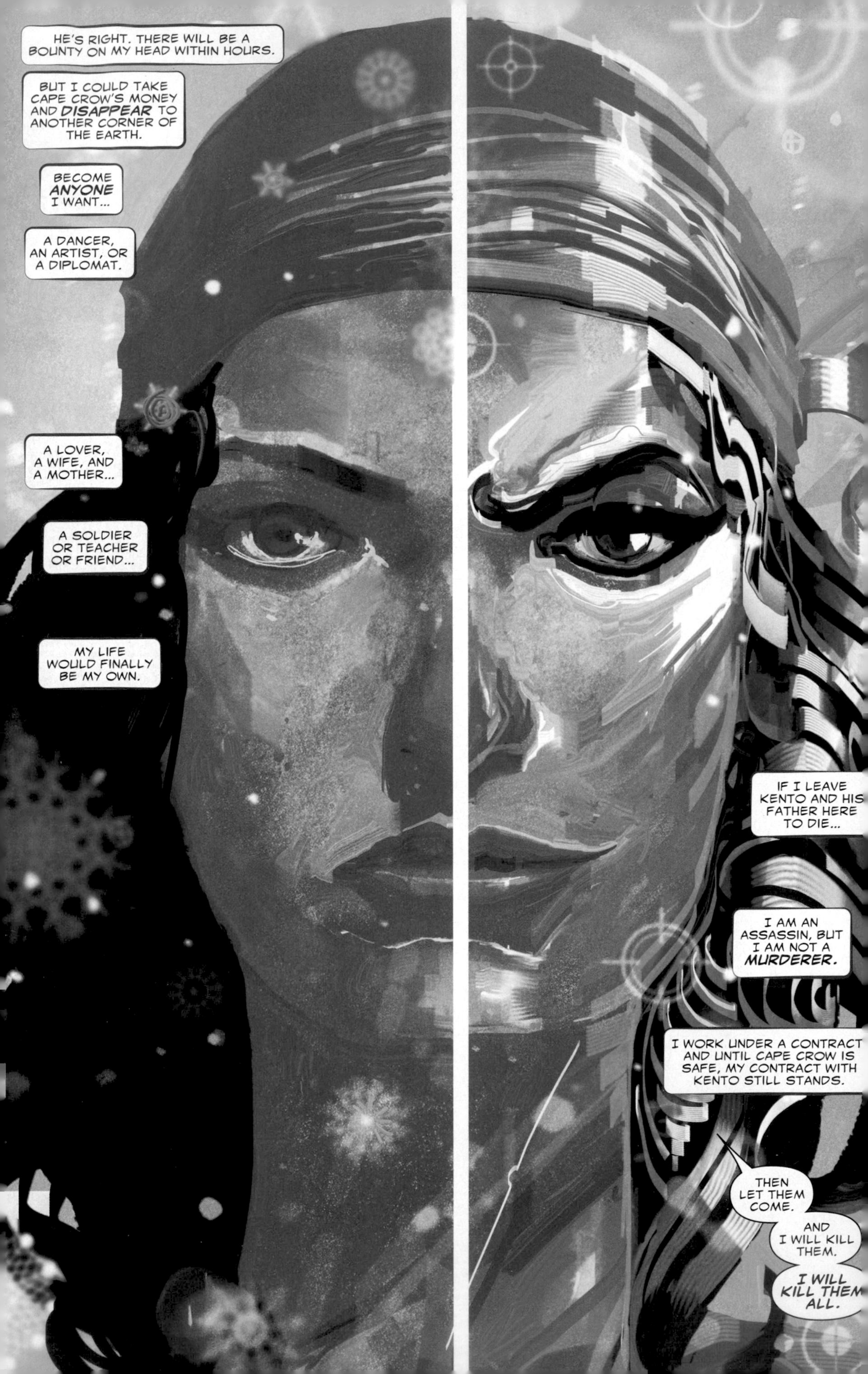
HE'S RIGHT. THERE WILL BE A BOUNTY ON MY HEAD WITHIN HOURS.
BUT I COULD TAKE CAPE CROW'S MONEY AND *DISAPPEAR* TO ANOTHER CORNER OF THE EARTH.
BECOME *ANYONE* I WANT...
A DANCER, AN ARTIST, OR A DIPLOMAT.
A LOVER, A WIFE, AND A MOTHER...
A SOLDIER OR TEACHER OR FRIEND...
MY LIFE WOULD FINALLY BE MY OWN.
IF I LEAVE KENTO AND HIS FATHER HERE TO DIE...
I AM AN ASSASSIN, BUT I AM NOT A *MURDERER.*
I WORK UNDER A CONTRACT AND UNTIL CAPE CROW IS SAFE, MY CONTRACT WITH KENTO STILL STANDS.
THEN LET THEM COME.
AND I WILL KILL THEM.
I WILL KILL THEM ALL.

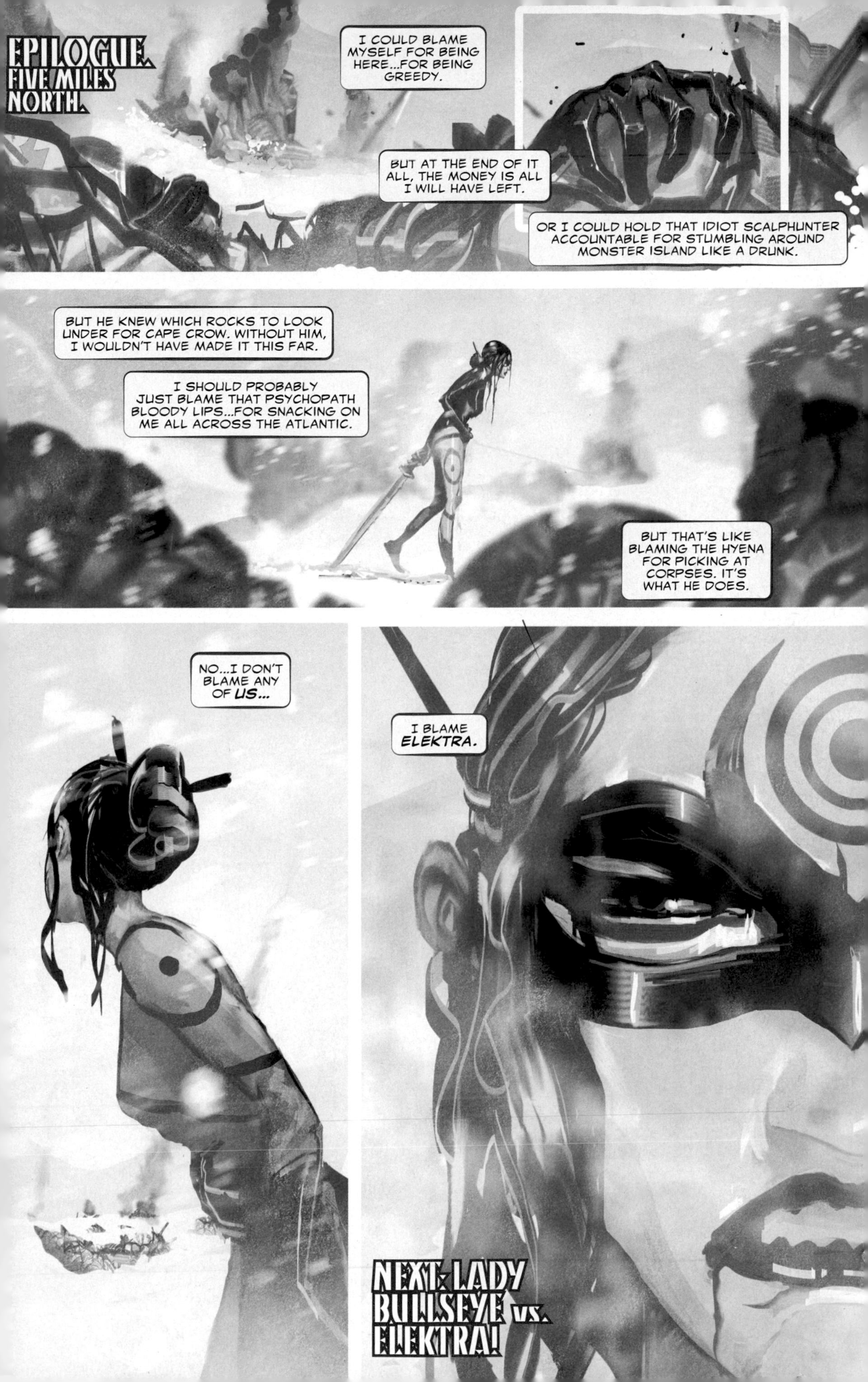
EPILOGUE. FIVE MILES NORTH.
I COULD BLAME MYSELF FOR BEING HERE...FOR BEING GREEDY.
BUT AT THE END OF IT ALL, THE MONEY IS ALL I WILL HAVE LEFT.
OR I COULD HOLD THAT IDIOT SCALPHUNTER ACCOUNTABLE FOR STUMBLING AROUND MONSTER ISLAND LIKE A DRUNK.
BUT HE KNEW WHICH ROCKS TO LOOK UNDER FOR CAPE CROW. WITHOUT HIM, I WOULDN'T HAVE MADE IT THIS FAR.
I SHOULD PROBABLY JUST BLAME THAT PSYCHOPATH BLOODY LIPS...FOR SNACKING ON ME ALL ACROSS THE ATLANTIC.
BUT THAT'S LIKE BLAMING THE HYENA FOR PICKING AT CORPSES. IT'S WHAT HE DOES.
NO...I DON'T BLAME ANY OF US...
I BLAME ELEKTRA.
NEXT: LADY BULLSEYE vs. ELEKTRA!

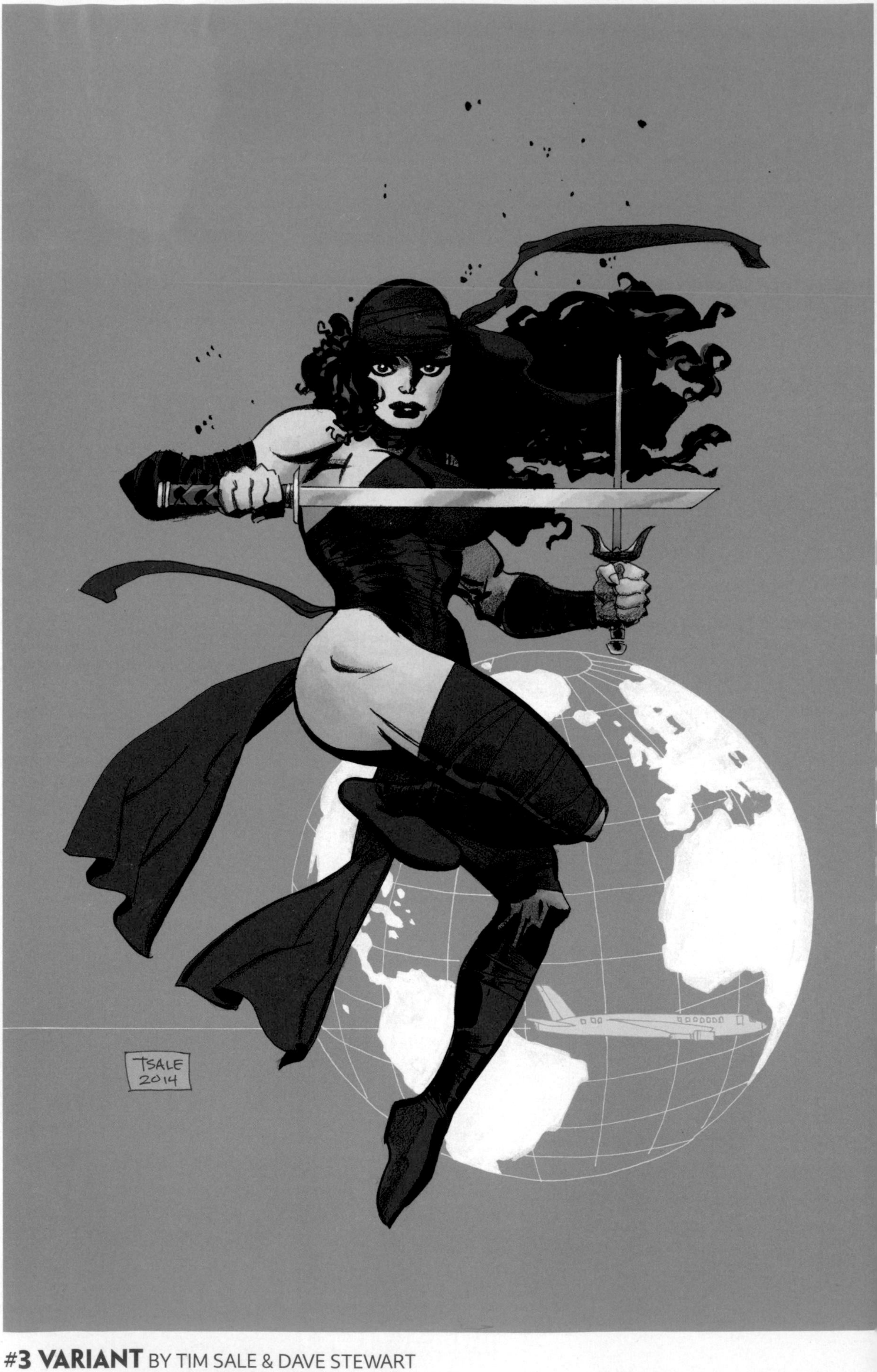
TSALE
2014

#3 VARIANT BY TIM SALE & DAVE STEWART